The Digital Transformation of Auditing and the Evolution of the Internal Audit

The main objective of this book is to provide both academics and practitioners with a global vision of the evolution of internal auditing in a fast-changing business landscape driven by digital transformation.

Digital transformation has been first associated with the emergence and the development of new technologies (artificial intelligence, blockchain, cloud computing, data analytics, predictive analytics, robotic process automation, IOT, drones etc.). Beyond the technological dimensions, this transformation has several impacts on businesses, organizations and processes and raises several questions for auditing activities. This book explores how digitalization not only has an impact on the audit environment, but also on internal audit practices and methodologies, information technology (IT)/information system (IS) audit, IT governance and risk management.

The auditing profession also has to face the same challenges. Auditors should develop new skills. To continue to provide high-quality service in such an environment, the methodologies, the process and the tools used for conducting an audit have progressively changed from those applied to the traditional audit. The internal audit has gradually moved from a monitoring – passive function – to a strategic and dynamic function in organizations.

Finally, the book also investigates the impact of the COVID-19 pandemic on internal auditing. The author highlights the need for a new vision and renewed forecasting tools. The post-COVID-19 business and corporate world has changed. Internal audit, as a key strategic function, must evolve too.

Nabyla Daidj (PhD, HDR) is Associate Professor of Strategic Management and Management Information Systems (MIS) at Institut Mines-Télécom Business School, Paris, France.

Finance, Governance and Sustainability
Challenges to Theory and Practice Series
Series Editor
Professor Güler Aras, Yildiz Technical University, Turkey; Georgetown University, Washington DC, USA

Focusing on the studies of academicians, researchers, entrepreneurs, policy makers and government officers, this international series aims to contribute to the progress in matters of finance, good governance and sustainability. These multidisciplinary books combine strong conceptual analysis with a wide range of empirical data and a wealth of case materials. They will be of interest to those working in a multitude of fields, across finance, governance, corporate behaviour, regulations, ethics and sustainability.

Management Scholarship and Organisational Change
Representing Burns and Stalker
Miriam Green

Ethics, Misconduct and the Financial Services Industry
Towards a Theory of Moral Business
Barbara Fryzel

Foundations of a Sustainable Economy
Moral, Ethical and Religious Perspectives
Edited by Umar Burki, Toseef Azid and Robert Francis Dahlstrom

Biolaw, Economics and Sustainable Governance
Addressing the Challenges of a Post-Pandemic World
Erick Valdés and Jacob Dahl Rendtorff

The Digital Transformation of Auditing and the Evolution of the Internal Audit
Nabyla Daidj

For more information about this series, please visit www.routledge.com/Finance-Governance-and-Sustainability/book-series/FINGOVSUST

The Digital Transformation of Auditing and the Evolution of the Internal Audit

Nabyla Daidj

Routledge
Taylor & Francis Group
LONDON AND NEW YORK

First published 2023
by Routledge
4 Park Square, Milton Park, Abingdon, Oxon OX14 4RN

and by Routledge
605 Third Avenue, New York, NY 10158

Routledge is an imprint of the Taylor & Francis Group, an informa business

British Library Cataloguing-in-Publication Data
A catalogue record for this book is available from the British Library

Library of Congress Cataloging-in-Publication Data
Names: Daidj, Nabyla, 1964- author.
Title: The digital transformation of auditing and the evolution of the internal audit / Nabyla Daidj.
Description: Milton Park, Abingdon, Oxon; New York, NY: Routledge, 2023. | Includes bibliographical references and index.
Identifiers: LCCN 2022023206 (print) | LCCN 2022023207 (ebook) | ISBN 9781032103914 (hardback) | ISBN 9781032103921 (paperback) | ISBN 9781003215110 (ebook)
Subjects: LCSH: Auditing, Internal. | Auditing—Technological innovations.
Classification: LCC HF5668.25 .D35 2023 (print) | LCC HF5668.25 (ebook) | DDC 657/.458—dc23/eng/20220525
LC record available at https://lccn.loc.gov/2022023206
LC ebook record available at https://lccn.loc.gov/2022023207

ISBN: 978-1-032-10391-4 (hbk)
ISBN: 978-1-032-10392-1 (pbk)
ISBN: 978-1-003-21511-0 (ebk)

DOI: 10.4324/9781003215110

Typeset in Bembo
by codeMantra

Contents

Figures

Tables

Exhibits

Appendices

Introduction

The main objective of this book is to provide for both academics and practitioners a global vision of the internal audit function and the main challenges it must face in the context of a fast-changing business landscape with the development of information technology (IT) and the digital transformation (Chapter 1).

Digital transformation has been first associated with the emergence and the development of new technologies (artificial intelligence, blockchain, cloud computing, data analytics, predictive analytics, robotic process automation, IOT, drones, etc.). Beyond the technological dimensions, this transformation has several impacts on business, organizations, and processes, and raises several questions. It could also lead audit regulators to revise audit standards in order to consider technological developments. "A digital transformation strategy impacts a company more comprehensively than an IT strategy and addresses potential effects on interactions across company borders with clients, competitors and suppliers" (Hess et al., 2016, p. 1). In brief, the digital transformation is a multidimensional phenomenon that can be explored from many different perspectives.

Information technology refers to "the automated means of originating, processing, storing, and communicating information, and includes recording devices, communication systems, computer systems (including hardware and software components and data), and other electronic devices" (AICPA 2007, AU 319.02).

Almost all organizations, private and public, in most industries use IT to support their operations (Bharadwaj et al., 2013). They are relying heavily on IT in conducting their day-to-day operations, resulting in changes in the nature of the work and the business relationships. IT has played a fundamental and powerful role in facilitating business activities and has become a catalyst for fundamental changes in the structure, operations, and management of organizations.

The auditing profession has been also exposed to the same challenges. To continue to provide high-quality service in such environment, the procedures, the tools, and the methods of conducting the audit have progressively

DOI: 10.4324/9781003215110-1

changed from those applied to the traditional audit (Chapter 4). Richard Chambers' (2019) words have been

> to sustain and build on our successes of the past two decades, internal auditors will need to pivot yet again to address the changing needs driven by high-tech disruptions that fundamentally impact how work gets done. To successfully adapt, internal auditors will need to embrace technology like never before.

For internal auditors, understanding the evolving risk landscape related to the business and learning to use technology in their work is a must (Chapters 5 and 6).

In addition, internal audit function has gradually moved from a monitoring– passive function in organization – to a strategic and dynamic function in organizations (Chapters 3 and 5). It has been considered for decades as the "organizational policeman and watchdog" (Morgan, 1979). Internal audit, as a value-added function, could play a central role in helping organizations and stakeholders by improving the operations of the organization and the effectiveness of the organization's risk management, control, and governance processes (Chapter 3).

Internal auditors could help management achieve company's goals, deliver not only assurance, but also to advise and anticipate risk. According to Drogalas et al. (2016), the new approach of internal auditing approach, the consulting role of internal audit, in line with strategic management, is emphasized. Precisely, strategic and IT alignment issues will be further explored in this book (Chapter 2).

Even if academic researches confirm that the internal auditor should play a greater strategic role within the organization, the practice of internal auditing has received relatively little academic attention. Roussy and Perron (2018) state that internal audit research is "far from comprehensive" (p. 345). While some internal auditing topics have been investigated in multiple research papers, a host of topics, especially related to new and emerging internal audit activities using technology, remain unexamined.

In summary, this book raises key questions emerging from academic research and professional business publications and debating in the auditing context. We have systematically favored a transversal approach mobilizing concepts in strategy, organization theory, and information systems management. Indeed, the issue of the evolution of the internal audit function cannot be addressed at the company level exclusively. Internal audit, and, in particular, IT audit, refers to several dimensions such as company strategy and alignment (strategy-organization-IT), corporate governance (whose rules and codes may vary from one country to another), IT governance, agility, risk management, and compliance (Chapters 3 and 4). This book contributes by clarifying and expanding upon these emerging concerns and by suggesting opportunities for future research. The literature review of academic literature and professional reports (white papers, surveys etc.) and websites is performed to identify various themes accordingly.

This book is divided into six chapters and proceeds in the following way:

Chapter 1 introduces and gives the salient features of the digital transformation.

The term "digital transformation" can be applied to changes at both the industry and organizational levels. Digital transformation simultaneously affects multiple areas within an organization, and there are many stakeholders involved in defining a transformation strategy (e.g., marketing, IT, product development, strategy, or HRM). Since the end of the 2000s, internal audit functions are under pressure to adapt to this "new" business environment, which is predominantly driven by technology. In this context, internal auditing is a key activity whose role must evolve. Digitalization not only has an impact on the audit environment, but also on internal audit practices, risk management, and information systems.

In this chapter, research on internal auditing and IT audit in a historical perspective combined with the current challenges of a dynamic and complex global business landscape will also be presented (Spencer Pickett, 2010).

Chapter 2 examines the successful conditions of strategic planning and the factors influencing the achievement of business-IT alignment (Nicho & Khan, 2017).

Over the years, the aims of strategic planning – setting overall goals, development of a plan to achieve them, and most efficient resource allocation – have remained constant. Internal audit has played a significant, useful, and valuable role in process of strategic planning.

In parallel, rapid changes in competition, demand, technology, and regulations make it more important than ever for organizations to be able to respond and adapt to their environment through the adoption of agile practices. In this context, the pressure on firms for aligning their business strategy with the technological changes in the environment has significantly increased with the emergence and growing importance of new digital technologies. IT scope cannot be separated from business scope. Achieving alignment is evolutionary and dynamic. Increasingly, the internal audit function is becoming strategic and reflects the need for alignment.

Chapter 3 addresses IT governance (ITG) issues.

The need for ITG is growing. ITG can refer to the management of the IT function including various layers (infrastructure, software applications, and operations) in order to ensure that key business objectives are met and IT is in alignment with business strategy. ITG can be considered as an enabler for business-IT alignment while minimizing IT risks. Van Grembergen (2002) emphasized, "IT governance is a combination of factors including leadership, structure, and processes that ensure that the organization achieves integration of business and IT" (p. 20).

What is the role of internal audit in IT governance? As explained by the IIA (2018),

> the role of internal audit in IT governance has become increasingly important in the wake of global financial crises and high-profile information security breaches. (…). Internal audit's role includes the responsibility to assess and make recommendations to improve the organization's governance processes (Standard 2110 – Governance) to help prevent governance failures and improve strategic performance as part of the third line of defense (…). Internal audit represents the third line of defense and is responsible for providing independent assurance that risk management and controls are operating effectively, and advise senior management and the board when deficiencies are identified.
>
> (p. 7)

Chapter 4 covers the main internal audit methodologies with a specific focus on IT audit techniques.

Audit approaches are the methods or techniques that auditors use in their audit assignments. They are numerous. The analysis, in particular, of the white papers written by audit firms has revealed several main themes debated by professionals coping alongside with the challenges of digital transformation in the auditing context. The traditional IT audit approaches are briefly presented. An analysis of three specific approaches is provided: the risk-based framework, the IT governance audit methodology, and the fundamentals of agile auditing. The digital maturity model (DMM) is also analyzed as it has been applied for internal audits leading to the development of new practices in auditing called continuous auditing.

Chapter 5 provides an overview of advanced technologies referring to both the tools available to auditors and the systems that need to be audited.

Auditors have to work more and more in an automated IT environment and accordingly modify their audit processes to cope with the new updated technologies. We explore to what extent new technologies and their developments open up new opportunities for internal auditing and the audit process itself leading to several opportunities for enhancing value and reducing costs. These technologies have currently an impact on or are likely to affect the audit profession in the near future. Increasing the use of IT can improve the efficiency and effectiveness of audit procedures, aid in the identification of fraud, and lower litigation costs.

The use of new technologies in the auditing field (e.g., computerized applications for auditing, data analytics, artificial intelligence, robotic process automation, etc.) is a contemporary issue emerging from auditors' awareness of the importance of them, in particular, in continuous internal auditing. For example, the use of data analytics allows the automation of routine procedures and can greatly expand the breadth and the scope of audit coverage.

Finally, this chapter could give some insights for higher education institutions and training institutes on new skills of auditors in technological matters, which auditors must have or develop to be in line with new market needs, and to face tomorrow's challenges.

Chapter 6 focuses on internal auditing in a COVID-19 era and on post-COVID 19 considerations.

The COVID-19 crisis has exposed the vulnerabilities of individuals, societies, and economies and has raised questions about the future and the 'long term' (prospects and scenarios). The term crisis is a multidimensional and multifaceted concept that assumes a number of forms and multiple levels of analysis. There is a need for a new vision and new monitoring and diagnostic tools.

The post-COVID 19 world has changed. Internal audit must change too. Internal audit has to evolve with the 'new normal'. The use of technology will be more critical to conducting internal audits in the future. The future of audit work should be analyzed in part in the light of remote working, process automation, and predictive analytics. More broadly, internal audits should contribute to strategic decision-making, and organizations will rely more and more on internal auditors to provide timely insights while guiding their businesses through a dynamic risk landscape.

References

AICPA (2007). *AICPA professional standards.* New York: AICPA.

Bharadwaj, A., et al. (2013). Digital business strategy: Toward a next generation of insights. *MIS Quarterly, 37*(2), 471–482.

Chambers, R. (2019). The road ahead for internal audit: 5 bold predictions for the 2020s. AuditBeacon. https://www.richardchambers.com/the-road-ahead-for-internal-audit-5-bold-predictions-for-the-2020s/

Drogalas, G., Arampatzis, K., & Anagnostopoulou, E. (2016). The relationship between corporate governance, internal audit and audit committee: Empirical evidence from Greece. *Corporate Ownership & Control, 14*(1–4), 569–577.

Hess, T., Matt, C., Wiesböck, F., & Benlian, A. (2016). Options for formulating a digital transformation strategy. *MIS Quarterly Executive, 15*(2), 103–119.

The Institute of Internal Auditors (IIA) - International Professional Practices Framework (2018). *Supplemental guidance. Global Technology Audit Guide (GTAG).* Auditing IT Governance. Retrieved January 15, 2022 from: https://www.iia.nl/SiteFiles/GTAG%2017%20Auditing%20IT%20Governance.pdf

Morgan, G. (1979). Internal audit role conflict: A pluralist view. *Managerial Finance, 5*(2), 160–170. https://doi.org/10.1108/eb013444

Nicho, M., & Khan, S. (2017). IT governance measurement tools and its application in IT-business alignment. *Journal of International Technology and Information Management, 26*(1), 81–111.

Roussy, M., & Perron, A. (2018). New perspectives in internal audit research: A structured literature review. *Accounting Perspectives, 17*(3), 345–385.

Spencer Pickett, K.H. (2010). *The internal auditing handbook.* 3rd edition. Chichester: John Wiley & Sons.

Van Grembergen, W. (2002). Introduction to the minitrack IT governance and its mechanisms. *Proceedings of the 35th Hawaii International Conference on System Sciences (HICSS), 5*, 3097. IEEE. https://ieeexplore.ieee.org/xpl/conhome/7798/proceeding

1 A historical perspective of internal audit

The impact of digital transformation

Introduction

This chapter highlights the key role of technology and the major related changes in the last three decades. Digital technology remains the key enabling technology of the current era of globalization. It has removed market barriers and transformed cost structures radically. In many cases, a disruptive technology can be seen as a technology that replaces the incumbent technology. It is the case with digital technology (OECD, 2017, 2019, and 2020). The 2000s have been characterized by technological and industrial convergence (between telecommunications, IT, and media). Then, new entrants with their digital platforms led to the spread of uberization in the economy. Finally, since the mid-2010s, it is the turn of the digital transformation to affect the entire economy, business sectors, and their main players (The World Economic Forum, 2016; Bockshecker et al., 2018).

In this context, internal auditing is a key activity whose role must evolve (KPMG, 2016; PWC, 2020). Digitalization has an impact not only on the audit environment but also on internal audit practices, risk management, and information systems. Internal audit is also evolving in its practices, which are gradually incorporating agile approaches and continuous improvements with data processing and analysis at the center of the system thanks to increasingly high-performance tools and technologies.

The challenges of internal auditing in the context of digital transformation are outlined with a focus on two levels of analysis: the audit industry and the internal level of companies. But before presenting the main impacts of digital transformation, we will first define the internal audit function and related missions. Finally, the main insights and main perspectives of research on internal auditing will be summarized.

The emergence and development of the audit function

The origin of auditing... and of auditors

Etymologically, audit, an ancient term, comes from the Latin 'audire' (to listen) / 'auditus' (heard).

DOI: 10.4324/9781003215110-2

The Roman Empire is supposed to have put in place a kind of procedure to detect fraud as early as the 3rd century BC. However, the first auditing activities (accounting) were recorded in England as early as the 17th century with the objective of validating financial statements. Auditing really developed in the 19th century with the growth of industry and trade, insurance companies, and the rise of investment banks, leading to the elaboration of the first professional standards.

At the beginning of the 20th century, it was the 1929 crisis with its series of bankruptcies, the collapse of economic activity, and the growing complexity of the business world that led to the need for the creation of systematic monitoring mechanisms and control processes in order to prevent risks such as fraud, corruption, and bankruptcy. The SEC (Securities and Exchange Commission), the stock market regulator in the United States, requires all companies to be audited.

In parallel with the evolution of audits, the missions of auditors have changed over time (Table 1.1). However, they still follow certain principles that remain unchanged.

What is internal auditing and their main related missions?

At a general level, the International Organization for Standardization (ISO), a worldwide federation of national standards bodies (ISO member bodies), provides a definition of audit included in its Guidelines for auditing management systems (ISO 19011:2011). It is

> a systematic, independent and documented process for obtaining audit evidence (records, statements of fact or other information which are relevant to the audit criteria and verifiable) and evaluating it objectively to determine the extent to which the audit criteria (set of policies, procedures or requirements used as a reference against which audit evidence is compared) are fulfilled.
>
> (https://www.iso.org/obp/ui/fr/#iso:std:iso:19011:ed-2:v1:en:fr)

According to ISO, audit activities are divided into two main categories as shown in Tables 1.2 and 1.3:

- Internal audits are also named first-party audits. They are conducted by the organization itself, or on its behalf, for management review and other internal purposes (e.g., to confirm the effectiveness of the management system or to get information for the improvement of the management system). "Internal audits can form the basis for an organization's self-declaration of conformity. In many cases, particularly in small organizations, independence can be demonstrated by the freedom from responsibility for the activity being audited or freedom from bias and conflict of interest.

Table 1.1 Evolution of auditing missions and positions through the ages

Period	*Authorities (bodies) demanding audit*	*Auditors*	*Main purposes*
2000 to 1700 BC	Kings, Emperors Churches, and States	Clerics and writers	Sanctioning thieves for embezzlement Protecting the heritage
1700–1850	States, commercial courts, and shareholders	Accountants	Suppressing fraud and punishing fraudsters Protecting the heritage
1850–1900	States and shareholders	Accounting and legal professionals	Avoiding fraud and certifying the balance sheet
1900–1940	States and shareholders	Accounting and legal professionals	Avoiding fraud and errors and certifying the balance sheet
1940–1970	States, banks, and shareholders	Accounting and legal professionals	*Certifying the regularity,* fairness, and *truthfulness* of *financial statements*
1970–1990	States, third parties, and shareholders	Accounting, auditing, and consulting professionals	Certifying the quality of internal control and compliance with accounting and auditing standards
1990–2010	States, third parties, and shareholders	Auditing and consulting professionals	Certifying the financial statements and the quality of internal control in accordance with the standards Expanding the scope of the internal audit (IT, IS, etc.) Protecting against international fraud Fighting against corruption
Since 2010	States, third parties, and shareholders	Auditing and consulting professionals	Certifying the financial statements and the quality of internal control in accordance with the standards Protecting against international fraud Fighting against corruption Using of non-financial metrics in relation to CSR (Corporate Social Responsibility activities involving social and environmental measures) reporting and auditing

Source: Adapted from Collins and Vallin (1992) and updated by the author.

Table 1.2 Scope of the international standard

Internal auditing	*External auditing*	
	Supplier auditing	*Third party auditing*
Sometimes called first-party audit	Sometimes called second-party audit	For legal, regulatory, and similar purposes For certification (see also the requirements in ISO/IEC 17021:2011)

Source: ISO (2021).

Table 1.3 Internal audit versus external audit

External audit		*Internal audit*
From outside the organization	Status	Employees of the organization
True and fair view of financial statements	Objective	Varies according to the audit
Historical	Focus	Forward-looking
Shareholders, Board of Directors and Audit Committee	Reports go to	Management and audit committee
External audit standards	Standards	Internal audit standards
Mandatory	Qualifications	Not mandatory

Source: IIA – Australia (2020, p. 6).

- External audits include second- and third-party audits. Second-party audits are conducted by parties having an interest in the organization, such as customers, or by other persons on their behalf. Third-party audits are conducted by independent auditing organizations, such as regulators or those providing certification."

Relationship between internal audit and internal control

Before addressing internal auditing issues more specifically, it is necessary to consider another important function, that of internal control. Internal control is sometimes confused with internal auditing, but these are two distinct but complementary activities (Petraşcu & Tamas, 2013).

The internal control has been defined by several institutes among them, the Committee of Sponsoring Organizations of the Treadway Commission (COSO), the Institute of Internal Auditors (IIA), and the American Institute of Certified Public Accountants (AICPA).

We will quote here the COSO (2013) definition, which states the following:

Internal Control is a process, effected by an entity's board of directors, management and other personnel, designed to provide "reasonable assurance regarding the achievement of objectives in the following categories:

operations, reporting, and compliance" (COSO, 2013, p. 3). This definition reflects certain fundamental concepts. Internal control is:

- Geared to the achievement of objectives in one or more categories – operations, reporting, and compliance
- A process consisting of ongoing tasks and activities – a means to an end, not an end in itself
- Effected by people – not merely about policy and procedure manuals, systems, and forms, but about people and the actions they take at every level of an organization to affect internal control
- Able to provide reasonable assurance – but not absolute assurance, to an entity's senior management and board of directors
- Adaptable to the entity structure – flexible in application for the entire entity or for a particular subsidiary, division, operating unit, or business process" (COSO, 2013, p. 3).

In light of the definitions presented previously of internal control and internal audit, there is a complementary relationship between them. The internal control determines the controls based on which a strategic business unit (SBU) or another kind of entity (business group, division, team, etc.) according to organizational structure should be managed while the internal audit aims at checking the implementation of internal controls.

Digital transformation: main insights

Digital transformation has led to numerous debates in both the academic sphere and the business world. To date, many research papers and white papers have been conducted on digital transformation.

From digitization to digital transformation

Digital transformation has given rise to several definitions (Daidj, 2019). Until now, there is no real consensus on the meaning of digital transformation (Gray & Rumpe, 2017; Kane, 2017). Digital transformation could be explored from several perspectives: organization, information systems, technologies, processes, business models, customers, etc. However, it is admitted that digital transformation is often seen as the stage that follows that of digitization, dematerialization, and digitalization (Table 1.4). Digital transformation is a very long journey that can lead to the last stage known as digital maturity, a natural process through which a company learns how to respond appropriately to the emerging digital competitive environment (Kane, 2017).

The main layers of digital transformation

Digital transformation is the basis of many reflections and is the focus of academic research as well as of case studies in sectors as varied as services

Table 1.4 Digitization versus digitalization versus digital transformation

Digital/digitization	*Digitalization*	*Digital transformation*
Technical conversion from analog information into a digital form or format (Autio, 2017; Bogush, 2021). "Digital" suggests that many changes in society, business, and industry will be driven by information technologies that allow data to be processed in real-time and even used to intelligently derive information to finally provide stakeholders with improved knowledge about their processes and products. Downstream digitization would also allow optimization, automation activities, and production techniques of various forms (Gray & Rumpe, 2017).	Digitalization is the process of leveraging digitization to improve business processes. Digitalization means making digitized information work for you. This term refers to the use of digital technologies and data to create revenue, improve business, and create a digital culture where digital information is at the core. It converts processes to be more efficient, productive, and profitable (Hapon, 2020). Exploiting digital technologies to change business processes and workflows to improve business models (Bogush, 2021). In relation to the "socio-technical processes surrounding the use of (a large variety of) digital technologies that have an impact on social and institutional contexts" (Tilson et al., 2010, p. 749).	Reorientating multiple processes, workflows, by leveraging several digital technologies, to deliver organizational objective(s) (Bogush, 2021) Digital transformation can be considered as "a process where digital technologies create disruptions triggering strategic responses from organizations that seek to alter their value creation paths while managing the structural changes and organizational barriers that affect the positive and negative outcomes of this process" (Vial, 2019, p. 118).

Source: Adapted from Daidj (2019).

(banking and insurance), transportation, retail, education, and training. Digitalization affects all sectors of the economy and the stakes are huge for companies whatever their size and turnover (large groups, intermediate-sized enterprises/ETI, and small-medium enterprises/SME as defined by INSEE in 2021) but also for public institutions, hospitals, universities, etc.

Since the end of the 2000s and especially in the early 2010s, digital transformation has been the focus of numerous academic papers and white papers written by major consulting and/or audit firms including Capgemini (2018), Capgemini Consulting & MIT (2011), Deloitte (2015), Bain & Company (2017), McKinsey (2021), and PWC (2020).

Digital transformation takes many forms and can affect all of the players within a company (business activities, organizational structure, operational processes and procedures, talents and skills of the workforce). It can also change relations with all the external stakeholders (customer, supplier, service provider, partner, etc.) through existing inter-organizational networks such as clusters and value networks coexisting with more recent systems such as business ecosystems and platforms. Digital transformation is a multifaceted and therefore complex phenomenon with a number of consequences at several levels as shown in the following table (Table 1.5). A number of issues are identified accordingly.

> The three "traditional" sectors are all affected with the primary sector (extraction such as mining, agriculture, and fishing), the secondary sector (manufacturing), and the tertiary sector (services). According to the INSEE definition, the tertiary sector covers a wide range of activities

Table 1.5 The main layers of digital transformation

	Country	*Sector*	*Market*	*Corporate level*
Changes	Evolution of macroeconomic conditions (economic, legal, political, social, environmental, technological factors, etc.)	New applications of digital technology in the three traditional sectors (Agriculture-Industry – Services) + "quaternary and quinary sectors"	Transformation of the external environment and markets in which companies operate	Organizational changes within firms
	Innovation policies driven by digitalization Public research Rules/standards Anti-trust laws Intellectual property (IP) systems Education (training) Investment/Infrastructure	Use of digital technology in a number of sectors. Agriculture 4.0. (smart farming) Industry 4.0. (digital factories)	Structure/competition (Prices) Barriers to entry/to exit (new entrants, incumbents) Two-sided markets/ Digital platforms Relationships between stakeholders (alliances, clusters, business and innovation ecosystems) Business models	Structure, strategic and digital business units, functions (e.g., HR, internal audit), talents, skills Innovation (digital) & open-innovation Co-creation/co-design new products/services (customer journey and experience) Culture (acculturation to digital) Operations (Information technology/ Information systems, process, etc.) Data management (creation, capture, and monetization)

Source: Elaborated by the author.

from commerce to administration, transport, financial and real estate activities, business and personal services, education, health and social work. It is made of:

- the market services sector (trade, transports, financial operations, business services, personal services, accommodation and food service activities, real estate, information-communication) and
- the non-market sector (public administration, education, human health, social work activities).

Over the past century, the service sector has rapidly expanded.

More recently, according to some economists, a fourth sector named "quaternary" has been often emerged in some publications in relation to industries providing information-based or knowledge-oriented products and services. Information systems (IS) and information technology (IT) are the core of these quaternary activities and services (computing services, media, information and communication technology, consulting, and research and development).

More occasionally, there is also some discussion about a fifth sector in the literature. Both the fourth and the fifth are closely related to the tertiary sector. As explained by Lisch (2014),

> (…) it shall be mentioned that sometimes this three-sector classification is further extended to a quaternary and quinary sector although there is little consensus with regard to their definitions except that both sectors provide a further breakdown of the tertiary sector. (…). The quinary sector (…) encompasses in some definitions categories like tourism, leisure, wellness and health whereas others use the term for the disposal and waste management industry. Obviously, these additional sectors pay tribute to the growing importance of the tertiary sector by emphasizing specific areas that have gained particular importance.

The impact of digital transformation on internal auditing: what is at stake?

Since the beginning of the 2010s, changes in the economic conditions, the technological environment, and the regulatory landscape have impacted how the audit industry operates (Mazars, 2021). In addition, the evolving digital transformation has started to affect internal auditing (and more specifically IT audit) at several levels:

- on the audit sector as a whole and the major players involved;
- on internal audit function (within large companies);
- on internal audit methodology;
- on auditors' tools and working methods; and
- on auditors' role, missions, and skills.

All these issues will be analyzed in depth in the next chapters. In the sections below, only the salient points are highlighted. The current trends in the audit industry and the internal audit function are first presented.

Current trends in the audit industry

The sector of large audit firms, mostly Anglo-Saxon, progressively concentrated at the international level in the 1980s and 1990s with large-scale mergers and acquisitions. The Big 8 became the Big 6 in 1989 (with the creation of Deloitte and Ernst & Young), then the Big 5 with PWC, and since 2002 the Big 4: Deloitte, Ernst & Young (E&Y), KPMG, PricewaterhouseCoopers (PWC). As Table 1.6 and Figures 1.1 and 1.2 show, their revenues have been steadily increasing since 2016.

Table 1.6 The evolution of the Big Four revenue (2016–2021)

In billion U.S. dollars	*2016*	*2017*	*2018*	*2019*	*2020*	*2021*
DELOITTE	36.9	38.8	43.2	46.20	47.60	50.20
PWC	35.4	37.7	41.3	42.45	43.03	45.14
EY	29.6	31.4	34.8	36.40	37.20	40.00
KPMG	25.4	26.4	28.9	29.75	29.22	32.13

Source: The Big Four and Statista.
Fiscal years: Deloitte ends May 31; PwC and EY end June 30; KPMG ends September 30. Values have been rounded.

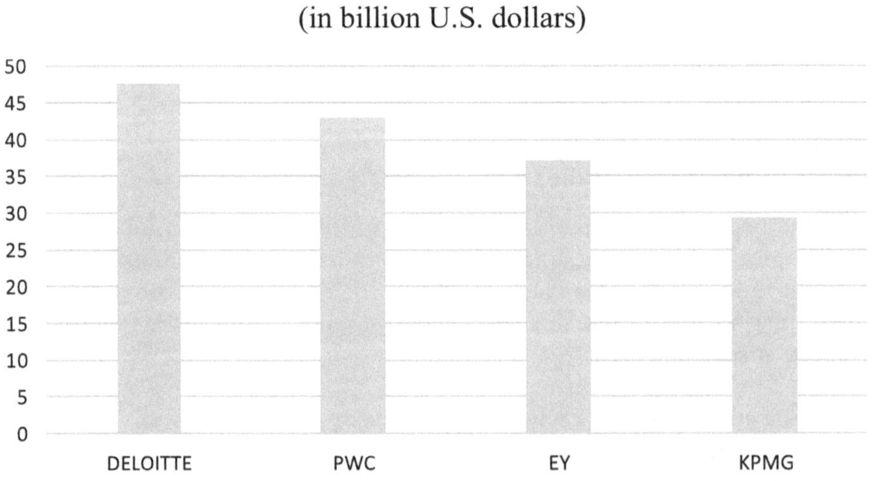

Figure 1.1 Revenue of the Big Four accounting/audit firms worldwide in 2020
Source: Adapted from Statista (2021).

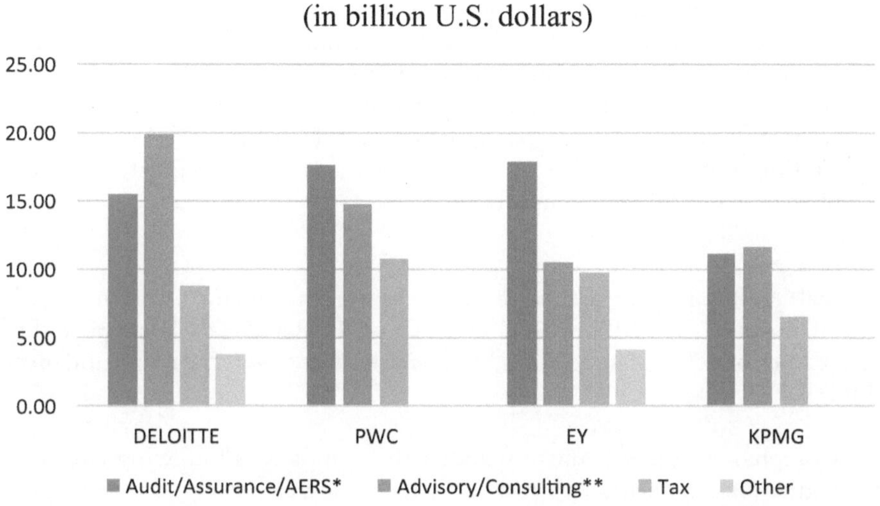

Figure 1.2 Revenue of the Big Four accounting/audit firms worldwide in 2020, by function. * PwC, Ernst & Young – "Assurance"; KPMG – "Audit"; Deloitte – "AERS – Audit and enterprise risk services." ** Deloitte – "Consulting"; Ernst & Young, PwC & KPMG – "Advisory." Other (Deloitte – "Financial Advisory"; Ernst & Young – "Transaction Advisory Services"). Fiscal years: Deloitte ends May 31; PwC and EY end June 30; KPMG ends September 30. Values have been rounded

Source: Adapted from Statista (2021).

The evolution of internal audit function in large companies in the context of digital transformation

Today, several trends are emerging, some of which are already well established in the auditing landscape, while others are more recent and should shift the way in which audits are carried out, as well as the associated means and resources as follows:

- Audits meet specific requirements and are standardized processes (see above the definition of the ISO 19011:2011 standard). ISO certifications are voluntary but demand periodic compliance audits (see below).
- As mentioned previously, internal audits ensure that a company follows its own procedures. Internal audits occur throughout the fiscal year. They are linked to the identification and analysis of risks and the implementation of control mechanisms. Several reports highlight the fact that internal audits will play a key role in digital business transformation.

In addition, integrated internal audits are conducted to meet changes in IT and business processes. An audit assesses the interactions between financial, operational, and technology processes on the achievement of control objectives. According to the definition of the IIA (2012),

> an integrated audit differs from a non-integrated audit in terms of scope and overall complexity. A traditional audit and an integrated audit differ in scope and depth and breadth of coverage. For example, a traditional audit may focus on financial or operational aspects while an integrated audit will take a more global approach that looks at several aspects including, but not limited to, financial, operational, IT, regulatory, compliance, environmental, and fraud.
>
> (p. 12)

Internal audit functions are traditionally viewed as an organization's third line of defense (The IIA, 2017). ECIIA and FERMA (2011) support the "three lines of defense" model as a benchmark for future regulatory guidance (Table 1.7).

- Compliance audits evaluate whether the company is following external regulations in relation to financial, technological, safety, and environmental issues. Several regulations could be examined during compliance auditing missions. Various national, European, and international regulations exist such as the Sarbanes-Oxley Act (SOX), the Generally Accepted Auditing Standards (GAAS), the protection of natural persons with regard to the processing of personal data and the free movement of such data, and repealing Directive 95/46/EC General Data Protection Regulation (GDPR) and the European payment services Directive 2nd version (PSD 2).

Table 1.7 The three lines of defense model

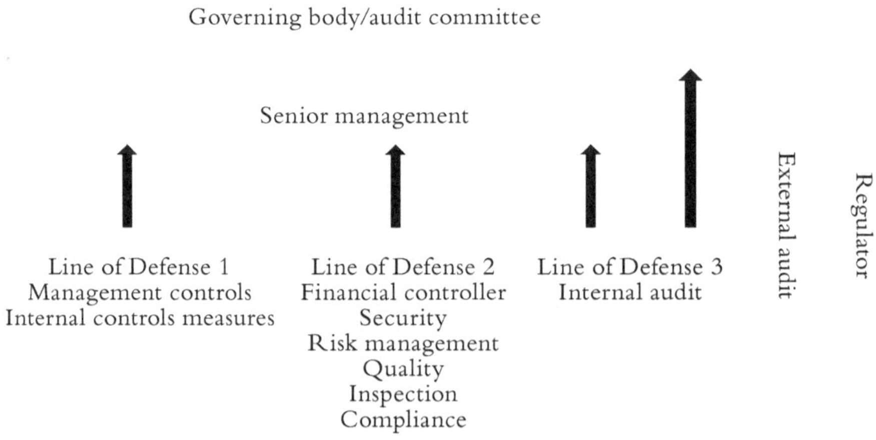

Source: Adapted from ECIIA (2021).

- There are many audit methodologies (Chapter 4). They are often specific and differ from one audit and consulting firm to another, and over time, they have developed their own approaches and tools.

The development of IT audit

The broader scope of internal audit

The scope of internal audits has increased considerably over the past few years while initially audits mainly involved a company's accounting and financial activities. Today, they can cover the organization as a whole, all activities, the different areas of the company (R&D, purchasing, production, manufacturing, supply chain, IS/IT, data quality, customer relations, etc.), and the related processes, but also all outsourced functions and all associated risks (Table 1.8). In an audit process, follow-up audits are also performed after an initial audit to ensure that corrective action has been implemented properly.

IT (internal) audit versus audit IT

As seen previously, internal audits may serve various objectives and multiple parties within an organization. One of them, and probably one of the most significant today, is called IT internal audit. IT audit is the process of

Table 1.8 The scope of internal audit

Finance department	*Executive management*		*Audited entity/ department/ function*	
Risk management		Specific audits	Quality Corporate Social Responsibility (CSR) IS (information system)/IT (information technology)	Transversal activities
	Internal audit			
Internal control External audit →		Missions	Procurement Sales Inventory HR Cash management Accounting	Processes

Source: Adapted from SiaPartners (2016).

evaluating and reporting on IT infrastructure (including computers, software, applications, etc.), policies, procedures, and operations for an organization. In a highly competitive and increasingly connected world with the development of new technologies (Chapter 5), the IT environment should be better controlled. An IT audit allows an organization to get a better understanding of whether the existing IT controls efficiently protect its assets, ensuring data integrity and alignment with the business and financial controls. An IT auditor is in charge of elaborating, implementing, testing, and evaluating the IT audit review procedures.

IT internal audit must not be confused with audit IT. Audit IT use refers to the extent auditors employ or use IT throughout the audit process, to "the auditor's tool kit" (Elliott & Jacobson, 1987) and audit technology support tools (Rosli et al., 2013). Elliott and Jacobson (1987) argue, "A tool may be thought of as anything that enhances an individual's capacity to perform a task. Audit IT consists of all the things designed to enhance the auditor's capacity to perform an audit task." (p. 198). Audit IT encompasses audit applications, productivity tools, work paper review technology, and the use of IT specialists (Janvrin et al., 2008).

The development of the IT audit universe

An audit universe refers to the potential range of all audit activities and includes a number of auditable entities. This assessment provides a systematic approach for prioritizing the audit entities identified in the audit universe. Maintaining an audit universe is not mandatory. However, it has been proven to be a professional audit good practice. Audit universe is also known as risk-based auditing (Chapter 4).

The IT audit universe is a part of the global audit universe. It should be built with a holistic perspective. It must be defined in order for the risk assessment process to be an effective driver for the creation of the IT audit plan (Table 1.9). Before developing an audit plan within the enterprise, an analysis of its corporate and business strategy must be done. The IT audit plan should be closely aligned with the business strategy and management (Chapter 2). Enterprise strategy is realized by the achievement of several goals that could be structured along the balanced scorecard (BSC) dimensions, an example being business service continuity and availability (Chapter 2).

The global technology audit guide (GTAG) has developed another version of IT audit plan. Quoted by the Chartered Institute of Internal auditors (2020), the GTAG promotes the following approach based on six steps: understand the business model, understand the supporting technologies, understand the business strategy and IT strategy, understand the model of the IT function, understand the IT support processes, understand the laws and regulations.

What is interesting in the two previous approaches is their converging views on the key role of strategy and its influence on IT decisions and IT audit plan elaboration.

Table 1.9 Audit plan design workflow

Step 1	*Step 2*	*Step 3*	*Step 4*
Understand the enterprise context and strategy	Determine the components of the IT audit universe	Risk assess the IT audit universe	Conclude and validate the IT audit plan
Understand enterprise strategy Understand the risk profile Understand current I&T-related issues	Consider the components of a governance system Determine the IT audit portfolios Define the IT audit universe	Consider the COBIT® 2019 design factors as risk factors	Resolve inherent priority conflicts Conclude the IT audit plan Publish the IT audit plan

Source: Adapted from ISACA® COBIT® 2019.

The Institute of Internal Auditors (2013) considers that IT audit universe is based on four main layers as follows:

- IT management. It includes a set of staff, policies, procedures, and processes that manage the IT environment. Both the facilities and the management process have to be audited. Various components are covered in such an audit (system monitoring, vendor management, IT project management, disaster recovery, service management, security management, IT governance, etc.).
- Technical infrastructure. It includes the underlying technology in supporting major applications for businesses (operating systems, files and databases, networks, data centers). Technical infrastructure audits focus on the review of technical configuration settings combined with their related management processes.
- Business applications (both transactional and support applications). They refer to computer programs that perform specific tasks related to the business operations. As they are an integral part of business processes, they cannot be considered from the process they support.
- External connections. The corporate network is connected to several external networks (such as the Internet, cloud computing, and software as a service provider).

The ever-rising importance of internal auditing and IT audits in the literature

Research on internal auditing

At a theoretical level, research on the evolution of internal auditing is rather limited, as several authors have pointed out. At a general level, DeFond and Zhang (2014) have stated that "internal audit research is still in its infancy"

(p. 278). However, Bailey et al. (2003) have presented research opportunities in internal audits as follows: internal audit and organizational/corporate governance, auditing risk assessment and risk management processes, impact of IT on internal auditing, etc. Ten years after Bailey et al.'s (2003) study, Lenz and Hahn (2015) have reviewed what academic literature has found about internal audit effectiveness. Kotb et al. (2020) have also attempted to evaluate and identify avenues through which future research can help to advance internal audits in order to address emerging challenges in the field.

> Future research could develop a comprehensive model based on stakeholders' perceptions of the determinants of internal audit effectiveness and examine the extent to which these determinants interact with each other in response to internal/external changes. Further research may also investigate how these determinants could possibly be mandated through regulatory or professional requirements and examine who judges internal audit effectiveness.
>
> (p. 1980)

The literature review suggests also a variety of research questions for exploration and investigation (The IIA, 2003; Lesage & Wechtler, 2010; Roussy & Perron, 2018; Christ et al., 2021). Internal auditing has been thus studied from various perspectives, including:

- Focus on audit quality. There is an increasingly important construct of internal audit quality (Behrend & Eulerich, 2019). DeFond and Zhang (2014) have defined higher audit quality and have provided a framework for systematically choosing among the commonly used audit quality proxies and evaluating their results. The two authors have encouraged future researchers to continue expanding knowledge of client demand-side factors, and further explore additional factors related to both auditor and client competencies defined as clients' abilities to meet their incentive-driven demand for audit quality. These abilities consist of mechanisms that facilitate meeting their demand for audit quality and are typically integral parts of the corporate governance system.
- Internal auditing and corporate governance (Chapter 3). Several scholars have underlined the fact that internal audit could add value and/or improve corporate governance (Gramling et al., 2004; Goodwin-Stewart & Kent, 2006; Archambeault et al., 2008; Cassell et al., 2012). In practice, internal auditing can be considered as one of the central pillars of good corporate governance (Eulerich & Eulerich, 2020).
- Digital transformation combined with an increasing use of new technologies. It has an impact on the internal audit process and practices (Betti et al., 2021). Betti and Sarens (2021) have shown that

  > a digitalised business environment affects the internal audit function in three respects. First, it impacts its scope. The agility of the internal

> audit planning and the required digital knowledge are expected to increase and information technology (IT) risks gain importance, especially cybersecurity threats. Second, the demand for consulting activities performed by internal auditors is higher and third, digitalisation modifies the working practices of internal auditors in their day-to-day tasks. New technologies such as data analytics tools are being implemented progressively in internal audit departments and digital skills are considered a critical asset.
>
> (p. 872)

The identification of specific factors for IT audit

Regarding more specifically IT audits, several scholars have also identified their importance and have called for further research on this topic (Weidenmier & Ramamoorti, 2006; Curtis et al., 2009).

This attention to IT audit has been driven by two primary reasons. The first one can be explained by the increased spending and dependence on IT for business operations. The second one is due to legislation and professional requirements related to the audit of these operations. Stoel et al. (2012) have added that

> within the IT audit literature, there are a variety of resources to guide practitioners at the operational level. For example, the Information Systems Audit and Control Association's (ISACA) Control Objectives for Information and related Technology (COBIT®) provides a detailed series of potential controls and checklists. Additionally, there are many publications (e.g., Davis, 1997; Bagranoff and Vendrzyk, 2000; Petterson, 2005; Brody and Kearns, 2009) and textbooks (e.g., Hunton et al., 2004a; Hall and Singleton, 2005) which provide overviews of IT audit processes and specific direction for audit tasks.
>
> (p. 63)

At a general level, researchers should use creative settings and research designs to open up the black box of the audit process (DeFond & Zhang, 2014; Lenz et al., 2018). This perspective is closely related to the use of IT in auditing activities and audit IT as presented previously. As explained by Ramamoorti and Weidenmier

> the notion of relinquishing the "black box" approach (i.e., looking at inputs and outputs but ignoring the processing) and instead, "auditing through the computer," required an intimate understanding of the logic behind computer operations, code review, as well as other sophisticated approaches for verifying general controls, application controls, and processing results.
>
> (2003, p. 306)

At a theoretical level, several topics have been explored as summarized in Table 1.10. A focus on more recent research in the context of technological changes and digital transformation has been provided. Several concepts have moved from theory into practice (e.g., continuous auditing).

Table 1.10 Main insights on IT audit: current research and perspectives (2010–2022)

Topics	*Authors*
IT audit (challenges and opportunities in the era of digital transformation/impact of IT on internal audit)	Dzuranin and Mălăescu (2016); Moorthy et al. (2011)
IT audit process assessment	Popa (2011)
IT audit quality	Stoel et al. (2012); Alagic et al. (2018)
IT audit and compliance by design	Julisch et al. (2011)
IT audit governance	Gheorghe (2010); Putri et al. (2017); Iliescu (2010)
IT security audit	Herat and Herat (2014)
IT and continuous auditing (CA)	Kuhn and Sutton (2010); Chan and Vasarhelyi (2011)
IT audit and IT risk assessment	Goosen (2016)
IT and maturity model	Dutta et al. (2022)
IT audit training/education	Barkhi and Kozlowski (2017)
IT auditing and strategy	Skrynkovskyy (2018)

Source: Elaborated by the author.

Conclusion

For decades, the internal audit function has changed in response to the shifts in global business practices. The issue of the evolution of internal auditing in the context of digital transformation has been addressed by several authors. The IT audit area is in a state of constant innovation driven both by technology and stakeholder demands. These innovations combined with regulatory compliance requirements, the increased volume of available data, and emerging management challenges are changing the practice environment (Weidenmier & Ramamoorti, 2006; Dzuranin & Mălăescu, 2016).

The digital transformation not only opens opportunities for IT audit to play a more positive role but also raises challenges for IT audit practices, especially regarding the efficiency and effectiveness of IT as audit IT is more and more combined with new technologies (Chapters 4 and 5). In this context, as IT risk is one of the main concerns for top management, "defining IT audit universe and IT audit characteristics becomes a key element in driving the changing role of IT audit in order to become more relevant, forward-looking, and risk-focused" (Aditya et al., 2018).

Questions for discussion

What is digital transformation?

What are the effects of digital transformation on internal audit?

What is the role of IT audit in the era of digital transformation?

How can internal audit (and IT audit) drive digital value?

Internal audit and compliance in focus. Based on the LVMH group (Appendix 1), explain the primary function of the internal audit and discuss the Group compliance program on the protection of personal data (GDPR).

Recommended reading

Christ, M.H., Eulerich, M., & Wood, D.A. (2019). *Internal auditors' response to disruption and innovation*. Altamonte Springs, FL: The IIA Research Foundation. Retrieved January 13, 2022 from: http://theiia.mkt5790.com/ResponsetoDisruptiveInnovation.

Ramamoorti, S. (2003). Internal auditing: History, evolution, and prospects. In A. Bailey, A. Gramling, & S. Ramamoorti (Eds.), *Research opportunities in internal auditing* (pp. 1–23). Altamonte Springs, FL: The Institute of Internal Auditors.

Zaoui, F., & Souissi, N. (2020). Roadmap for digital transformation: A literature review. *Procedia Computer Science, 175*, 621–628. https://doi.org/10.1016/j.procs.2020.07.090

References

Aditya, B.R., Hartanto, R., & Nugroho, L.E. (2018). *The role of IT audit in the era of digital transformation*. IOP Conference Series: Materials Science and Engineering. International Conference on Informatics, Engineering, Science and Technology (INCITEST). Bandung, Indonesia. https://doi.org/10.1088/1757-899X/407/1/012164

Alagic, A., Turulja, L., & Bajgoric, N. (2018). IT audit quality factors identification in the function of business continuity: A systematic literature review. *Proceedings of the International Conference of the Faculty of Economics Sarajevo* (pp. 1–30). University of Sarajevo, School of Economics and Business. http://www.efsa.unsa.ba/ices2018/sites/default/files/ICES2018%20Conference%20Proceedings%20final%20version%20%282%29.pdf

Archambeault, D., DeZoort, F.T., & Holt, T. (2008). The need for internal auditor report to external stakeholders to improve governance transparency. *Accounting Horizons, 22*(4), 375–388. https://doi. org/10.2308/acch.2008.22.4.375

Autio, E. (2017). *Digitalisation, ecosystems, entrepreneurship and policy*. Policy Brief 20. Retrieved November 14, 2021 from: https://tietokayttoon.fi/documents/1927382/2116852/20_2017_Digitalisation%2C+ecosystems%2C+entrepreneurship+and+policy/6b383210-70de-491f-b0df-38de52699458?version=1.0

Bailey, D., Gramling, A.A., & Ramamoorti, S. (2003). *Research opportunities in internal auditing*. Altamonte Springs, FL: The Institute of Internal Auditors Research Foundation. Retrieved October 15, 2021 from: https://jabatanfungsionalauditor.files.wordpress.com/2016/06/research-opportunities-in-internal-auditing1.pdf

Bain & Company (2017). *Orchestrating a successful digital transformation. Business Insights.* Retrieved February 13, 2018 from: http://www.bain.com/publications/articles/-orchestrating-a-successful-digital-transformation.aspx.

Barkhi, R., & Kozlowski, S. (2017). ERP in the classroom: Three SAP exercises focused on internal controls. *Journal of Emerging Technologies in Accounting, 14*(1), 77–83.

Betti, N., & Sarens, G. (2021). Understanding the internal audit function in a digitalised business environment. *Journal of Accounting & Organizational Change, 17*(2), 197–216. https://doi.org/10.1108/JAOC-11-2019-0114

Betti, N., Sarens, G., & Poncin, I. (2021). Effects of digitalization of organisations on internal audit activities and practices. *Managerial Auditing Journal, 36*(6), 872–888. https://doi.org/10.1108/maj-08-2020-2792 Behrend, J., & Eulerich, M. (2019). The evolution of internal audit research: A bibliometric analysis. *Accounting History Review, 29*(1), 103–139.

Bockshecker, A., Hackstein, S., & Baumöl, U. (2018). Systematization of the term digital transformation and its phenomena from a socio-technical perspective – A literature review. *Research Papers* 43. ECIS. Retrieved August 29, 2021 from: https://aisel.aisnet.org/ecis2018_rp/43

Bogush, P. (2021). *Digitalization vs digitization – Knowing the difference.* Last updated 22 June, 2021. https://www.businesstechweekly.com/operational-efficiency/digital-transformation/digitalization-vs-digitization/

Capgemini (2018). *Digital transformation review series.* Retrieved March 11, 2020 from: https://www.capgemini.com/consulting/digital-transformation-institute/digital-transformation-review.

Capgemini Consulting & MIT (2011). *Digital transformation: A roadmap for billion-dollar organizations.* Retrieved April 5, 2018 from: https://www.capgemini.com/wp-content/uploads/2017/07/Digital_Transformation__A_Road-Map_for_Billion-Dollar_Organizations.pdf

Cassell, C.A., Giroux, G.A., Myers, L.A., & Omer, T.C. (2012). The effect of corporate governance on auditor–client realignments. *Auditing: A Journal of Practice and Theory, 31*(2), 167–188.

Chan, D.Y. & Vasarhelyi, M.A. (2011). Innovation and practice of continuous auditing. *International Journal of Accounting Information Systems, 12*(2), 152–160.

The Chartered Institute of Internal auditors (2020). *How to derive an IT audit universe*? 21 September 2020. Retrieved May 25, 2021 from: https://www.iia.org.uk/resources/managing-internal-audit/audit-universe/how-to-derive-an-it-audit-universe/?downloadPdf=true

Christ, M.H., Eulerich, M., Krane, R., & Wood, D.A. (2021). New frontiers for internal audit research. *Accounting Perspectives, 20*(4), 449–475. https://doi.org/10.1111/1911-3838.12272

Collins, L. & Vallin, G. (1992). *Audit & contrôle interne, aspects financiers, opérationnels et stratégiques.* Paris: Dalloz.

Committee of Sponsoring Organizations of the Treadway Commission (COSO) (2013). *2013 Internal control – Integrated framework.* Executive Summary. Retrieved October, 21, 2021 from: https://www.coso.org/Documents/990025P-Executive-Summary-final-may20.pdf

Curtis, M.B., Jenkins, J.G., Bedard, J.C., & Deis, D.R. (2009). Auditors' training and proficiency in information systems: A research synthesis. *Journal of Information Systems, 23*(1), 79–96. http://dx.doi.org/10.2308/jis.2009.23.1.79

Daidj, N. (2019). Strategic and Business-IT alignment under digitalization: Towards new insights? In K. Mezghani & W. Aloulou (Eds.), *Business transformations in the era of digitalization* (pp. 93–105). Hershey: IGI Global.

DeFond, M., & Zhang, J. (2014). A review of archival auditing research. *Journal of Accounting and Economics 58*(2–3), 275–326. http://dx.doi.org/10.1016/j.jacceco.2014.09.002

Deloitte (2015). Building your digital DNA. Digital transformation in progress. https://www2.deloitte.com/content/dam/Deloitte/be/Documents/technology/deloittedigital/Deloitte-Digital-BE_Building-your-digital-DNA_download_HR.pdf

Dutta, A., Roy, R., & Seetharaman, P. (2022). An assimilation maturity model for IT governance and auditing. Information & Management, 59(1). [103569]. http://dx.doi.org/10.1016/j.im.2021.103569

Dzuranin, A.C., & Mălăescu, I. (2016). The current state and future direction of IT audit: Challenges and opportunities. *Journal of Information Systems, 30*(1), 7–20. https://*doi*.org/10.2308/isys-51315

Elliott, R.K., & Jacobson, P.D. (1987). Audit technology: A heritage and a promise. *Journal of Accountancy, 163*(5), 198–217.

Eulerich, A.K., & Eulerich, M. (2020). What is the value of internal auditing? – A literature review on qualitative and quantitative perspectives. *Maandblad Voor Accountancy en Bedrijfseconomie, 94*(3/4), 83–92.

European Confederation of Institutes of Internal Auditing (ECIIA) (2021). *What is internal auditing?* Retrieved January 12, 2022 from: https://www.eciia.eu/what-is-internal-auditing/

European Confederation of Institutes of Internal Auditing (ECIIA)/The Federation of European Risk Management Associations – (FERMA) (2011). Guidance on the 8th EU Company Law Directive (article 41). Retrieved January 12, 2022 from: https://www.iia.nl/SiteFiles/ECIIA%20FERMA%20-2.pdf

Gheorghe, M. (2010). Audit methodology for IT governance. *Informatica Economica, 14*(1), 32–42.

Goodwin-Stewart J., & Kent, P. (2006) Relation between external audit fees, audit committee, characteristics and internal audit. *Accounting and Finance, 46*(3), 387–404. https://doi.org/10.1111/j.1467-629X.2006.00174.x

Goosen, R. (2016). The development of an integrated risk assessment questionnaire for internal auditor's use. *Southern African Journal of Accountability and Auditing Research – SAJAAR, 18*(1), 63–71.

Gramling, A.A., Maletta, M.J., Schneider, A., & Church, B.K. (2004). The role of the internal audit function in corporate governance: A synthesis of the extant internal auditing literature and directions for future research. *Journal of Accounting Literature, 23*, 194–244.

Gray, J. & Rumpe, B. (2017). Models for the digital transformation. *Software and Systems Modeling, 16*(2), 307–308.

Hapon, M. (2020). What is the difference between digitization, digitalization and digital transformation [updated, September 28, 2020]. https://www.netguru.com/blog/digitization-and-digitalization

Herath, H., & Herath, T. (2014). IT security auditing: A performance evaluation decision model. *Decision Support Systems, 57*, 54–63.

Iliescu, F.-M. (2010). Auditing IT governance. *Informatica Economica, 14*(1), 93–102.

INSEE (2021). *Definitions. Intermediate-sized enterprises / ETI. Small and medium enterprises / SME*. Retrieved October 15, 2021 from: https://www.insee.fr/en/metadonnees/definition/c2034 and https://www.insee.fr/en/metadonnees/definition/c1962

The Institute of Internal Auditors – (IIA) (2017). *Issue 8. Global perspectives and insights. Internal audit and external audit distinctive roles in organizational governance*. Retrieved October 17, 2021 from: https://global.theiia.org/knowledge/Public%20Documents/GPI-Distinctive-Roles-in-Organizational-Governance.pdf

The Institute of Internal Auditors – (IIA) (2013). *Global Technology Audit Guide 4-Management of IT auditing 2nd Edition*. Retrieved October 17, 2021 from: https://www.iia.nl/SiteFiles/IIA_leden/Praktijkgidsen/GTAG-4-2nd-Edition[1].pdf

The Institute of Internal Auditors (IIA) (2012). *Integrated auditing*. Retrieved October 17, 2021 from: https://www.iia.nl/SiteFiles/IIA_leden/Praktijkgidsen/PG%20Integrated%20Auditing[1].pdf

The Institute of Internal Auditors (IIA) – Australia (2020). *Internal audit standards*. Retrieved October 17, 2021 from: https://www.iia.org.au/sf_docs/default-source/quality/presentation-internal-audit-standards.pdf?sfvrsn=4

The Institute of Internal Auditors Research Foundation (2003). *Research opportunities in internal auditing*. Retrieved December 21, 2021 from: https://jabatanfungsionalauditor.files.wordpress.com/2016/06/research-opportunities-in-internal-auditing1.pdf

ISACA (2019). *COBIT® 2019 Design Guide: Designing an information and technology governance solution*. Retrieved June 19, 2021 from: https://www.isaca.org/-/media/files/isacadp/project/isaca/articles/journal/2019/volume-3/developing-the-it-audit-plan-using-cobit-2019_joa_eng_0519

ISO (2021). *ISO (19011:2011). Guidelines for auditing management systems*. Retrieved November 5, 2021 from: https://www.iso.org/obp/ui/fr/#iso:std:iso:19011:ed-2:v1:en:fr

Janvrin, D., Bierstaker, J., & Lowe, D. (2008). An examination of audit information technology use and perceived importance. *Accounting Horizons, 22*(1), 1–21. https://doi.org/10.2308/acch.2008.22.1.1

Julisch, K., Suter, C., Woitalla, T., & Zimmermann, O. (2011). Compliance by design – Bridging the chasm between auditors and IT architects. *Computers & Security, 30*(6–7), 410–426.

Kane, G.C. (2017). Digital maturity, not digital transformation. MIT Sloan Management Review, April 4. Retrieved September 16, 2021, from: https://sloanreview.mit.edu/article/digital-maturity-not-digital-transformation/

KPMG (2016). *Transforming internal audit: A maturity model from data analytics to continuous assurance*. Retrieved November 2, 2021 from: https://assets.kpmg/content/dam/kpmg/pdf/2016/05/Transforming-Internal-Audit.pdf

Kotb, A., Elbardan, H., & Halabi, H. (2020). Mapping of internal audit research: A post-Enron structured literature review. *Accounting, Auditing & Accountability Journal, 33*(8), 1969–1996. https://doi.org/10.1108/AAAJ-07-2018-3581

Kuhn, J.R., & Sutton, S.G. (2010). Continuous auditing in ERP system environments: The current state and future directions. *Journal of Information Systems, 24*, 91–112.

Lenz, R., & Hahn, U. (2015). A synthesis of empirical internal audit effectiveness literature pointing to new research opportunities. *Managerial Auditing Journal, 30* (1), 5–33. https://doi.org/10.1108/MAJ-08-2014-1072

Lenz, R., Sarens, G., & Jeppesen, K. (2018). In search of a measure of effectiveness for internal audit functions: An institutional perspective. *EDPACS: The EDP Audit, Control, and Security Newsletter, 58*(2), 1–36.

Lesage, C., & Wechtler, H. (2010). An inductive typology of auditing research. *Contemporary Accounting Research, 29(*2), 487–504. http://dx.doi.org/10.2139/ssrn.1173054

Lisch, R. (2014). *Measuring service performance: Practical research for better quality*. London: Routledge.

LVMH (2020). 2020 Universal Registration Document. Fiscal year ended December 31, 2020. Retrieved October 21, 2021 from: https://r.lvmh-static.com/uploads/2020/06/lvmh-document-denregistrement-2020-va-interactif.pdf

Mazars (2021). *The future of audit: Market view. Myths, realities and ways forward*. Retrieved November 6, 2021 from: https://www.mazars.com/content/download/1036511/54076648/version//file/The%20Future%20of%20Audit%20Market%20view.pdf

McKinsey (2021). *Building the internal-audit function of the future*. February 18. Retrieved October 17, 2021 from: https://www.mckinsey.com/business-functions/risk-and-resilience/our-insights/building-the-internal-audit-function-of-the-future

McKinsey (2018). *Unlocking success in digital transformations*. Survey. Retrieved October 17, 2021 from: https://www.mckinsey.com/business-functions/people-and-organizational-performance/our-insights/unlocking-success-in-digital-transformations

Moorthy, M.K., Mohamed, A.Z., Gopalan, M., & San, L. (2011). The impact of information technology on internal auditing. *African Journal of Business Management, 5*(9), 3523–3539.

OECD (2020). Digital innovation: Cross-sectoral dynamics and policy implications. In OECD (Ed.), *The digitalisation of science, technology and innovation: Key developments and policies* (pp. 99–118). Paris: OECD Publishing. https://doi.org/10.1787/ee2a2c2f-en

OECD (2019). *Digital innovation: Seizing policy opportunities*. Paris: OECD Publishing. https://doi.org/10.1787/a298dc87-en

OECD (2017). *The next production revolution: Implications for governments and business*. Paris: OECD Publishing. https://doi.org/10.1787/9789264271036-en

Petraşcu, D., & Tamas, A. (2013). Internal audit versus internal control and coaching. *Procedia Economics and Finance, 6*, 694–702.

Popa, M. (2011). Framework for evaluation of the IT&C audit metrics impact. *Informatica Economica, 15*(4), 119–133.

Putri, M.A., Lestari, V.A., & Aknuranda, I. (2017). Audit of information technology governance using COBIT 4.1: Case study in PT.XY. *Internetworking Indonesia, 9*(1), 47–52.

PWC (2020). *Digital Factories 2020. Shaping the future of manufacturing*. Retrieved March 17, 2021 from: https://www.pwc.de/de/digitale-transformation/digital-factories-2020-shaping-the-future-of-manufacturing.pdf

Ramamoorti, S., & Weidenmier, M.L. (2003). The pervasive impact of information technology on internal auditing. In A. Bailey, A. Gramling, A. & S. Ramamoorti (Eds.), *Research opportunities in internal auditing* (pp. 301–373).Altamonte Springs, FL: The Institute of Internal Auditors.

Rosli, K., Yeow, P., & Eu-Gene, S. (2013). Adoption of audit technology in audit firms. In H. Deng & C. Standing (Eds.), *Information systems: Transforming the future: Proceedings of the 24th Australasian Conference on Information Systems* (pp. 1–12),

Melbourne, Australia, 4–6 December. Melbourne: Royal Melbourne Institute of Technology (RMIT) University.

Roussy, M., & Perron, A. (2018). New perspectives in internal audit research: A structured literature review. *Accounting Perspectives, 17*(3), 345–385. https://doi.org/10.1111/1911-3838.12180

SiaPartners (2016). *From our experts.* Retrieved November 28, 2019 from: https://www.sia-partners.com/fr/actualites-et-publications/de-nos-experts/quelle-strategie-pour-laudit-interne

Statista (2021). *Revenue of the Big Four accounting / audit firms worldwide in 2020.* Retrieved on November 2, 2021 from: https://www.statista.com/statistics/250479/big-four-accounting-firms-global-revenue/

Stoel, D., Havelka, D., & Merhout, J.W. (2012). An analysis of attributes that impact information technology audit quality: A study of IT and financial audit practitioners. *International Journal of Accounting Information Systems, 13*, 60–79.

Skrynkovskyy, R. M. (2018). An IT audit as a tool for strategic enterprise management. *The Problems of Economy, 1*, 231–236.

Tilson, D., Lyytinen, K., & Sørensen, C. (2010). Research commentary—Digital infrastructures: The missing IS research agenda. *Information System Research, 21*(4), 748–759.

Vial, G. (2019). Understanding digital transformation: A review and a research agenda, *The Journal of Strategic Information Systems, 28*(2), 118–144. https://doi.org/10.1016/j.jsis.2019.01.003

Weidenmier, M.L., & Ramamoorti, S. (2006). Research opportunities in information technology and internal auditing. *Journal of Information Systems, 20*(1), 205–219. https://doi.org/10.2308/jis.2006.20.1.205

World Economic Forum (2016). *Digital transformation of industries. Demystifying digital and securing $100 trillion for society and industry by 2025.* Retrieved April 3, 2021 from: http://reports.weforum.org/digital-transformation/wp-content/blogs.dir/94/mp/files/pages/files/wef-digital-transformation-2016-exec-summary.pdf

Appendix 1.1

Audit and internal control practices in the LVMH group (As December 31, 2020)

As an insight into the respective roles of control and audit activities, it is interesting to note in the LVMH 2020 financial document, internal audit is mentioned 14 times while internal control is quoted 113 times. The following excerpts illustrate the extent to which these core activities are intertwined at several levels.

Second line of defense

The Internal Control Department, which reports to the Audit & Internal Control Director, coordinates the implementation of internal control and risk management systems. It monitors and anticipates regulatory changes in order to adapt mechanisms. It coordinates a network of internal controllers responsible, within the Maisons and under the responsibility of their Management Committees, for ensuring compliance with the Group's internal control procedures and preparing controls tailored to their businesses. They also spearhead various projects related to the internal control and risk management systems and promote the dissemination and application of guidelines.

Third line of defense

The Audit & Internal Control Department covers the entire Group and operates according to an audit plan, which is revised annually. The audit plan is used to monitor and reinforce the understanding and correct application of expected control activities. The audit plan is prepared on the basis of an analysis of potential risks, either existing or emerging, by type of business (such as size, contribution to profits, geographical location, quality of local management, etc.) and on the basis of meetings held with the operational managers concerned; it can be modified during the year in response to changes in the political and economic environment or internal strategy.

The audit teams conduct internal control assessments covering various operational and financial processes. They also undertake accounting audits as well as audits of cross-functional issues within a given business segment. Regular follow-ups are run on the internal control recommendations resulting from past audits at subsidiaries with the most significant internal control issues. (...)

The main features of the audit plan, the primary conclusions of the current year, and the follow-up of the principal recommendations of previous assignments are presented to the Performance Audit Committee.

The main responsibilities of the Performance Audit Committee are to:

- monitor the process of preparing financial and non-financial information, in particular, the parent company and consolidated financial statements and, where applicable, make recommendations to ensure their integrity;
- monitor the work of the Statutory Auditors, taking into account, where applicable, the observations and findings of the Haut Conseil du Commissariat aux Comptes (the supervisory body for the French audit industry) on checks carried out by it pursuant to Articles L. 821-9 et seq. of the French Commercial Code;
- ensure the existence, pertinence, application and effectiveness of internal control, risk management including risks of a social and environmental nature, and internal audit procedures; monitor the ongoing effectiveness of those procedures; and make recommendations to Executive Management on the priorities and general direction of the work of the Internal Audit function;
- analyze the Company's and the Group's exposure to risks, and, in particular, to those risks identified by internal control and risk management systems, including those of a social and environmental nature, as well as material off-balance sheet commitments of the Company and the "Group."

Source: LVMH (2020). Extracts (https://r.lvmh-static.com/uploads/2020/06/lvmh-document-denregistrement-2020-va-interactif.pdf).

Given the acute sensitivity of civil society with regard to security and use of personal data, the tightening of rules and the greater severity of penalties, as well as the fragmentation of laws and their increasing complexity, it is essential to ensure adequate governance.

In an era of innovation for the Group, which is moving ahead with an ambitious digital strategy, resolutely focused on its customers and their aspirations, LVMH must offer services that guarantee perfect compliance. This means building and promoting a personal data protection culture that permeates all the Group's business lines and activities as well as taking into account the resulting technical and methodological developments. To ensure a consistent, effective approach, a data protection policy is proposed to all Maisons in order to provide them with a common framework of rules and recommendations, helping ensure that appropriate measures are taken suitable to protect personal data within the LVMH group worldwide, in compliance with applicable regulations.

Source: LVMH (2020). Extracts (https://r.lvmh-static.com/uploads/2014/10/extract-from-the-2018-reference-document-ethics-responsibility.pdf).

2 Aligning internal audit with the organization's strategy

Introduction

This chapter focuses on several key concepts in relation to strategic planning and business IT alignment. How has internal audit addressed these issues over the past decades?

Over the years, the aims of strategic planning – strategic fit and most efficient resource allocation – have remained constant. However, the environment in which companies run and plan their business has changed significantly, becoming more dynamic, very competitive, and global. Improvements in information processing have led to major changes in most industries. The extremely competitive business environment in which companies operate today in the digital economy requires them to use strategic planning to manage more efficiently.

Internal audit has accurate knowledge of systems and controls in organizations. As such function in organizations, it should play a key role in the process of strategic planning. Decision makers should have reliable source of information (including reports and recommendation made by internal auditors) to use in process of strategic planning. The position of internal audit in the process of strategic planning is significant, useful, and valuable for the organization.

As the balanced scorecard (BSC) is a strategic planning system and methodology, its main insights are presented here. Since its introduction in the early 1990s, the BSC has evolved from a performance measurement tool to a strategic management tool. It is a common tool to measure internal audit performance.

From strategic/IT planning to strategic/IT alignment, there is just a step forward. Strategic alignment of IT with the business objectives is a critical success factor for many companies (Bodnar, 2006; Daidj, 2019). Strategy and business-IT issues are closely related and should be more combined in order to achieve a competitive advantage that might be called a 'digital competitive advantage'. Several scholars have stressed the need for companies to take into account all these dimensions in a digital strategy (Bharadwaj et al., 2013; Drnevich & Croson, 2013; Mithas et al., 2013; Pagani, 2013). Increasingly,

DOI: 10.4324/9781003215110-3

the audit function is becoming strategic and reflects the need for alignment for a given company at all levels: strategy – organization – functions – business lines – information systems – processes.

Following this introduction, the remainder of this chapter is structured as follows. The first section surveys past research on the state of strategic planning and internal audit. The subsequent section introduces the BSC in relation to auditing activities, and the third section raises the question of strategic IT/IS alignment. Several authors have conducted various analyses with different research scopes to detect and correct misalignment. The theoretical approaches mainly focus on how organizations can achieve alignment, but with less contribution on how the internal audit could be aligned.

Strategic planning and internal audit

Back to basics

Robert N. Anthony is the author of *Planning and Control Systems* (1965), one of the books that laid the foundation for strategic planning. The traditional strategic planning model is the fit model of strategy making aiming at achieving a fit between internal resources and external environment. This "fit issue" will be addressed in the strategic IS alignment models that will be analyzed in the next section of this chapter.

The strategic planning models take into consideration available resources and analyze the feasibility of alternative strategies using existing internal resources and competencies. Strategic planners should then conduct analyses of internal and external diagnosis. Strategic planning must take into account both the company's complexity and its relevant environment.

Strategic planning focuses on managing interaction with environmental forces, which include competitors, government, suppliers, customers, various interest groups, and other stakeholders. Managers have then to collect and analyze information about the business environment but also to have an in-depth and accurate knowledge of their company (core business and internal characteristics) in order to develop a clear mission, goals, and objectives (current and future) and to effect long-term planning.

Long-range (or strategic) planning is the function that involves setting goals and deciding how to achieve them. It helps the organization to move in a direction while operating in an efficient and effective manner. Planning could aid in the anticipation of major strategic issues and in the recognition of environmental (industry, technology) changes (see below). Eadie (1991) has defined a strategic issue as a "major change challenge – opportunities and problems that appear to demand an organizational response, so a successful balance can be maintained between the organization's internal and external environments" (pp. 292–293). Strategic planning gives direction to action. The strategic management process allows the best allocation of resources and identifies future costs and returns from various alternatives.

Links between strategic planning and internal audit

Several academia have highlighted the linkages between internal audit and strategic planning adopting accordingly a strategic perspective. Audit and/or consulting firms have also proposed several definitions. "The strategic planning process for internal audit begins with the development of the strategic vision – a picture of what the internal audit function would look like at the end of its two- to five-year strategic planning horizon" (Wolters Kluwer, 2019, p. 7). As internal auditors provide information for the decision-making process, which in some level involves internal auditors in the process of decision-making. Internal auditors should be also more involved in process of strategic planning (Table 2.1).

> In our disruptive environment, strategic planning has become a logical candidate for increased Internal Audit involvement. Boards are recognizing that their role goes beyond approving management's plan, to assisting in development, ensuring communication, and overseeing the results of the strategy. In this context, the board needs assurance that an appropriate planning process exists and has been utilized.
>
> (Deloitte, 2016, p. 6)

In addition, various tools have been elaborated to further integrate internal auditing into a strategic planning perspective. PWC (2015) suggests, for example, the adoption of an approach based on six steps for developing an internal audit strategic plan. A strategic plan includes generally prescription for internal audit's evolution for maintaining its relevance and value as the business transform (Exhibit 2.1).

Table 2.1 The internal auditor's role

Although achieving and maintaining IT-business alignment is really a management issue, the internal audit department can help. Internal audit evaluation of an organization's strategic planning efforts, including how IT supports the business priorities, can provide valuable feedback to the board and senior management. An audit of IT investment processes should determine whether:

- significant business priorities are appropriately identified and assessed on an ongoing basis;
- changes to those priorities are monitored;
- significant investment management controls are operating effectively and consistently;
- risk-management techniques are in place and effective;
- management and staff have the processes in place to recognize and respond to new business opportunities as they arise; and
- IT-related investments are effectively and efficiently managed.

Source: Spencer Pickett (2010, p. 590).

Exhibit 2.1 Internal audit's strategic planning process: phases and objectives

Phase 1 – Develop mission and set vision
Phase 2 – Understand organizational plans and assess needs
Phase 3 – Perform a SWOT analysis to identify gaps
Phase 4 – Define initiatives to fill gaps and develop a roadmap
Phase 5 – Ensure stakeholder alignment and develop communication plan
Phase 6 – Identify key performance indicators (KPIs) to measure success

Source: Adapted from PWC (2015, p. 3).

Finally, the internal audit could also review the strategic planning process. In its report entitled: "Nine ways to strengthen Internal Audit's impact and influence in the organization," Deloitte (2016) has devoted a chapter to the review of the strategic planning process. The expression of strategic planning is mentioned more than once. As explained by Deloitte (2016),

> In many organizations, internal audit will be prompting the audit committee to ensure that the board is fully engaged in strategic planning. It's a key governance and oversight issue, particularly with regard to the data that management relies upon, the models planners use, and the assumptions management makes. (p. 6)

A renewed debate on strategic planning

Limitations of the concept of strategic planning

Many scholars have questioned the notion of strategic planning for a long time. Mintzberg et al. (1998) have analyzed the five types of management (strategy as a plan, ploy, pattern, position, and perspective) into "10 schools of thought." They describe for each of them, its history and origins, basic concepts, applications, advantages, and disadvantages. The ten schools are the following:

The Design School – Strategy formation is a process of conception
The Planning School – Strategy formation as a formal process
The Positioning School – Strategy formation as an analytical process
The Entrepreneurial School – Strategy formation as a visionary process
The Cognitive School – Strategy formation as a mental process
The Learning School – Strategy formation as an emergent process
The Power School – Strategy formation as a collective process

The Cultural School – Strategy formation as a collective process
The Environmental School – Strategy formation as a reactive process
The Configuration School – Strategy formation as a process of transformation

Regarding more precisely the planning school, it has been considered as a prescriptive approach based on strategy formation seen as a formal process, which follows a rigorous set of steps from analysis of the situation to the development and exploration of various alternative scenarios. The strategic planning approach aiming at enhancing the performance of the organization has been questioned, for example, for public organizations (Bovaird, 2008; George et al., 2018) or criticized at a more general level (Mintzberg, 1994; Martin, 2014).

In his famous paper and book entitled *The Rise and Fall of Strategic Planning* (1994), Mintzberg has explained that strategic planning in its conventional form is not the same as strategic thinking. He has described "three fallacies": the fallacy of prediction, the fallacy of detachment, and the fallacy of formalization.

> According to the premises of strategic planning, the world is supposed to hold still while a plan is being developed and then stay on the predicted course while that plan is being implemented (…). How in the world can any company know the period for which it can forecast with a given accuracy? (…). Contrary to what traditional planning would have us believe, deliberate strategies are not necessarily good, nor are emergent strategies necessarily bad. I believe that all viable strategies have emergent and deliberate qualities, since all must combine some degree of flexible learning with some degree of cerebral control. (. . .) Formal procedures will never be able to forecast discontinuities, inform detached managers, or create novel strategies. Far from providing strategies, planning could not process without their prior existence. All this time, therefore, strategic planning has been misnamed. It should have been called strategic programming, distinguished from other useful things that planners can do, and promoted as a process to formalize, when necessary, the consequences of strategies that have already been developed. In short, we should drop the label "strategic planning" altogether.
>
> (pp. 111–112)

Toward agile practices

Limitations of strategic planning are numerous as summarized above. Strategic planning does not identify all critical issues related to the organization. The dominance of a structured strategy process is questionable in a context where uncertainty and ambiguity predominate and where it is difficult to articulate strategic intent (Ciborra, 1997).

> In the vast majority of companies, strategic planning is a calendar-driven ritual (. . .) [which assumes] that the future will be more or less like the present' (. . .). The essential problem in organizations today is a failure to distinguish planning from strategizing.
>
> (Hamel, 1996, pp. 70–71)

Several authors such as Salmela et al. (2000) have then asserted that even in turbulent environments, comprehensive planning can be beneficial, Grant (2003) showed that planning systems could even foster adaptation and responsiveness. But more and more companies have developed several responses to the planning challenges in order to have a more "agile" strategic planning process.

The "agility" concept was created in 1991 by a group of researchers at the Iacocca Institute (Lehigh University, USA). They defined it as "a manufacturing system with extraordinary capabilities (Internal capabilities: hard and soft technologies, human resources, educated management, information) to meet the rapidly changing needs of the marketplace (speed, flexibility, customers, competitors, suppliers, infrastructure, responsiveness). A system that shifts quickly (speed and responsiveness) among product models or between product lines (flexibility), ideally in real-time response to customer demand (customer needs and wants)."

Principles of agility have been then applied to other functions of enterprise, and the "agile enterprise" concept was created (Goldman et al., 1995). Doz and Kosonen (2010) have defined strategic agility "as the 'thoughtful and purposive interplay' on the part of top management between three 'meta-capabilities'."(p. 371). These capabilities are linked with strategic sensitivity (the sharpness of perception of, and the intensity of awareness and attention to, strategic developments), leadership unity (the ability of the top team to make bold, fast decisions, without being bogged down in top-level 'win-lose' politics), and resource fluidity (the internal capability to reconfigure capabilities and redeploy resources rapidly).

Internal and external obstacles can impede companies from meeting these "agility" requirements. At the internal level, within a company there are a range of elements that may reduce the effectiveness of these practices, such as divergent goals and priorities, risk-averse cultures and silo-based information and organizational structure. Agile approaches are recognized as being more productive than traditional approaches (Chapters 3 and 4).

Information technology (IT)/information system (IS) strategic planning

In parallel to research on strategic planning, other scholars have combined the topic of planning with IT and IS dimensions. Practitioners as well as researchers have consistently considered IT and IS planning as a very important topic.

> Despite a history of neglected planning, IS needs effective strategic planning as much as, and perhaps more than, other functional areas. (...) Systems without planning will mean, for most organizations, not only financial losses but additional hidden, and often greater, costs such as lowered staff morale, missed opportunities, continuous management fire-fighting, and customer dissatisfaction.
>
> (Robson, 1994, p. 81)

At a general level, IT strategic planning aims at determining strategic directions for technology decisions, providing adequate tools and involving the entire organization where everyone is aware that his/her mission/job is a part of the IT process. Strategic planning for information systems (IS) is defined as the process of identifying a portfolio of computer-based applications that will support an organization in executing its business plan and consequently achieving its business and strategic goals (King & Teo, 2000). Linkages between IS and business strategy in correlation with strategic planning have been recognized by several scholars (Porter & Millar, 1985; Ward et al., 1990). IS strategy can impact business strategy and the IS planning process can impact the business planning process (see below the presentation of alignment models).

Several expressions have then emerged in the 1980s and 1990s (Amrollahi et al., 2013) to refer to the integration of IT and IS in strategic planning frameworks as follows:

- strategic information system planning (SISP),
- information system planning (ISP),
- information technology planning (ITP),
- information resource planning (IRP).
- strategic information management (SIM) planning,

Table 2.2 presents the main insights of the literature review.

At this stage, it is possible to make some preliminary comments:

- The definition of each expression has many variations and has evolved since the end of the 1980s. There is a parallel evolution between technology and IT environment changes and the development of renewed strategic/IT planning concepts and models. New requirements must be taken into account (fierce market competition, disruptive technology, strict compliance, etc.). As mentioned by Doherty et al. (1999), "differences between SISP, and the planning practices that pre-dated it, are in terms of its explicit emphasis on strategic alignment and competitive impact" (p. 264).
- There is a need for IT or IS systems planning whatever the appellation used (SISP, ISP, ITP, etc.). Successful planning is important to the realization of the potential strategic impact of information systems.
- To provide a comprehensive view of IT/IS planning, several studies have emphasized the need to start with the identification of the business

Table 2.2 Various definitions and expressions in the literature

Authors/ reference	*Term*	*Definition*
Lederer and Sethi (1988)	Strategic information system planning (SISP)	SISP is "the process of deciding the objectives for organizational computing and identifying potential computer applications which the organization should implement" (p. 445).
Hevner et al. (2000)	Strategic information system planning (SISP)	SISP "is the process of aligning an organization's business strategy with effective computer-based information systems to achieve critical business objectives" (p. 1).
Teo and King (1997)	Information system planning (ISP)	ISP can be defined "as the process of establishing objectives for organizational computing and identifying potential applications that the organization should implement (Lederer & Sethi, 1991 and 1992). ISP has become increasingly important as organizations attempt to leverage information systems (IS) applications to improve efficiency, reengineer business processes, gain competitive advantage, and compete more effectively. For ISP to be effective, it is crucial that IS plans be aligned with business plans so that IS can more effectively support business strategies." (pp. 185–186).
Fergerson (2012)	Information system planning (ISP)	It is "a set of activities directed toward achieving three objectives: (a) recognizing organizational opportunities and problems where IS might be applied successfully; (b) identifying the resources needed to allow IS to be applied successfully to these opportunities and problems; and (c) developing strategies and procedures to allow IS to be applied successfully to these opportunities and problems. (Hann & Weber, 1996, p. 1044)" (p. 9).
Boynton and Zmud (1987)	Information technology planning (ITP)	ITP is defined as "organizational activities directed toward (1) recognizing organizational opportunities for using information technology, (2) determining the resource requirements to exploit these opportunities, and (3) developing strategies and action plans for realizing these opportunities and for meeting the resource needs. Information technology resources include the hardware, software and personnel used in supporting electronically based information processing, including data, text, voice and image forms of information." (p. 59).

Fallshaw (2000)	Information technology planning (ITP)	"Identification of the external factors that would affect and influence strategic directions; consideration of IT trends and emerging technologies; a review and assessment of the current IT environment; and finally identifying the strategies and actions required to implement this vision" (p. 195)
Singh and Beyer (1990)	Information resource planning (IRP)	"IRP is an integration of the process-driven and data-driven approaches for planning the implementation of information technology in support of business goals and objectives. Using a disciplined yet flexible approach, IRP develops a migration strategy for smooth transition from the business environment to the automated environment" (p. 634).
Lin et al. (2012)	Information resource planning (IRP)	"IRP refers to the comprehensive planning, including collection, processing, transmission to the usage, for the information that the governments or enterprises need. It is the overall planning focusing on analysis of data, to integrate information resources, to eliminate islands of information and to achieve the sharing of information resources (Gao, 2002). Information resource planning can be briefly described as "five criteria, three models, and two stages." Five criteria are: data element standard, information classification coding standard, standard user view standards, concept database standards and logical database standards; three models are: system function model, system data model, system architecture model; two stages are: requirements analysis phase and system modeling phase" (p. 1497).

Source: Based on the articles cited.

process of an organization (management, core, support). The second step is to establish clear criteria for selecting specific processes for improvement. Several tools can be used to optimize processes such as Business process management (BPM) which is a software solution to automate repetitive tasks and to analyze process workflows.

- Planning has been itself characterized as a learning process.
- Alignment is mentioned in most definitions as well. Not surprisingly, alignment between business and IT has been often considered as the key objective of SISP (Chen et al. 2010; Karanja & Patel, 2012; Silvius & Stoop, 2013; Maharaj & Brown, 2015).

Strategic planning, BSC, and internal audit

Strategic Planning and BSC are among the approaches and models that focus on planning and performance assessment of organizations. The BSC provides a framework for strategic planning and performance management. The BSC has been also often considered as a methodology for strategic planning. It has been selected as one of the 75 most influential business ideas of the 20th century by the Harvard Business Review as Niven (2005, p. 16) has pointed out. The second part of this section is dedicated to the usage of the BSC model to measure the performance of the internal audit function.

The initial BSC concept

The BSC is an effective strategic planning tool that gives managers a general overview of how well the organization is succeeding in meeting its mission and vision. The concept of the BSC was developed in the early 1990s by Kaplan and Norton (1992). It has broader applications on the planning side even if it was originally conceived as an improved performance measurement system in order to determine if the organization is properly aligned and to improve shareholder value. "If you can't measure it, you can't manage it" (Kaplan & Norton, 1996, p. 21).

The BSC focuses on both financial and non-financial performance targets and outcomes (customer satisfaction, business process, and learning measures). Kaplan and Norton have basically distinguished between lagging (measuring results) and leading indicators (predictive measurement). There should be then a balance between performance drivers (leading indicators) and outcome measures (lagging indicators). Well-designed balanced scorecards can be very effective in ensuring consistency of objectives through the utilization of both financial and nonfinancial measures. Performance drivers communicate the way to achieve goals, and they indicate early on whether strategies are being implemented successfully. Outcome measures could enable the business unit to make long-term operational improvements and to enhance financial performance (Wu, 2012). The optimal model of BSC should have an appropriate mix of performance drivers and outcome measures that have been tailored to the business unit's strategy (Frigo et al., 2000).

The BSC is a logical strategic framework organized across four key perspectives (Kaplan & Norton, 2000) leading to the identification of the critical drivers of success:

- Financial perspective increases value from new products and customers, increases customer value, improves cost structure, and improves asset utilization (the financial perspective could be measured by numerous indicators as operating income (OI), return on equity, economic value added (EVA), cash flow, earnings per share (EPS), revenue growth, sales growth, inventory turnover, market share, etc.).

- Customer perspective includes customer value proposition (the customer perspective is measured in part by indicators of customer satisfaction, on-time delivery, customer loyalty, number of new customers, etc.).
- Internal perspective focuses on processes that create new products and services, customer management processes, operations and logistics processes, and regulatory and environmental processes (the internal business perspective is measured in part by indicators such as cycle time, unit cost, yield, number of defects produced, quality, etc.).
- Organizational learning and growth perspective include employee competencies, technology, corporate culture (the innovation and learning perspective is measured in part by indicators such as percent of sales from new products, number of employee suggestions that are adopted, turnover rates, hours of employee training, employee skill development, scope of process improvements, etc.).

The BSC provides the answer to four basic questions:

- How does the company appear to its shareholders?
- How do customers view the company?
- What business processes must the firm improve and exceed at?
- Can the company continue to learn, to innovate, and create value?

The BSC can be considered as a prescriptive framework that translates the organization's strategy into several perspectives, with a balance between short-term and longer-term strategic goals, internal and external measures, performance results, and the drivers of future results. Figge et al. (2002) have added that the BSC is a management tool that supports the successful implementation of corporate strategies.

Linkages between the IT BSC and alignment

Several authors have attempted to provide an integrated framework for linking the BSC to other concepts. It is in relation to strategic/IT alignment that the contributions of BSC are most noteworthy. The BSC could be used as an effective framework to improve the strategic alignment process in an organization. "The importance of strategic alignment has been stated frequently (Earl, 1996; Labovitz and Rosansky, 1997; Corrall, 2000), indeed, Galliers and Newell (2003) call it a central tenet of much of the theory and practice of IS strategy" (Avison et al., 2004, p. 224). Alignment issues will be addressed in-depth below.

Traditional strategic management involves a search for the strategic fit between business portfolios, market niches and products, customers, and distribution channels. Strategic fit represents the degree to which a company is matching its resources and competencies with the opportunities in the external environment. Strategic fit is closely related to the resource-based view (RBV) of the firm which explains that the key to profitability is rather through unique characteristics of the company's resources and competencies. Several broad definitions have been formulated by scholars from the strategy field. "Strategy is the act of aligning a company and its environment" (Porter, 1991, p. 4).

In parallel, since the end of the 1990s, the BSC has been progressively applied to the IT function, and its processes, as Gold (1992, 1994) and Willcocks (1995) have conceptually described it. It has been further developed by Van Grembergen and Van Bruggen (1997), Van Grembergen and Timmerman (1998), Van Grembergen (2000) and Van Grembergen et al. (2003). BSC can be applied for the IT function within an organization in order to assess its performance along the four perspectives of the scorecard. The impact of IT investments can be traced, directly or indirectly, to changes in the financial performance of the organization (Addo et al., 2004).

Van Grembergen (2000) has defined the relationships between IT scorecards and the BSC (Exhibit 2.2). These relationships have to be defined throughout the scorecard to address all elements and to link with the business through the business contribution perspective. The author uses the term of "cascade" to describe theses links.

> The IT Development BSC and the IT Operational BSC both are enablers of the IT Strategic BSC that in turn is the enabler of the Business BSC. This cascade of scorecards becomes a linked set of measures that will be instrumental in aligning IT and business strategy and that will help to determine how business value is created through IT
>
> (p. 42)

The IT balanced scorecard can also support the governance process, because it bundles the business with IT (Van Grembergen, 2000; Son et al., 2005).

Van Grembergen (2000) has presented the standard IT BSC based on four orientations (user orientation, business contribution, operational excellence, and future orientation) for which a specific mission and various strategies are defined (Table 2.3). Each orientation should be combined with

Exhibit 2.2 The representation of the IT BSC

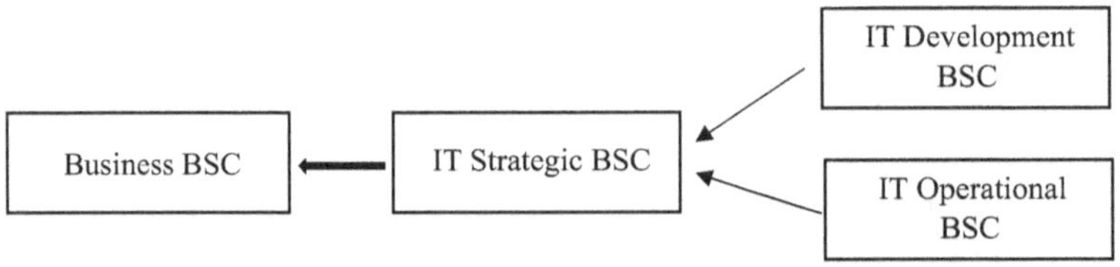

Source: Adapted and based on Van Grembergen (2000, p. 43).

Table 2.3 Standard IT BSC

	Perspective questions	*Mission*	*Strategies*
User/customer orientation	How do users view the IT department? / How should IT appear to business unit executives to be considered effective in delivering its services?	to be the preferred supplier of information systems	preferred supplier of applications preferred supplier of operations vs. proposer of best solution, from whatever source partnership with users user satisfaction
Operational excellence	How effective and efficient are the IT processes? At which services and processes must IT excel to satisfy the stakeholders and customers?	to deliver effective and efficient IT applications and services	efficient and effective developments efficient and effective operations
Business / corporate contribution	How does management view the IT department? How should IT appear to the company executive and its corporate functions to be considered a significant contributor to company success?	to obtain a reasonable business	control of IT expenses business value of IT projects provide new business capabilities
Future orientation	How well is IT positioned to meet future needs? How will IT develop the ability to deliver effectively and to continuously learn and improve its performance?	to develop opportunities to answer future challenges	training and education of IT staff expertise of IT staff research into emerging technologies age of application portfolio

Source: Adapted and based on Van Grembergen (2000, p. 43) and Van Grembergen, De Haes & Guldentops (2003, p. 26).

corresponding metrics and measures that assess the current situation. These assessments should be conducted on a regular basis to adjust the IT strategy and the targeting of measures if necessary.

In 2016, the IT Governance Institute (ITGI) published the second edition of its report entitled "Board Briefing on IT governance" based, in particular, on *Control Objectives for Information and related Technology* (COBIT) one of the most adopted IT control frameworks internationally (Chapter 4). The authors of the report have adopted a similar approach to that described and analyzed by Van Grembergen (2000) and Van Grembergen et al. (2003). To apply the balanced scorecard concepts to the IT function, the four perspectives need to be redefined. To demonstrate the value IT delivers to the business requires cause-and-effect relationships between two types of measures throughout the scorecard: outcomes measures (measuring what you have done) and performance drivers (measuring how you are doing). A well-developed IT BSC contains a good mix of these two types of measures and should link to the higher-level business scorecards (Table 2.4).

In a book chapter published in 2003, Van Grembergen, Saull, and De Haes have combined the IT BSC with the requirements with alignment (Figure 2.1). The main insights of their research can be summarized as follows:

- The elaboration of both scorecards should start simultaneously as it requires both IT and senior management to discuss the opportunities of information technologies which support the IT/business alignment and IT governance process.
- The IT scorecard technique must be considered as a supportive mechanism for IT/business alignment and IT governance.

The BSC perspectives for internal auditing?

Several scholars have mentioned the links between the BSC and internal auditing. Amongst the seminal research on this topic, we can mention Frigo (2002, 2014) who was one of the first authors to highlight the fact that the BSC could give the internal auditing function the ability to play a strategic

Table 2.4 Sample IT BSC measures

Corporate contribution		
Ensuring effective IT governance *Align IT with business objectives* *Deliver value* *Manage costs* *Manage risks* *Achieve intercompany synergies*		
Customer orientation		Future orientation
Measuring up to business expectations *Service provider* *Strategic contributor*	*Information*	*Building the foundation for future delivery and continuous learning and growth*
Operational excellence		
Performing the IT functions with increasing credibility and impact *Operational excellence* *Business partnership* *Technology leadership*		

Source: Adapted from IT Governance Institute (2016, p. 32). Extracts.

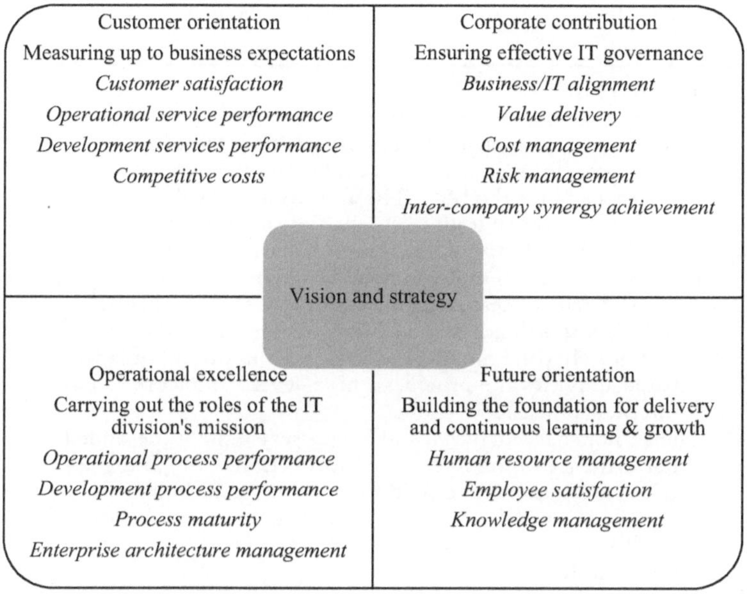

Figure 2.1 IT strategic scorecard framework
Source: Adapted and based on Van Grembergen, Saull and De Haes (2003, p. 31).

role in the organization. Several principles, based on stakeholder satisfaction (internal audit customers such as audit committee, management, and the audited), audit processes, and internal audit innovation and capabilities, should be adopted in order to achieve the internal auditing function's strategic enhancement process.

According to Frigo (2002), there are some key elements of this model that could be applied for the internal audit departments based on:

- the measure of the performance from customer's point of view;
- the determination of certain indicators for the quantifying of the internal audit performance;
- the connection between internal audit and customer' expectation;
- the focus on general strategies of the department; and
- the innovation and capabilities of internal audit.

Koutoupis et al. (2018) have also discussed the main theoretical and conceptual findings on the usage of the BSC model to measure the performance of the internal audit function. The papers they have mentioned in their literature review are summarized in Table 2.5.

In one of its reports, the IIA (2010) has presented a framework drawing from Frigo' work including the four main pillars mentioned above in relation to IIA Standards Departmental Outcomes and Priorities Legislation/Policy (Figure 2.2).

Table 2.5 The BSC and the measure of the performance of the internal audit function

Authors	*Main insights*
Bota-Avram et al. (2011)	One of the main metrics used by international leading companies for measuring and evaluating the performance of internal audit is the BSC. The authors have explored data for nine international leading companies contained in the study published by Protivi Knowleadgeleader (2010).
Feizizadeh (2012)	Internal audit needs to demonstrate its own effectiveness using a performance measurement system tied to the expectations of its key stakeholders. The author recommends the BSC that goes beyond numbers to examine important, broad-based activities and provides a high-level framework to assess internal audit effectiveness.
Baiden et al. (2016)	The authors have analyzed and have assessed the value-added performance of the internal audit function through the use of the BSC methodology in the mist of the turbulence and volatile business landscape confronting the internal audit profession. The results are quite mixed. The study has revealed that: • Most respondents do not perceive the internal audit function as providing value-addition services to their organizations based on IIA's internal audit performance assessment criteria. • To assess the performance of the internal audit practice using an adaptation of the BSC methodology to ascertain whether the function is providing value-addition or destroying shareholder value.

Source: Developed by the author, based on the articles cited.

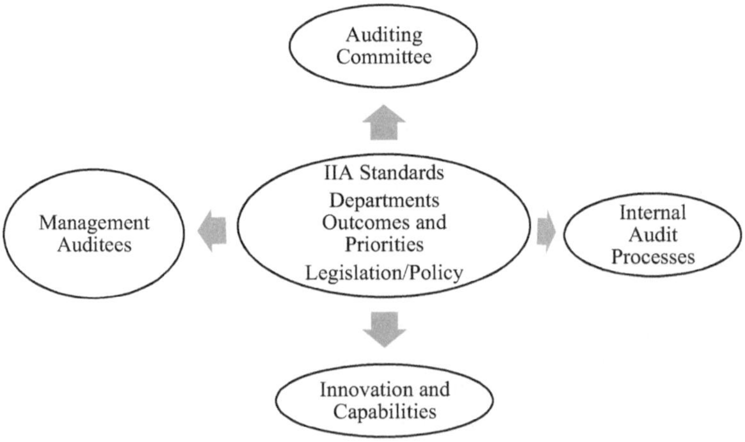

Figure 2.2 A balanced scorecard framework for internal auditing
Source: Adapted from the IIA (2010, p. 6).

Both quantitative and qualitative metrics are important in demonstrating an internal audit activity's performance to key stakeholders. In addition to compliance with the standards, specific measures for internal auditing's performance measurement objectives are suggested as follows:

- Audit Committee (satisfaction survey, risk concerns, plan input)
- Management/Auditees (satisfaction survey, average number of recommendations per audit, percent of recommendations implemented by corrective action date, cost savings, changes to processes)
- Internal Audit Processes (risk coverage, percent completed vs. planned audits, number of recommendations/audits, actual vs. planned costs, elapsed audit time start to finish, conformance to policy and standards, quality assurance techniques developed)
- Innovation and Capabilities (staff experience, training hours/auditor, percentage of staff holding relevant designations, number of innovative improvements implemented, number of process improvements, percentage of surprise risk events).

In a more recent white paper (2019), the IIA-Australia, quoting Turner (2019) definition of BSC for internal audit, has underlined that

> balanced scorecards are designed to translate internal audit strategy into action with the aim of helping to manage and measure the performance of the internal audit function, and, consequently, achieving alignment with organizational strategies. They are becoming an increasingly well-established means for reporting quantitative and qualitative KPIs to the audit committee in a balanced way.
>
> (p. 3)

What is really at stake in this approach are both quantitative and qualitative performance metrics as shown in Table 2.6.

In a publication entitled "Ten steps to a strategically focused internal audit function," PWC (2003) developed a BSC metric used to assess internal audit performance as shown in Tables 2.7 and 2.8.

From strategic planning to strategic alignment

This section further discusses the concept of strategic and IT alignment, one of the most widespread theoretical approaches. As we have already mentioned it, IT has played a fundamental and powerful role in facilitating business activities and has become a catalyst for fundamental changes in the structure, operations, and management of organizations including auditing function (Brown & Magill, 1994; Kearns & Sabherwal, 2006; Luftman et al., 2006) and alignment issues. The alignment challenge is being strengthened today in the context of digital transformation (Chapter 1).

Table 2.6 Examples of KPIs included in balanced scorecard reports

Balanced scorecard element	*Examples of internal audit function key performance indicators (KPIs)*	*Measure type*	*Inward or outward facing measure*
Partnering with the audit committee	Board (or audit committee) expectations met	Qualitative	Outward (delivers value for critical stakeholders)
	Percentage of audit plan complete	Quantitative	Inward
Supporting senior management	Client satisfaction goals – value added	Qualitative	Outward (delivers value for critical stakeholders)
	Client satisfaction goals – usefulness of recommendations	Qualitative	Outward (delivers value through useful recommendations for critical stakeholders)
	Cycle times (duration period of audits)	Quantitative	Outward (drives timely reporting for stakeholders)
Managing internal audit processes	Performance against the internal audit financial budget	Quantitative	Inward
	Availability of current and relevant internal audit charter, intranet, audit manual	Qualitative	Outward (provides useful resources for stakeholders)
	Budget to actual audit times	Quantitative	Inward
	Conformance with quality assurance and improvement standards (based on internal and external quality assessments)	Qualitative	Outward (adds to credibility of work for stakeholders
Managing Innovation and capabilities	Internal auditor workforce satisfaction	Qualitative	Inward
	Completion of initiatives in professional development plan	Quantitative	Inward
	Optimizing innovative practices and utilization of internal audit resources (to conduct audits while minimizing 'administration')	Quantitative	Inward

Source: Internal Auditing Foundation (2019, p. 175) quoted by the IIA-Australia (2019, p. 4).

Table 2.7 Internal audit balance scorecard metric

25% People	25% Internal Audit Process Effectiveness
Quality of professional staff Ability to address specialized and technical needs Understanding of the business and the global business environment Interaction and communication with the management executives Development of management talent for the organization	Rapid and effective start-up Effective and timely communications Development and delivery of practical recommendations to improve internal controls and corporate governance Results of auditee satisfaction questionnaire
25% Risk management	**25% Value Added to the Business**
Timely and effective identification of key business risks Percentage of audit activities and resources allocated to addressing key business risks Adaptability and responsiveness to emerging risks • Understanding and fulfilment of the needs to of: • The audit committee • Executive management	Protection of shareholder value through an imposed control environment Enhanced shareholder value through: • Cost reductions • Reduced revenue leakage • Reduced working capital • Enhanced cash flow

Source: Adapted from ECIIA (2020).

Table 2.8 Example: Internal audit planning balanced scoreboard

Quantitative measures	*Strategic plan status*	*Tactical plan status*
Client satisfaction ratings Internal audit KPIs	Achievement of stakeholder Expectations Management of client expectations Building strong client relationships Update of plan, expectations	Status Project 1 Status Project 2 Status Project 3 Carryover projects status
Current Annual Audit Plan Status	*Human Capital*	*Financial Metrics*
Number of audits scheduled Number of audit completed Status of open audit responses	Coaching/timeliness of feedback Development Mentoring Training/CPE hours Recruiting Staff turnover/retention	Status re annual budget Status re strategic initiatives budget

Note: Headings cover status of plans plus status of annual audit plan
Source: Adapted from Wolters Kluwer (2019, p. 17).

Strategic IT/IS alignment: definitions

The fit between strategy and organization has become a key success factor in relation to corporate governance issues (Chapter 3). Since the late 1970s, the alignment between strategy (business) and IT has become a key research topic. Since then, the importance of strategic IT/IS alignment has been well known and documented by several scholars (Table 2.9). Alignment is considered "a nebulous concept that is difficult to understand" (Chan et al. 1997, p. 126). It is a multidimensional concept that can be defined according to several criteria as follows:

Table 2.9 IT/IS alignment definitions

Authors	*Definitions*
Benbya and McKelvey (2006, p. 287)	"IS alignment is a continuous co-evolutionary process that reconciles top-down 'rational designs' and bottom-up 'emergent processes' of consciously and coherently interrelating all components of the Business/IS relationship at three levels of analysis (strategic, operational and individual) in order to contribute to an organization's performance over time."
Chan and Reich (2007, p. 300)	"The degree to which the business strategy and plans, and the IT strategy and plans, complement each other."
Coltman et al. (2015, p. 96)	"If the definition of IT alignment is revised to reflect both the extent of IT support for business strategy *and* the extent to which IT is deployed/leveraged in facilitating current and future business strategy, it may be possible to spot instances of misalignment that are because of underutilized IT capabilities (Tallon, 2000; Tallon and Kraemer 2003). This is consistent with prior calls in the literature to explicitly account for the bidirectional link between business and IT as articulated in the original work by Henderson and Venkatraman (1993) and what Rockart et al. (1996) and others term two-way strategic IT alignment (Rockart et al., 1996; Hirschheim and Sabherwal, 2001; Philip and Booth, 2001)."
Henderson & Venkatraman (1993, 1999, pp. 472–473)	"Our concept of strategic alignment is based on two fundamental assumptions: One, economic performance is directly related to the ability of management to create a strategic fit between the position of an organization in the competitive product-market arena and the design of an appropriate administrative structure to support its execution. The assumption is consistent with the generally accepted axiom that strategic choices in the external and internal domains should be consistent. Two, we contend that this strategic fit is inherently dynamic. The choices made by one business enterprise or firm (if fundamentally strategic), will over time evoke imitative actions, which necessitate subsequent responses. Thus, strategic alignment is not an event but a process of continuous adaptation and change."

Hirschheim and Sabherwal (2001)	"The notion of strategic alignment is based on three arguments: (1) an organization's performance is related to its attaining the appropriate structure and capabilities to execute its strategic decisions; (2) alignment is a two way street: the business strategy influences IT and IT influences business strategy; and (3) strategic alignment is not an event but a process of continuous adaptation and change."
Reich and Benbasat (1996, p. 56)	"The degree to which the information technology mission, objectives, and plans support and are supported by the business mission, objectives, and plans."
Luftman et al. (2008, p. 2)	"Alignment addresses both how IT is aligned with the business and how business should or could be aligned with IT. Terms such as harmony, link, fuse, fit, match, meld, converge, and integrate are frequently used synonymously with the term alignment (perhaps another reason why alignment has been so evasive). Whatever term you prefer, it is a persistent/pervasive problem that demands an ongoing process to ensure that IT and business strategies adapt effectively and efficiently together."

Source: Based on the articles cited.

- level of analysis (strategic, functional, operational, individual, social);
- conceptualization as a state *versus* as a process; and
- dynamic *versus* static vision.

Alignment theoretical frameworks

The seminal paper published by Henderson and Venkatraman (1989, 1990) presents a model used by the two authors in many of their publications in the 2000s (Table 2.10). They have been the first to describe clearly the relationship between business strategies and information technology strategies. The well-known strategic alignment model (SAM) is built on four quadrants, each consisting of three components as shown in Table 2.10. All of the components combined determine the degree of alignment. At least, as important are the linkages between the quadrants. The two authors highlight the linkages (represented with crosses in Table 2.10) between the four blocks (business strategy, IT strategy, organizational infrastructure, and IT infrastructure) and the interdependencies between related items. Strategic fit is the result of alignment business and IT strategy at an external level. Functional integration is about internal level based on alignment between business and IT infrastructures and processes. Finally, the cross-integration is the alignment between the four blocks.

The SAM model has raised a great interest in the academic community, especially because of its easy-to-use representation and the fact that it takes

Table 2.10 The strategic alignment model (SAM)

Strategic fit		Business strategy			IT strategy	
	External			×		
		Business scope			Technology scope	
		Distinctive competencies	Business governance		Systemic competencies	IT governance
		×	×			
Functional integration	Internal	Organizational infrastructure and processes		×	IS infrastructure & processes	
		Administration infrastructure			Architecture	
		Processes	Skills		Processes	Skills

Crosses represent linkages
Source: Adapted from Henderson & Venkatraman (1990, p.7).

into account the two levels of analysis (external and internal) that are essential for understanding a company's strategy. The closely related strategic and IT alignment perspectives are analyzed in equal measure.

Many authors (Luftman et al., 1993; Reich & Benbasat, 1996; Luftman, 2000; Avison et al., 2004; Chan & Reich, 2007; Bhattacharya, 2018) have extended and/or revisited the concept of business-IT alignment based on Henderson and Venkatraman's SAM (1989, 1990) in two main ways: those who analyze mostly the internal alignment level within organization (Smith & McKeen, 2003) and those who focus on the external environment such as uncertainty, technological uncertainty, and regulatory uncertainty (Camponovo & Pigneur, 2006; Mithas & Rust, 2016).

As explained by Luftman and Brier (1999), IT has been frequently treated as a "cost centre" or viewed as an "expense" rather than an enabler or driver of business value. Strategic alignment sheds new light on IT and its role in the development of business strategies. In 1996, Luftman has presented its first alignment framework based on 12 components (Exhibit 2.3).

Strategic alignment can be also viewed as a process. Luftman and Brier (1999) have then proposed a six-step approach (Exhibit 2.4) that incorporates organizational assessment using a strategic alignment based on the Henderson and Venkatraman model.

Luftman (2000) has developed a renewed framework called the Strategic Alignment Maturity Model (SAMM) consisting of 41 factors (business practices) aggregated in the six components of communications, value measurement, technology scope, partnership, governance, and skills. Luftman (2000) has postulated that alignment between the business and IT is the result of these six components acting together.

> Alignment addresses both how IT is in harmony with the business, and how the business should, or could be in harmony with IT. Alignment maturity evolves into a relationship where the function of IT and other business functions adapt their strategies together. Achieving alignment is evolutionary and dynamic. IT requires strong support from senior management, good working relationships, strong leadership, appropriate

Exhibit 2.3 The 12 components of alignment

Business strategy

Business Scope – Includes the markets, products, services, groups of customers/clients, and locations where an enterprise competes as well as the competitors and potential competitors that affect the business environment.

Distinctive Competencies – The critical success factors and core competencies that provide a firm with a potential competitive edge. This includes brand, services, research, manufacturing and product development, cost and pricing structure, and sales and distribution channels.

Business Governance – How companies set the roles and relationship between management stockholders, and the board of directors. Also included are how the company is affected by government regulations and how the firm manages its relationships and alliances with strategic partner.

Organization infrastructure and processes

Administrative Structure – The way the firm organizes its businesses. Examples include central, decentralized, matrix, horizontal, vertical, geographic, federal, and functional. Processes – How the firm's business activities (the work performed by employees) operate or flow. Major issues include value-added activities and process improvement.

Skills – H/R considerations such as how to hire/fire, motivate, train/educate, and culture.

IT strategy

Technology Scope – The important information applications and technologies.

Systemic Competencies – Those capabilities (e.g., access to information that is important to the creation/achievement of a company's strategies) that distinguishes the IT services.

IT Governance – How the authority for resources, risk, conflict resolution, and responsibility for IT is shared among business partners. IT management and service providers. Project selection and prioritization issues are included here.

IT infrastructure and processes

- Architecture – The technology priorities, policies, and choices that allow applications, software, networks, hardware, and data management to be integrated into a cohesive platform.

- Processes – Those practices and activities carried out to develop and maintain applications and manage IT infrastructure.
- Skills – IT human resource considerations, such as how to hire/fire, motivate, train/educate, and culture.

Source: Luftman (2000, pp. 7–8).

Exhibit 2.4 Six-step process for alignment

Set the goals and establish a team
Understand the business-IT linkage
Analyze and prioritize gaps
Specify the actions (project management)
Choose and evaluate success criteria
Sustain alignment

Source: Luftman and Brier (1999, p. 115).

> prioritization, trust, and effective communication, as well as a thorough understanding of the business and technical environments.
>
> (Luftman, 2000, pp. 6–7)

Guldentops (2003) has also suggested a model leading to some pragmatic practices to achieve alignment and makes a distinction between vertical and horizontal alignment. He has considered that there are two types of practices, underlying the fact that alignment is not only required at the strategic level but also at the operational level. Vertical alignment is primarily driven by repeatedly communicating an integrated business and IT strategy down into the organization, and translating it at each organizational layer into the language, responsibilities, values, and challenges at that level. Furthermore, this 'cascading down' of the strategic objectives should be clearly linked to performance measures that are reported upwards. Horizontal alignment is primarily driven by cooperation between business and IT upon integrating the strategy, developing and agreeing on performance measures (e.g., IT BSC), and sharing responsibilities (e.g., IT project co-responsibility).

Since the beginning of the 1990s, several scholars have highlighted the fact that the business and IT strategies alignment can be a key success factor. Chan et al. (1998) have thus indicated that is alignment has positive impact on business performance, which has been confirmed by other studies (Kearns and Lederer, 2000, 2003; Tallon et al., 2000; Sabherwal & Chan, 2001; Cragg et al., 2002; Tallon, 2003; Avison et al., 2004; Chan et al., 2006).

Internal audit and strategic IT/IS alignment. What lessons for practitioners?

Challenges in achieving alignment in practice

Key issues emerge when it is time to define the best practices in alignment for businesses. Several authors have pointed out the difficulties in setting up an effective alignment strategy based on frameworks that are inspired by a theoretical vision that is often necessary but not sufficient and that should meet the requirements of business life as experienced by companies in the short and long term.

Despite attempts to develop various alignment models presented in the former section, many authors consider that their practical use and adoption by practitioners are still limited. For Coltman et al. (2015), for example,

> strategic IT alignment has been defined using such distinct terms as 'matched with', 'in harmony with', 'complement each other', 'contingent upon', and 'congruent with' or more simply as 'aligned', 'fit', 'support', 'integrated', 'synergy', 'linked', or 'co-aligned'. Guidelines for translating these verbal statements into operational measures and specific empirical tests are not universally available.
>
> (p. 92)

This view has been also shared by Van Grembergen, De Haes and Guldentops (2003):

> Although the Strategic Alignment model clearly recognizes the need for continual alignment, it does not provide a practical framework to implement this (Van Der Zee & De Jong, 1999). In that case, the question of how to realize strategic alignment is still not solved. Van Der Zee and De Jong (1999) have proposed the Balanced Scorecard as an implementation solution.
>
> (p. 10)

Sledgianowski and Luftman (2005) have also explained that if there is a need for alignment, the conditions of alignment can be questioned:

> both information technology (IT) and business leaders are continually looking for management practices to help them align their IT and business strategies. Alignment seems to grow in importance as companies strive to link IT and business in light of dynamic business strategies and continuously evolving technologies. Importance aside, what is not clear is how to achieve and sustain harmony among business and IT, how to assess the maturity of alignment, and what the impact of misalignment might be on the firm
>
> (p. 102)

It should be noted that several researchers have attempted, from a practitioner perspective, to test the SAM model (Avison et al., 2004), assess the effects of IT-business alignment on organizational performance (Gerow et al., 2015), and appreciate the dynamic nature of alignment (Campbell et al., 2005; Walsh et al., 2013).

Internal audit and alignment: a complex assignment?

The problem becomes even more difficult when it comes to integrating internal audit perspectives. How to achieve alignment between organizational goals and the internal audit function's objectives? As mentioned previously, one of the reasons for this is the lack of templates dedicated to the specific relationship between the internal audit function and the alignment imperative. What are the main objectives for the internal audit function in light of corporate alignment? The viewpoints may differ in terms of the perspective chosen (Table 2.11).

Table 2.11 Internal audit and alignment: the vision of the Big Four

Deloitte (2010, p. 14)	"Remember that the alignment of internal audit needs to be regularly revisited. A changing competitive landscape, evolving needs of the business, turnover of personnel, and other factors necessitate constant review and refreshing. It can never be "set and forget."
EY (2021)	"Internal Audit (IA) transformation services range from performing strategic and tactical diagnostics to building a transformation road map that is focused on digitalization and increased value. When working with EY clients, our focus is on supporting them through IA Disrupted by Design, an approach where we help companies transform internal audit holistically (people, process and technology) to build or maintain trust. Further, through outsourcing, teaming or performing elements as a managed service, we help to provide new solutions that assist in aligning the IA function to the business strategy in a rapidly changing risk landscape."
KPMG (2018, p. 18)	"Alignment of operations to organization's strategy and objectives. How Internal Audit can help: • Assess whether resource allocation is aligned with the organization's key strategic objectives and initiatives. • Perform audits of the process of strategy development, e.g., evaluate strategy formulation, the degree to which strategy is translated into objectives and key performance measures and evaluate whether delivery has resulted in the desired performance and results. • Assess the differences between the defined strategy and the actual, emerging strategy, and assess effectiveness of execution against the actual, emerging strategy. • Review change management processes in operational areas that are heavily impacted by business transformation and may not typically be associated with the IA function, e.g., IT and data management and business as usual processes.

	• Participate proactively in Enterprise Risk Management (ERM) activities with Executive Management and Risk Management in order to provide insights into emerging strategic and operational risks and determine a plan for integration into the annual audit plan if necessary."
PWC (2012, p. 9)	"The need for alignment between business and internal audit. Why is alignment around risks so important? For internal audit to be truly effective, an organization must create a culture whereby stakeholders and chief audit executives (CAEs) hold robust dialogue around enterprise risks, share their objective perspectives, and reach a common viewpoint on the role of internal audit around the most critical risks. Given the number of risks facing organizations today, alignment around the most critical risks is essential to prioritize and enable effective allocation of resources. Absent this alignment, CAEs may fail to target resources to those areas stakeholders consider most critical – thereby missing the opportunity to deliver value to the business."

Source: Deloitte (2010), EY (2021), KPMG (2018), PWC (2012).

If the focus is on strategy (corporate level), the audit function should support alignment strategy in order to enable the company to achieve two main objectives as follows: developing sustainable competitive advantage (cost and/or differentiation) and creating value.

In a report entitled "The future of internal audit is now" (2012), EY has underlined the need to realize strategic alignment of the internal audit function. There are four steps leading internal audit functions need to take to realize strategic alignment, increase its relevance to the business and help the company achieve a risk maturity that accelerates stronger financial performance.

Conclusion

The evolution of strategic planning and IT/IS strategic alignment has been analyzed by several scholars. Business and IT performance are closely related. The growing importance of digital technology for organizations is also reflected in the alignment between IT and business, specifically in the integration of IT-strategy and business strategy in a common digital business strategy (Bharadwaj et al. 2013). Misalignment could lead to a failure of strategy and bad corporate governance (see Chapter 3).

The internal audit plays also a key role in the process of strategic planning and strategic IT/IS alignment. The alignment between the strategic goals and the internal audit, particularly in this current environment that is changing constantly, is crucial. Internal auditors need to "stay dynamic" in order to develop a plan and conduct audits and internal auditing activities that are aligned to the business changes (Betti & Sarens, 2018). Internal audits should also regularly revise the plan or shorten the time between the risk assessment and the beginning of the audit. These practical actions will be also very useful and valuable for the organization to achieve more strategic objectives.

Questions for discussion

How does IT strategy relate to business strategy?

How might the concepts of IS strategy, strategic planning, IT strategic planning be differentiated?

What is the actual practice of BSC in the internal audit?

The chapter describe several models to IT strategic planning and IT strategic alignment in organizations. What are the relative strengths of the models in (a) their applicability to describe actual situations, and (b) in their usefulness for managers of IT?

How aligning internal audit to deliver value?

Recommended reading

Aversano, L., Grasso, C., & Tortorella, M. (2012). A literature review of business/IT alignment strategies. *Procedia Technology, 5*, 462–474. https://doi.org/10.1016/j.protcy.2012.09.051

Hinkelmann, K., Gerber, A., Karagiannis, D., Thoenssen, B., Van der Merwe, A., & Woitsch, R. (2016). A new paradigm for the continuous alignment of business and IT: Combining enterprise architecture modelling and enterprise ontology. *Computers in Industry, 79*, 77–86. https://doi.org/10.1016/j.compind.2015.07.009

Karanja, E., & Patel, S.C. (2012). A review of research trends in strategic information systems planning. *International Journal of Business Information Systems, 10*(2), 151–177. http://dx.doi.org/10.1504/IJBIS.2012.047145

References

Addo, T.B.A., Chow, C.W., & Haddad, K.M. (2004). Development of an IT balanced scorecard. *Journal of International Information Management, 13*(4), 219–238.

Amrollahi, A., Ghapanchi, A.H., & Talaei-Khoei, A. (2013). A systematic literature review on strategic information systems planning: Insights from the past decade. *Pacific Asia Journal of Association for Information Systems, 5*(2), 39–66.

Anthony, R.N. (1965). *Planning and control systems: A framework for analysis*. Boston, MA: Graduate School of Business Administration, Harvard University.

Avison, D., Jones, J., Powell, P., & Wilson, D. (2004). Using and validating the strategic alignment model. *Journal of Strategic Information Systems, 13*(3), 223–246. https://doi.org/10.1016/j.jsis.2004.08.002

Baiden, N.E., Baiden, Y.P., & Ayariga, C. (2016). Assessing the balance score card of the internal audit performance-value addition or destruction: An empirical study of firms in Sekondi-Takoradi, Ghana. *European Journal of Business and Management, 8*(20), 75–89.

Bhattacharya, P. (2018). Aligning enterprise systems capabilities with business strategy: An extension of the Strategic Alignment Model (SAM) using Enterprise Architecture. *Procedia Computer Science, 138*, 655–662.

Benbya, H., & McKelvey, B. (2006). Using coevolutionary and complexity theories to improve IS alignment: A multi-level approach. *Journal of Information Technology, 21*(4), 284–298. https://doi.org/10.1057/palgrave.jit.2000080

Betti, N., & Sarens, G. (2018). *Aligning internal audit activities and scope to organizational strategy. How the business environment and organizational strategy impact internal audit.* Lake Mary, FL: Internal Audit Foundation. Retrieved March 23, 2021 from: http://felaban.s3-website-us-west-2.amazonaws.com/documentos_comites/archivo20190117150601PM.pdf

Bharadwaj, A., El Sawy, O., Pavlou, P.A., & Venkatraman, N. (2013). Digital business strategy: Toward a next generation of insights. *MIS Quarterly, 37*(2), 471–482. https://doi.org/10.25300/MISQ/2013/37:2.3

Bodnar, G.H. (2006). What's new in COBIT 4. *Internal Auditing, 21*(4), 37–44.

Bota-Avram, C., Popa, I., & Stefanescu, C. (2011). Methods of measuring the performance of internal audit. *The USV Annals of Economics and Public Administration, 10*(3), 137–146.

Bovaird, T. (2008). Emergent strategic management and planning mechanisms in complex adaptive systems—The case of the UK best value initiative. *Public Management Review, 10*(3), 319–340.

Boynton, A.C., & Zmud, R.W. (1987). Information technology planning in the 1990's: Directions for practice and research. *MIS Quarterly, 11*(1), 59–71. https://doi.org/10.2307/248826

Brown, C.V., & Magill, S.L. (1994). *Alignment* of the IS functions with the enterprise: Toward a model of antecedents. *MIS Quarterly, 18*(4), 371–403.

Campbell, B., Kay, R., & Avison, D. (2005). Strategic alignment: A practitioner's perspective. *Journal of Enterprise Information Management, 18*(6), 653–664.

Camponovo, G., & Pigneur, Y. (2006). *Conceptual foundations for designing information systems supporting the strategic analysis of technology environments.* Pre-ICIS SIGDSS Research Workshop, Milwaukee.

Chan, Y.E., Huff, S.L., Barclay, D.W., & Copeland, D.G. (1997). Business strategic orientation, information systems strategic orientation, and strategic alignment. *Information Systems Research, 8*(2), 125–150.

Chan, Y.E., & Reich, B.H. (2007). IT alignment: What have we learned? *Journal of Information Technology, 22*(4), 297–315. https://doi.org/10.1057/palgrave.jit.2000109

Chan, Y.E., Sabherwal, R., & Thatcher, J.B. (2006). Antecedents and outcomes of strategic IS alignment: An empirical investigation. *IEEE Transactions on Engineering Management, 53*(1), 27–47.

Chen, D.Q., Mocker, M., Preston, D.S., & Teubner, A. (2010). Information systems strategy: Reconceptualization, measurement, and implications. *MIS Quarterly, 34*(2), 233–259.

Ciborra, C. (1997). De profundis? Deconstructing the concept of strategic alignment. *Scandinavian Journal of Information Systems, 9*(1), 67–82.

Coltman, T., Tallon, P., Sharma, R., & Queiroz, M. (2015). Strategic IT alignment: Twenty-five years on. *Journal of Information Technology, 30*(2), 91–100. https://doi.org/10.1057/jit.2014.35

Cragg, P., King, M., & Hussin, H. (2002). IT alignment and firm performance in small manufacturing firms. *Journal of Strategic Information Systems, 11*(2), 109–132.

Daidj, N. (2019). Strategic and business-IT alignment under digitalization: Towards new insights? In K. Mezghani & W. Aloulou (Eds.), *Business transformations in the era of digitalization* (pp. 93–105). Hershey: IGI Global.

Deloitte (2010). The broken triangle? Improving the relationship between internal audit, management, and the audit committee. Retrieved January 18, 2019 from:

https://www2.deloitte.com/content/dam/Deloitte/uy/Documents/audit/El%20Tri%C3%A1ngulo%20roto_Auditoria%20Interna_Comite%20de%20auditoria_Gerencia.pdf

Deloitte (2016). *Where insights lead. Nine ways to strengthen Internal Audit's impact and influence in the organization*. Retrieved October 13, 2021 from: https://www2.deloitte.com/us/en/pages/risk/articles/internal-audit-strategic-plan.html

Drnevich, P.L., & Croson, D.C. (2013). Information technology and business-level strategy: Toward an integrated theoretical perspective. *MIS Quarterly, 37*(2), 483–509.

Eadie, D.C. (1991). Planning and managing strategically. In R.L. Edwards & J.A. Yankey (Eds.), *Skills for effective human services management* (pp. 285–301). Silver Spring, MD: NASW Press.

ECIIA (2020). *Keeping the internal audit function aligned*. Retrieved November 21, 2021 from: https://www.eciia.eu/wp-content/uploads/2020/02/Insurance-Guidelines-v9-4.2.20.pdf

EY (2012). The future of internal audit is now. Increasing relevance by turning risk into results. Insights on risk. June. Retrieved September 30, 2021 from https://www.argusdelassurance.com/mediatheque/6/4/7/000013746.pdf

Fallshaw, E.M. (2000). It planning for strategic support: Aligning technology and vision. *Tertiary Education and Management, 6(*3), 193–207.

Feizizadeh, A. (2012). Strengthening internal audit effectiveness. *Indian Journal of Science and Technology, 5*(5), 2777–2778.

Fergerson, B. (2012). *Key stages of Strategic Information System Planning (SISP) methods and alignment to strategic management planning concepts*. Retrieved September 30, 2021 from: https://core.ac.uk/download/pdf/36686889.pdf

Figge, F., Hahn, T., Schaltegger, S., & Wagner, M. (2002). The sustainability balance scorecard- linking sustainability management to business strategy. *Business Strategy and the Environment, 11*(5), 269–284. https://doi.org/10.1002/bse.339

Frigo, M.L. (2014). *The balanced scorecard: Applications in internal auditing and risk management*. Lake Mary, FL: Institute of Internal Auditors Research Foundation.

Frigo, M.L. (2012). The balanced scorecard: 20 years and counting. *Strategic Finance, 94*(4), 49–53.

Frigo, M.L. (2002). *A balanced scorecard framework for internal auditing departments*. Lake Mary, FL: Institute of Internal Auditors Research Foundation.

Frigo, M.L., Pustorino, P.G., & Krull, G.W. (2000). The Balanced Scorecard for community banks: Translating strategy into action. *Bank Accounting and Finance, 13*(3), 17–29.

Gao, F.X. (2002). *Information Resource Planning – Information foundation construction engineering*. Beijing: Tsinghua University Press.

George, B., Desmidt, S., Cools, E., & Prinzie, A. (2018). Cognitive styles, user acceptance and commitment to strategic plans in public organizations: An empirical analysis. *Public Management Review, 20*(3), 340–59. https://doi.org/10.1080/14719037.2017.1285112

Gerow, J., Thatcher, J.B., & Grover, V. (2015). Six types of IT-business strategic alignment: An investigation of the constructs and their measurement. *European Journal of Information Systems, 24*(5), 465–491.

Gold, C. (1994). *US measures — a balancing act*. Boston, MA: Research Note, Ernst & Young Center for Innovation.

Gold, C. (1992). *Total quality management in information services.* Boston, MA: Research Note, Ernst & Young Center for Business Innovation.

Goldman, S.L., Nagel, R.N., & Preiss, K., (1995). *Agile Competitors and Virtual Organizations: Strategies for Enriching the Customer.* New York: Van Nostrand Reinhold.

Grant, R.M. (2003), Strategic planning in a turbulent environment: Evidence from the oil majors. *Strategic Management Journal, 24*(6), 491–517.

Guldentops, E. (2003). *IT Governance: Part and Parcel of Corporate Governance.* CIO Summit, European Financial Management & Marketing (EFMA) Conference, Brussels.

Hamel, G. (1996). Strategy as revolution. *Harvard Business Review, 74*(4), 69–76.

Henderson, J., & Venkatraman, N. (1993). Strategic alignment: Leveraging information technology for transforming organizations, *IBM Systems Journal*, 32(1), 4–16 (Reprint in 1999, *38*(2&3), 472–484).

Henderson J., & Venkatraman N. (1990). *Strategic alignment: A model for organizational transformation via information technology*. Working Paper 3223–90. Sloan School of Management, Massachusetts Institute of Technology. Retrieved May 12, 2020 from: https://dspace.mit.edu/bitstream/handle/1721.1/49184/strategicalignme90hend.pdf?sequence=1&isAllowed=y

Henderson, J., & Venkatraman, N. (1989). Strategic alignment: A model for organisational transformation. In: T. Kochan & M. Unseem, M. (Eds.), *Transforming organisations.* (pp. 97–117). New York: Oxford University Press.

Hevner, A.R., Bernt, D.J., & Studnicki, J. (2000). Strategic information systems planning with box structures. *Proceedings of the 33rd Annual Hawaii International Conference on System Sciences* (pp. 1–11). https://doi:10.1109/HICSS.2000.926735

Hirschheim, R., & Sabherwal, R. (2001). Detours in the path toward strategic information systems alignment. *California Management Review, 44*(1), 87–108.

The Institute of Internal Auditors (IIA) (2019). Balance scorecard reporting. Retrieved November 21, 2021 from: https://iia.org.au/sf_docs/default-source/technical-resources/2018-whitepapers/iia-whitepaper_balanced-scorecard-reporting.pdf?sfvrsn=2

The Institute of Internal Auditors (IIA) (2010). *IPPF – Practice guide measuring internal audit effectiveness and efficiency.* Retrieved November 21, 2021 from: https://www.iia.nl/SiteFiles/IIA_leden/PG_Measuring-IA-Effectiveness_Nov2010[1].pdf

The Institute of Internal Auditors (IIA) – Australia (2019). *Balance scorecard reporting.* Retrieved January 12, 2022 from: https://iia.org.au/sf_docs/default-source/technical-resources/2018-whitepapers/iia-whitepaper_balanced-scorecard-reporting.pdf?sfvrsn=2

The Internal Audit Foundation (2019). *Sawyer's internal auditing: Enhancing and protecting organizational value.* 7th edition. Lake Mary, FL: Internal Audit Foundation.

IT Governance Institute (2016). *Board briefing on IT governance.* 2nd edition. Retrieved November 21, 2021 from: http://eventosfehosp.com.br/2017/material/sao_paulo/ti/jose/ITGI-Instrucoes-de-Governanca-de-TI-para-a-Alta-Administracao.pdf

Karanja, E., & Patel, S. (2012). A review of research trends in strategic information-systems planning. *International Journal of Business Information Systems, 10*(2), 151–177.

Kaplan, R.S., & Norton, D.P. (2000). Having trouble with your strategy? Then map it. *Harvard Business Review, 78*(5), 167–176.

Kaplan, R.S., & Norton, D.P. (1996). *The balanced scorecard. Translating strategy into action.* Harvard: Harvard Business School Press.

Kaplan R.S., & Norton, D.P. (1992). The balanced scorecard: Measures that drive performance. *Harvard Business Review, 70*(1), 71–79.

Kearns, G.S., & Lederer, A.L. (2003). A resource-based view of strategic IT alignment: How knowledge sharing creates competitive advantage. *Decision Sciences, 34*(1), 1–29.

Kearns, G.S., & Lederer, A.L. (2000). The effect of strategic alignment on the use of IS-based resources for competitive advantage. *The Journal of Strategic Information Systems, 9*, 265–293. https://doi:10.1016/S0963-8687(00)00049

Kearns, G.S., & Sabherwal, R. (2006). Strategic alignment between business and information technology: A knowledge-based view of behaviors, outcome, and consequences. *Journal of Management Information Systems, 23*(3), 129–162.

King, W.R., & Teo, T.S.H. (2000). Assessing the impact of proactive versus reactive modes of strategic information systems planning. *Omega, 28*(6), 667–679. https://doi:10.1016/S0305-0483(99)00079-1

KPMG (2018). *20 key risks to consider by Internal Audit before 2020. Are you aware of the risks concerning Internal Audit today and in the near future*? Retrieved May 12, 2020 from: https://assets.kpmg/content/dam/kpmg/ch/pdf/key-risks-internal-audit-2018.pdf

Koutoupis, A., Filos, J., Pappa, E., Pantelis, P., & Vousinas, G. (2018). *Implementing the balanced scorecard to internal audit function*. 6th European Academic Conference on Internal Audit and Corporate Governance, 18–20 April 2018, Naples.

Lederer, A.L., & Sethi, V. (1992). Root causes of strategic information systems planning problems. *Journal of Management Information Systems, 9*(1), 25–45. https://doi.org/10.1080/07421222.1992.11517946

Lederer, A.L., & Sethi, V. (1991). Critical dimensions of strategic information systems planning. *Decision Sciences, 22*(1), 104–119. https://doi.org/10.1111/j.1540-5915.1991.tb01265.x

Lederer, A.L., & Sethi, V. (1988). The implementation of strategic ISP methodologies. *MIS Quarterly, 12*(3), 445–461.

Lin, H., Sun, Y., & Wang, B. (2012). Research and application on information resources planning for university. *Proceedings of the 2nd International Conference on Computer and Information Application (ICCIA) 1497–1500*. https://citeseerx.ist.psu.edu/viewdoc/download?doi=10.1.1.915.9799&rep=rep1&type=pdf

Luftman, J. (2000). Assessing business-information technology alignment maturity. *Communications of the Association for Information Systems, 4*(1), 1–49. 10.4018/9781878289872.ch006

Luftman, J. (1996). *Competing in the information age: Practical applications of the strategic alignment model*. New York: Oxford University Press.

Luftman, J., & Brier, T. (1999). Achieving and sustaining business-IT alignment. *California Management Review, 42*(1), 109–122.

Luftman, J., Dorociak, J., Kempaiah, R., & Rigoni, E.H. (2008). Strategic alignment maturity: A structural equation model validation. *Proceedings of Americas Conference on Information Systems (AMCIS), 53*, 1–16. Toronto, Canada: AIS.

Luftman, J., Kempaiah, K., & Nash, E. (2006). Key issues for information technology executives 2005. *MIS Quarterly Executive, 5*(2), 81–99.

Luftman, J., Lewis, P., & Oldach, S. (1993). Transforming the enterprise: The alignment of business and information technology strategies. *IBM Systems Journal, 32*(1), 198–221.

Maharaj, S., & Brown, I. (2015). The impact of shared domain knowledge on strategic information systems planning and alignment. *South African Journal of Information Management, 17*(1), 12 pp. https://doi.org/10.4102/sajim.v17i1.608

Martin, R.L. (2014). The big lie of strategic planning. *Harvard Business Review, 92*(1–2), 79–84.

Mintzberg, H. (1994). *The rise and fall of strategic planning.* New York: Free Press.

Mintzberg, H., Lampel, J., & Ahlstrand, B. (1998). *Strategy safari: The complete guide through the wilds of strategic management.* London: FT Prentice Hall.

Mithas, S., & Rust, R.T. (2016). How information technology strategy and investments influence firm performance: conjecture and empirical evidence. *MIS Quarterly, 40*(1), 223–245.

Mithas, S., Tafti, A., & Mitchell, W. (2013). How a firm's competitive environment and digital strategy posture influence digital business strategy. *MIS Quarterly, 37*(2), 511–536.

Niven, P. R. (2005). *Balanced scorecard diagnostics: Maintaining maximum performance.* Hoboken, NJ: John Wiley & Sons, Inc.

Pagani, M. (2013). Digital business strategy and value creation: Framing the dynamic cycle of control points. *MIS Quarterly, 37*(2), 617–632.

Porter, M.E. (1991). Towards a dynamic theory of strategy. *Strategic Management Journal, 12*(S2), 95–117.

Porter, M.E., & Millar, V.A. (1985). How information gives you competitive advantage. *Harvard Business Review, 63*(4), 149–160.

PWC (2015). Internal audit strategic planning. Making internal audit's vision a reality during a period of rapid transformation. Retrieved September 26, 2021 from: https://www.pwc.com/gr/en/publications/internal-audit-strategic-planning-september-2015.pdf

PWC (2012). Aligning internal audit. Are you on the right floor? Retrieved September 26, 2021 from: https://www.pwc.com/gr/en/publications/assets/state-of-internal-audit-2-2012.pdf

PWC (2003). Ten steps to a strategically focused internal audit function. Retrieved September 26, 2021 from: https://www.pwc.com/us/en/services/consulting/cybersecurity-risk-regulatory/internal-audit/building-internal-audit-function.html

Reich, B., & Benbasat, I. (1996). Measuring the linkage between business and information technology objectives. *MIS Quarterly, 20*(1), 55–81.

Robson, W. (1994). *Strategic management and information systems.* London: Pitman.

Sabherwal, R., & Chan, Y.E. (2001). Alignment between business and IS strategies: A study of prospectors, analyzers, and defenders. *Information Systems Research, 12*(1), 11–33.

Salmela, H., Lederer, A.L., & Reponen T. (2000). Information systems planning in a turbulent environment. *European Journal of Information Systems, 9*(1), 3–15.

Silvius, A.J., & Stoop, J. (2013). The relationship between the process of strategic information systems planning and its success: An explorative study. *Proceedings of the 46th Hawaii International Conference on Systems Sciences* (pp. 4495–4501). http://dx.doi.org/10.1109/hicss.2013.536

Singh, I.B., & Beyer, R.C. (1990). Information resource planning methodology: A case study. *Systems Integration '90. Proceedings of the First International Conference on Systems Integration* (pp. 634–642). https://doi.org/10.1109/ICSI.1990.138729

Sledgianowski, D., & Luftman, J. (2005). IT-business strategic alignment maturity: A case study. *Journal of Cases on Information Technology, 7*(2), 102–120.

Son, S., Weitzel, T., & Laurent, F. (2005). Designing a process-oriented framework for IT performance management systems. *The Electronic Journal Information Systems Evaluation, 8*(3), 219–228.

Smith, H., & McKeen, J. (2003). Developments in practice IX: The evolution of the KM function. *Communications of the Association for Information Systems, 12*(4), 69–79.

Spencer Pickett, K.H. (2010). *The internal auditing handbook.* 3rd edition. Chichester: John Wiley & Sons.

Tallon, P.P. (2003, November 15). The alignment paradox. *CIO Insight.* http://www.cioinsight.com/c/a/Past-News/Paul-Tallon-The-Alignment-Paradox.

Tallon, P., & Kraemer, K., & Gurbaxani, V. (2000). Executives' perceptions of the business value of information technology: A process-oriented approach. *Journal of Management Information Systems, 16*(4), 145–174.

Teo, T.S.H., & King, W.R. (1997). Integration between business planning and information systems planning: An evolutionary-contingency perspective. *Journal of Management Information Systems, 14*(1), 185–214.

Turner, B.R. (2019). *New auditor's guide to internal audit: With insights, stories, and tips from expert practitioners from across the world.* Lake Mary, FL: Internal Audit Foundation.

Van der Zee, J.T.M., & De Jong, B. (1999). Alignment is not enough: Integrating business and information technology management with the balanced business scorecard. *Journal of Management Information Systems, 16*(2), 137–158. https://doi.org/10.1080/07421222.1999.11518249

Van Grembergen, W. (2000). The balanced scorecard and IT governance. *Information Systems Control Journal (previously IS Audit & Control Journal), 2,* 40–43.

Van Grembergen, W., De Haes, S., & Guldentops, E. (2003). Structures, processes and relational mechanisms for information technology governance: Theories and practices. In W. Van Grembergen (Ed.), *Strategies for information technology governance* (pp. 1–36). Hershey, PA: Idea Group Publishing.

Van Grembergen, W., Saull, R., & De Haes, S. (2003). Linking the IT balanced scorecard to the business objectives at a major Canadian financial group. In W. Van Grembergen (Ed.), *Strategies for information technology governance* (pp. 23–50). Hershey, PA: Idea Group Publishing.

Van Grembergen, W., & Timmerman, D. (1998). Monitoring the IT process through the balanced scorecard. *Proceedings of the 9th Information Resources Management (IRMA) International Conference* (pp. 105–116).Hershey, PA: Idea Group Publishing.

Van Grembergen, W., & Van Bruggen, R. (1997). Measuring and improving corporate information technology through the balanced scorecard technique. *Proceedings of the Fourth European Conference on the Evaluation of Information technology* (pp. 163–171). Delft: Delft University Press.

Walsh, I., Renaud, A., & Kalika, M. (2013). The translated strategic alignment model: A practice-based perspective. *Systèmes d'Information et Management, 18*(2), 37–68.

Ward, J., Griffiths, P., & Whitmore, P. (1990). *Strategic planning for information systems.* New York: John Wiley.

Willcocks, L. (1995). *Information management. The evaluation of information systems investments.* London: Chapman & Hall.

Wolters Kluwer (2019). Strategic planning for internal audit. A CAE's guide to driving value creation. Retrieved October 30, 2021 from: https://hpmgroup.co/wp content/uploads/2019/10/Strategic-Planning-for-Internal-Audit.pdf

Wu, H.-Y. (2012). Constructing a strategy map for banking institutions with key performance indicators of the balanced scorecard. *Evaluation and Program Planning, 35*(3), 303–332. https://doi.org/10.1016/j.evalprogplan.2011.11.009

3 IT governance, risks, and compliance

Introduction

This chapter focuses on governance, risks, and compliance issues. IT governance has a strategic orientation (what to do) while IT management is more tactical (how to do). To understand the concept of IT governance, one needs insight into the principles of corporate governance and its constituents (Weill & Ross, 2004). Corporate governance is the process and structure used to manage and run the business of the corporation in order to attain the objectives of the shareholders. Corporate governance as a set of rules and behavior according to which companies should be managed and monitored, contributes to the productivity and competitiveness of the whole economy. Governance practices of corporate boards of directors (composition, compensation, shareholder rights, and disclosure of information practices) and interlocked boards and general principles of corporate governance are described in the first section.

IT governance (ITG) is analyzed in-depth in section "Corporate governance: an historic debate". An overview of past and current research of ITG is presented. The concept of IT governance (ITG) emerged in academic research in the late 1990s (Brown, 1997; Sambamurthy & Zmud 1999; Peterson et al., 2000; Van Grembergen et al., 2003; De Haes & Van Grembergen, 2005). IT Governance control frameworks are also numerous in the professional existing literature. To implement good IT governance, IT governance methodologies, control frameworks, and standards have been provided such as COBIT (Control Objectives for Information and related Technology) and ITIL (Information Technology Infrastructure Library).

Today, several trends are taking shape, some of which are already well established in the audit landscape, while others are more recent and should reorient the way audits are carried out and the associated means and resources:

- Internal audits relate to the identification and analysis of risks and the implementation of control mechanisms.
- ITG, risk, and compliance activities are by nature interconnected, and they share generally common sets of information, methodology, processes, and technology.

DOI: 10.4324/9781003215110-4

- Audits comply more and more with the requirements of conformity (compliance) with regulations (e.g., General Data Protection Regulation – GDPR).

These issues will be discussed in the last section.

Corporate governance: a historic debate

An old theoretical debate

Corporate governance has focused for many decades on issues resulting from the separation of ownership and control. This governance addresses, in particular, the principal-agent relationship between shareholders and managers (potential agency conflict) and the maximization of shareholder value (Exhibit 3.1) and specifies the decision-making rules for the organization (Gill, 2008; Burtscher et al., 2009).

Exhibit 3.1 The evolution of corporate governance

The separation of ownership and control

The separation of ownership and control issue has a long story. As far back as 1776, Adam Smith wrote in his famous book An Inquiry into the Nature and Causes of the Wealth of Nations that the key to a firm's success is to deal with the separation of ownership and control:

> The directors of such companies, however, being the managers rather of other people‘s money than of their own, it cannot well be expected, that they should watch over it with the same anxious vigilance with which the partners in a private co-partnery frequently watch over their own. Like the stewards of a rich man, they are apt to consider attention to small matters as not for their master's honour, and very easily give themselves a dispensation from having it. Negligence and profusion, therefore, must always prevail, more or less in the management of the affairs of such a company. It is upon this account that joint stock companies for foreign trade have seldom been able to maintain the competition against private adventurers. (Book 5, Chapter 1, Part 3, Art. 1).
>
> (Smith, reprinted in 2008, p. 700)

The Agency theory

Jensen and Meckling (1976) have explained that the firm could be defined as a nexus of contracts, and therefore a legal fiction, and have described situations and relationships in which one party (the principal) delegates work to another (the agent). The main objectives of agency theory are to explain how explicit or implicit contracts can be drawn up between the two parties to take account of shirking, opportunism, bounded rationality, and imperfect and incomplete information to monitor agent behavior and to propose an optimal incentive structure. Agency theory has been applied to a variety of strategic management topics, such as corporate strategy and corporate governance. Modern corporations characterized by separation of ownership and control, the interests of shareholders (principals) and managers (agents) may diverge. In this context, managers will seek to maximize their own interests at the expense of shareholders. According to agency literature on corporate governance, the Board of Directors is a control instrument to protect shareholders' interests in the value distribution process.

In 1932, in their book *The Modern Corporation and Private Property*, Berle and Means considered that separation of ownership from control had become the norm. Several authors have studied organizations in which ownership and control are separated (Knight, 1921; Arrow, 1974; Chandler, 1977; Fama & Jensen, 1983). Berle and Means pointed out the rise of managerialism in the American economy. Since then, this book had become the reference work for studying the US model of corporate control. The two authors emphasized the importance of the separation of ownership from control because of the growing dispersal of stockholdings in large companies. Although stockholders had legal control of large American corporations, they had no real control. This control was henceforth performed by the group executive management through their managers engaged in day-to-day management and the Board of Directors. Berle and Means referred to this situation as "management control." In addition as Mizruchi (1996), mentioned:

> dating back to the Congressional investigations of the early 1900s, interlocks had been viewed by some observers as a means by which control of corporations could be traced. The assumption was that a firm that had extensive representation of banks and other corporations on its board was subject to control by those institutions.
>
> (p. 281)

But, the corporate scandals in the 2000s have shown the vulnerability of shareholder governance mechanisms in monitoring managerial behavior and the limits of the concept of shareholder value, which has started to lose relevance. Lazonick and Sullivan (2000) underline the fact that

> there are, however, many problems with this rosy view of the power of shareholder value in reshaping corporate governance and, indeed, the organization of the economy to deliver sustainable prosperity. In both theory and practice, the arguments for maximizing shareholder value ignore significant problems of US economic performance in the era of 'downsize and distribute' as well as important historical foundations of the current stock-market and economic booms. A consideration of these problems of economic performance and foundations of the current booms raises serious questions about the future sustainability of US prosperity in a shareholder-value regime.
>
> (p. 29)

As one might expect, this issue has generated considerable discussion and is subject to widely differing interpretations and critics. A very different approach is then proposed, called stakeholder theory, which focuses on the fact that managers should be concerned with all stakeholders of the firm. According to Freeman (1984), a stakeholder is someone who can affect (impact) or is affected by the corporation.

Source: Elaborated by the author.

Corporate governance and competitive advantage

The concept of governance is broad, including political stability, government and regulatory effectiveness, control of corruption, accountability, and disclosure. The globalization of economies and companies is also prompting changes in corporate governance systems. Governance is related to various actors, institutions, principles, and interactions.

Country-specific variables impact the efficiency of corporate governance in both developed and emerging market economies. Corporate governance systems are embedded in the unique economic, political, and cultural context of each country. The corporate governance structure is dynamic. Several countries have attempted to update their corporate governance code in order to take account of the constantly evolving international standards worldwide. In each country, corporate governance has been developed in response to country-specific factors and new market conditions. There are, however, more and more common principles and rules adopted by all countries in accordance with independent board members, audit independence, avoidance of conflict of interest, and transparency in information. Since the 2000s, important changes in external environments have affected the corporate governance practices of firms all around the world.

As several authors have mentioned, there is an important connection between corporate governance and the competitive strategy of firms. Corporate governance may (or may not) support strategic vision, organizational structure (including IT issues), and financial performance. Good corporate governance is an essential foundation for a successful business. Competitive strategy aims to establish a profitable position and sustainable competitive advantage. The development of this advantage depends on the industry within which the organization competes. But sustainability is also becoming an aspect of good corporate governance.

Governance should be then analyzed with a multi-level (macro-, meso-, and micro-perspective) and multi-disciplinary approach (economics, strategy, finance, IS, IT management, etc.). As De Brouwer (2003) has explained it,

> 'good' governance does not mean that firms should not fail. In market economies, firms enter and exit. The risk and cost of failure helps discipline and focus private decision making. In this regard, the aim of improving corporate governance is to reduce the likelihood that exit occurs because of managerial failure, self-interest or corruption, and to minimise contagion and flow-on effects to other firms and the economy in general. (p. 9)

The meso-level operates immediately below the national level and above the micro (corporate) level. It consists of bodies (professional), institutions, and processes, which influence the functioning of sector. Consequently, there are strong linkages between the different levels of governance (Table 3.1).

Various corporate governance practices

The concept of corporate governance refers to systems by which companies are directed and controlled and to the structures of control by which managers are held accountable to those who have a legitimate stake in an enterprise (Johnson et al., 2008). The different roles and responsibilities of shareholders, directors, and management are defined in the corporate governance system. The introduction of monitoring and control mechanisms has had also a significant impact on corporate governance rules.

Corporate ownership is closely related to corporate governance that attempts to regulate the decision-making power of executives to ensure that they do not serve their own interests to the detriment of shareholders, but also of creditors, employees, and the company, in general. It refers also to the activities of control and coordination that compose the internal regulation in compliance with external obligations (Solomon & Solomon, 2004).

Various mechanisms are used to ensure that managers act in accordance with shareholders' interests: monitoring and incentives devices (linking promotion or pay to the performance of the firm), indirect means of corporate control such as that provided through the discipline of the capital market and finally increasing shareholders' and creditors' role through their ability to monitor the company results or through their institutional rights such as the power to replace management.

Table 3.1 A multi-level governance system

At what level?	*Global level*	*Meso-level*	*Micro-level*	
Level of analysis of governance?	Global governance	Governance at sector level Corporate governance (private sector) Government governance (public sector)	Company	
	Country (or international scope*)	Sector of economic activity (e.g., agriculture, energy, finance, ICT, transportation)	Corporate governance	IT governance
Who is governing? (governance and responsibility role) Main players	Economic, political, and administrative authority (Governments, ministries, etc.)	Sectoral institutions Business organizations Professional bodies/ associations Public agencies	The responsibility of the Board of directors	Several levels of responsibility Strategic level The Board of Directors and executives (including the Chief information officer (CIO) and/or the Chief technology officer (CTO))
Main features/ principles	Governance policy Public governance Economic regulation Legal system Public procurement	Regulatory governance (accountability and performance of regulators in key sectors) (OECD, 2021)	Principles Ensuring the basis for an effective corporate governance framework, the rights of shareholders and key ownership functions, the equitable treatment of shareholders, the role of stakeholders in corporate governance, disclosure and transparency, the responsibilities of the board	IT principles, infrastructure strategies, architecture, business applications needs and investment

Codes (governance rules, law)	Legal and economic frameworks National corporate governance code Securities law Open government data governance Responsible business conduct (rbc) principles for multinational enterprises	Codes for private and public sectors	Code of best practices Codes designed for listed and non-listed companies or even for both of them Codes issued by individual firms	Corporate governance codes can address IT governance issues (De Haes et al., 2017) IT governance standards (ISO 38500, COBIT, ITIL, etc.)

* Note: International institutions (OECD, International Corporate Governance Network (ICGN)) promote the diffusion of good governance practices.
Source: Elaborated by the author.

As governance practices differ around the world depending on national laws and societal norms, the literature places emphasis on comparing countries from the most developed capital markets to the less developed capital markets. Several models of corporate governance have been identified by researchers with a special interest for three of them: the Anglo-US model (integrates mainly the UK, the US, Australia, Canada, and New Zealand), the German model (governs German and Austrian companies, some corporations in the Netherlands, Scandinavia, France, and Belgium have adopted some elements of the German model), and the Japanese model. Different elements have been identified to characterize each of them: key players, the share ownership pattern in the given country, the composition of the Board of Directors, the regulatory framework, disclosure requirements for publicity-listed stock corporations, corporate actions requiring shareholder approval, and interaction among key players.

In the 1990s, several countries launched programs of reform in corporate governance and business practices, which impacted patterns of corporate ownership, structures of Boards of Directors, and decision processes by managers.

Since the beginning of the 1970s, the issue of corporate governance has become prominent. Several questions have been identified and analyzed, such as the impact of the legal and regulatory framework (following several corporate scandals in the 2000s), the evolution of the separation of ownership and control, and the expansion of the organization's boundary (Daidj, 2016).

Linking corporate governance to IT governance

As the IT governance issue should be considered in relation to corporate and business governance, several models have been elaborated accordingly. In this section, we will refer to two of them that are converging.

The first interesting framework dates from the mid-2000s. According to AFAI-CIGREF (2005), the first layer is represented by the enterprise governance that includes corporate and business governance. IT governance is directly connected to these latter types of governance (Table 3.2). IT governance is defined as a management process based on best practices enabling the business to drive its IT function around seven pillars as follows: business value creation, IT customer, IT processes, IT finance, IT competencies, IT risk management, and transparency and relationships.

As mentioned in Table 3.2, the Sarbanes – Oxley Act (commonly referred to as "SOX") was enacted in 2002 by the United States Congress. This Act was designed by two Congressmen Paul Sarbanes and Michael Oxley to protect shareholders and stakeholders from fraudulent corporate practices, to make auditors more independent, to prevent conflict of interest by analysts, and finally to restore confidence in the markets after the collapse of large companies in the 2000s such as Enron and WorldCom (Chabrak & Daidj, 2007).

In addition, AFAI-CIGREF (2005) have then identified ten IT governance practices and combine them to the seven pillars mentioned above. As a result, a grid has been defined to develop the best practices (Table 3.3).

The second model presented in Table 3.4 has been elaborated by the IIA in its Supplemental Guidance part of The International Professional Practices Framework® (IPPF®).

Table 3.2 Positioning IT governance

Enterprise governance		
Sarbanes-Oxley Act (SOX)	Corporate governance Conformance processes Chairman / CEO Non-executive directors Audit committee Remuneration committee Risk management Internal audit Accountability Assurance	Business governance Performance processes Strategic planning and alignment Strategic decision-making Strategic risk management Scorecards Strategic enterprise systems Continuous improvement Value creation Resource utilization
COSO		
IT governance		
COBIT	Risk mitigation including security policy, review and control	Value creation Performance

Note added by the author.
The Committee of Sponsoring Organizations of the Treadway Commission (COSO), established in 1985, has developed an *Internal Control – Integrated framework* (1992), a model for corporate governance and internal controls. COBIT (see below and Chapter 4).

Table 3.3 Contribution of the ten practices to the seven pillars.

	Business value creation	*IT customers*	*IT processes*	*IT finance*	*IT competencies*	*IT risk management*	*Transparency and relationships*
IT planning	X	X			X	X	X
IT/business alignment	X	X				X	X
IT value creation-oriented project portfolio management	X	X				X	X
IT budgeting and controlling		X		X		X	X
IT project management		X	X			X	
IT customer-oriented Service Delivery and Process Optimization		X	X		X	X	X
IT risk management		X				X	X
IT future-oriented Competencies and solutions management			X		X		X
IT communication management	X	X					X
Relationships management							
IT performance and measurement management	X	X				X	X

Source: Adapted from AFAI-CIGREF (2005) and updated by the author.

Table 3.4 Organizational governance and IT governance relationship

Organizational governance			
Corporate governance	*Business governance*		*IT governance*
	Key organizational assets		
Human assets	Physical assets	Financial assets	IT assets IT governance Areas Structures Mechanisms

Source: The IIA's International Professional Practices Framework (2018, p. 5).

Main insights of IT governance (ITG) in the literature review

IT governance: definitions

IT governance (ITG) can be also referred to as governance of enterprise IT (GEIT) or corporate governance of IT. Practitioners and academics both agree that ITG is not a precise concept. It can then lead to multiple interpretations. ITG has therefore given rise to numerous publications and definitions. At a general level, ITG is closely related to corporate and business governance (Table 3.5).

To draw analogies or make comparisons with other disciplines both corporate and business levels are considered as well in the traditional strategic management approach. Business and corporate strategy represent today the basis for obtaining sustained competitive advantage, in particular, in dynamic and turbulent markets. The duration of competitive advantage is unpredictable. Business strategy is the way a business competes in a particular business sector. The strategic decisions made in business-level strategy are related to pricing, marketing, and manufacturing efficiency. Corporate strategy is focused on the way companies create value across different businesses. It is corporate strategy that should guide key decisions in the businesses and coordinate their business strategies. But, for most corporate enterprises, the corporate strategy is simply the sum of business strategies, with some broad objectives and statement of business mission. But corporate-level strategic processes enable dynamic strategic repositioning of enterprise and reconfiguration of corporate resources and competencies in order to strengthen competitive advantage.

As explained by Calder (2007), one of the main drivers of IT governance is precisely the search for competitive advantage – in the dynamically changing information economy – through intellectual assets, information, and IT.

ITG definitions are numerous and various elaborated by both practitioners (professional bodies) and academic scholars as presented in Table 3.5. Their content has evolved in the last few years in line with the theoretical debates and changes in professional practices.

Table 3.5 Evolving ITG definitions (1990–2020)

Professional bodies and public institutions	
The IIA (International Professional Practices Framework® – IPPF®) (2018, p. 4)	"Taking a strategic approach to implementing information technology (IT) governance helps organizations address the speed of technological advancements, IT services proliferation, and the greater dependency on IT to meet organizational objectives. Effective IT governance contributes to control efficiency and effectiveness, and allows the organization's investment in IT to realize both financial and nonfinancial benefits"
The IT Governance Institute (ITGI) (2003, p. 10)	"...the responsibility of the board of directors and executive management. It is an integral part of enterprise governance and consists of the leadership and organizational structures and processes that ensure that the organization's IT sustains and extends the organization's strategies and objectives"
The IT Compliance Institute (ITCI) (2007, p. 4)	"IT governance and strategy encompasses the core definitions, structures, and processes that shape all IT efforts and systems. Auditable functions of IT governance include: 1 Definition of what the IT organization is and does, including values and goals 2 IT risk definition and management 3 Definition of roles and responsibilities, including leadership structures 4 Strategic planning, monitoring, and continual improvement 5 Oversight of standards, policies, and procedures 6 Oversight of technical foundations, such as IT infrastructure, architectures, a semantic baseline or glossary, and data management, 7 Asset management, including staff, systems, media, networks, and content 8 Resource planning 9 Investment management"
Academic authors – Evolution of definitions	
In the 1990s	
Luftman and Brier (1999, p. 111)	Luftman (1996) has built a strategic alignment model based on four main components (i.e., business strategy, organization infrastructure and processes, IT strategy, IT infrastructure, and processes). The two authors mention this research of Luftman (1996) who has included ITG in the IT strategy block and has defined as follows: "How the authority for resources, risk, conflict resolution, and responsibility for IT is shared among business partners, IT management, and service providers. Project selection and prioritization issues are included here."

(*Continued*)

Academic authors – Evolution of definitions

In the 2000s	
Peterson (2004, pp. 7–9)	"IT governance is defined as: the distribution of IT decision-making rights and responsibilities among enterprise stakeholders, and the procedures and mechanisms for making and monitoring strategic decisions regarding IT. IT governance is thus the enterprise management system through which an organization's portfolio of IT systems is directed and controlled (...). IT Governance Focuses on Specific IT Decisions. IT Governance Is the Responsibility of the CIO (Chief Information Officer). IT Governance Is Concerned with Organizing the IT Function. IT Governance Is a New Form of "Old School" IT Management. IT Governance Focuses on the (De-) Centralization of IT."
Van Grembergen (2002, p. 1)	"IT Governance is the organisational capacity exercised by the Board, Executive Management and IT management to control the formulation and implementation of IT strategy and in this way ensure the fusion of business and IT"
Weill (2004, p.3)	"IT governance represents the framework for decision rights and accountabilities to encourage desirable behavior in the use of IT (...). IT governance is not about what specific decisions are made. That is management. Rather, governance is about systematically determining who makes each type of decision (a decision right), who has input to a decision (an input right) and how these people (or groups) are held accountable for their role. Good IT governance draws on corporate governance principles to manage and use IT to achieve corporate performance goals."
In the 2010s	
De Haes and Van Grembergen (2015, p. 2)	IT governance is "an integral part of corporate governance and addresses the definition and implementation of processes, structures and relational mechanisms in the organization that enable both business and IT people to execute their responsibilities in support of business/IT alignment and the creation of business value from IT-enabled business investments."
Joshi et al., (2013, p. 118).	IT governance transparency can be defined as "the ability of firms to provide adequate and relevant IT governance information in a timely and effective manner to their stakeholders, such as investors, policymakers, and regulatory bodies, so that they can assess management's behavior in using IT"

Source: Based on the articles cited.

ITG and main theoretical-related issues

The scope of ITG is very broad as it is related to several other concepts, frameworks, and practices. The complexity of ITG can be also explained partly by the fact that it can be viewed at several levels as shown in Figure 3.1. The interactions between the three main layers are crucial and should be analyzed accordingly. Scholars have studied all these dimensions and their main findings are summarized here.

ITG and IT/business alignment

One of the main targets of ITG is to achieve strategic/business/IT alignment (Chapter 2). ITG practices should:

- ensure that IT strategy is aligned with business strategy current and corporate strategy future objectives;
- ensure that IT delivers against the strategy through clear expectations and specific metrics;
- allocate IT investments budgets in line with the business objectives; and
- ensure that technology investment decisions are aligned with business goals (Gheorghe, 2010).

Several authors have focused on the fact that an effective ITG aligning the IT and business objectives could have a significant and positive impact on the global corporate performance (Luftman, 1996; Luftman & Brier, 1999; Webb et al., 2006; De Haes & Grembergen, 2008, 2009; Beimborn et al. 2009; Chaudhuri, 2011; De Haes et al., 2020). "The key element in IT governance

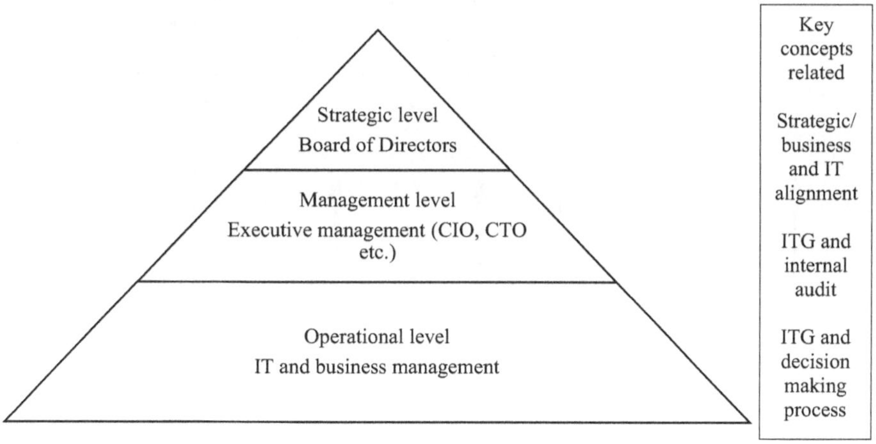

Figure 3.1 The three layers of ITG
Source: Adapted from Van Grembergen and De Haes (n.d., p. 6).

is the alignment of the business and IT to lead to the achievement of business value" (De Haes & Van Grembergen, 2004, p. 7).

ITG and internal audit

We have already presented in Chapter 1 the internal audit function from the "three lines of defense model perspective." "Internal audit's role includes the responsibility to assess and make recommendations to improve the organization's governance processes (Standard 2110 – Governance) to help prevent governance failures and improve strategic performance as part of the third line of defense" (The IIA, 2018, p. 7). In his position paper published in 2013 and entitled "The Three Lines of Defense in Effective Risk Management and Control," the IIA has adapted the model initially developed by ECIIA/FERMA (Guidance on the 8th EU Company Law Directive, article 41). This more specific model shows the responsibilities for the "Three lines of Defense model" as it relates to IT governance (Table 3.6).

The IT auditors in charge of the assessment of the ITG efficiency can perform a number of key roles (Hardy, 2009; Gheorghe, 2010):

- initiating IT governance programs: explain IT governance and its value to management;
- assessing the current state: provide advice and assist with current-state assessments;
- planning IT governance solutions;
- monitoring IT governance initiatives; and
- helping make IT governance business as usual.

Table 3.6 The three lines of defense model in reference to IT governance

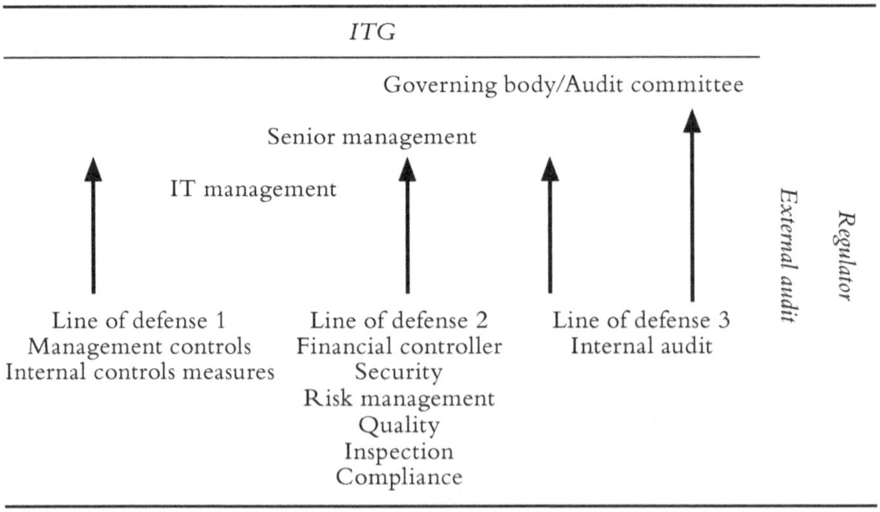

Source: Adapted from ECIIA (2022).

As explained by Dutta et al. (2022),

> the significant levels of investment in IT have naturally led organizations to seek ways to make efficient and effective use of this investment. Two related functions that address this need are IT audit and IT governance. An IT audit assesses a company's technological infrastructure to ensure processes and systems run accurately and efficiently remain secure and meet compliance regulation. IT governance, on the other hand, is a framework to align IT and business strategy with the objective of ensuring IT investments enhance business value.

ITG versus IT management

The model presented in Table 3.6 is interesting because it illustrates precisely what comes under IT governance and what is derived from IT management. For decades, ITG has been assimilated to IT management. In fact, they are not synonymous. The short sentence used by Beachboard et al. (2010) is quite interesting from this point of view: "there is a difference between IT management and IT governance that makes a difference" (p. 83).

There are subtle differences between them which have important implications. ITG has a wider scope than IT management (Figure 3.2.). As explained by Peterson (2004),

> IT Governance Is a New Form of "Old School" IT Management. Whereas the domain of IT management focuses on the efficient and effective supply of IT operations, services, and products, IT governance faces the dual demands of contributing to present business operations and simultaneously positioning the IT function for meeting future business

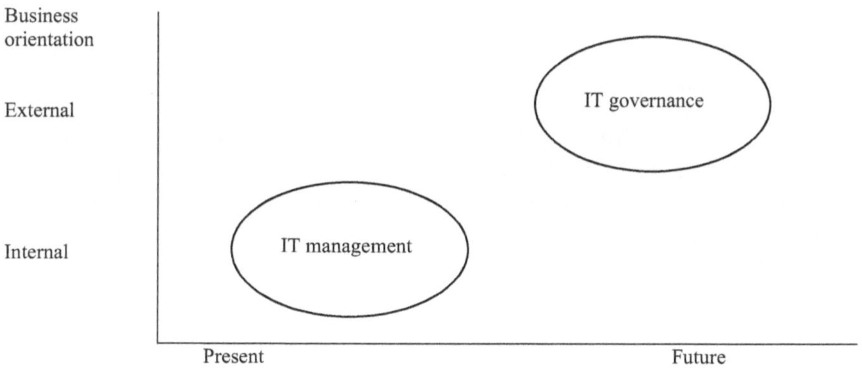

Figure 3.2 ITG versus IT management

Notes: IT management handles with the internal supply of IT services and products, and also the management of IT operations. IT governance focuses on performing and transforming IT to meet present and future demands of business

Source: Adapted from Peterson (2003).

> demands. This does not undermine the importance or complexity of IT management, but serves to indicate that IT governance is both internally and externally oriented, spanning both present and future timeframes.
> (p. 9)

Weill (2004) has also highlighted the gap between ITG and IT Management:

> IT governance is not about what specific decisions are made. That is management. Rather, governance is about systematically determining who makes each type of decision (a decision right), who has input to a decision (an input right) and how these people (or groups) are held accountable for their role. Good IT governance draws on corporate governance principles to manage and use IT to achieve corporate performance goals.
> (p. 3)

ITG and decision-making process

ITG is also closely related to who makes decisions whereas IT management is based on the process of making and implementing decisions (Weill & Woodham, 2002; Weill & Ross, 2004). IT governance is the responsibility of executives and the board of directors, and consists of the leadership, organizational structures, and processes that ensure that the enterprise's IT sustains and extends the organization's strategies and objectives (ITGI – COBITT). The IT Governance Institute (2005) states that

> attaining good IT governance does not happen by accident, or by telling the CIO to 'make it so'. It needs to be prepared, properly implemented and monitored, if value destruction is to be avoided and value creation achieved. The tone has to be set at the top.
> (p. 4)

ITG and transparency in information

Since the beginning of the 2010s, the debate on ITG has been renewed and a few scholars (Joshi et al., 2013; De Haes et al., 2019) have taken into consideration the transparency and disclosure issue in a general environment where the national corporate governance code has an impact on the level of IT governance disclosure. Joshi et al. (2013) have then defined IT governance transparency as "the ability of firms to provide adequate and relevant IT governance information in a timely and effective manner to their stakeholders, such as investors, policy makers, and regulatory bodies, so that they can assess management's behavior in using IT" (p. 118). IT governance transparency can be considered at two levels (external and internal).

The COBIT 5 process reference model (see below) has also highlighted the process named EDM05 Ensure stakeholder transparency explaining "the director's role in monitoring and evaluating IT governance and IT performance with a generic method for establishing goals and objectives and related metrics" (ISACA, 2012, p. 47). Efforts to achieve transparency should be also done in the way goals, metrics, and performance are expressed. In other words, the language should be meaningful to the stakeholders so that appropriate actions can be taken and decisions can be made (ISACA, 2012).

Perspectives for future research

For researchers, the contemporary model represents the beginning of the culmination of foundational research on IT governance frameworks. The building blocks of current research are being used, while new core concepts are also being proposed. Prior to Weill and Ross (2004), the two streams of research resulted in a complex web of theoretical models, many of which are too difficult to substantiate empirically. Researchers are now faced with the opportunity to build on the framework articulated in this paper, to examine the appropriateness of continuing research in one of the streams, or to heed the call for research put forth by Sambamurthy and Zmud (2000) attempting to separate IT governance structures from IT organizational structures.

This chapter is not based on a comprehensive literature review. Several topics in relation to ITG and more precisely the conditions of an effective ITG have not been analyzed in depth as follows:

- ITG organization: ITG is determined by the way the IT function is organized and where the IT decision-making authority is. Finally, can ITG structures be separated from organizational structures?
- The board-level ITG. In parallel with the Agency theory (described previously) or in contradiction to it, the question of the involvement of boards in ITG has been raised from various angles. The stewardship theory states, for example, that the relationship of the owners and management is built on trust. The interests of the stewards and the principals could converge accordingly. Given this perspective, "managers need less oversight, and more advice, because they are deemed to be trustworthy good stewards of the resources they manage. Boards can provide these services as well through the IT issues they discuss." (Turel & Bart, 2014, p. 227).

  The contingency theory is based on the idea that an organization's success is dependent on various internal and external factors (e.g., organization's size, strategy, distinctive resources and core competencies availability, adaptability to legal, technological, and social environment). Nolan and McFarlan (2005) have developed a model of dependence of the firm's current and future operations and activities on technology. In their strategic impact grid, they have represented four "IT use modes" (factory, strategic, support, and turnaround) along two axes (two contingencies: low (defensive) to high (offensive) need for new IT/ low to high need for reliable information technology). In each of these modes, the level and approach in board IT governance can be different.

- The linkages between ITG and new technologies such as robotic process automation (RPA). The literature review suggests that, to be organizationally effective, RPA needs to be aligned with the existing IT governance processes. However, requirements about cycle of implementation and delivery methods are quite different between RPA technology and traditional IT systems. While traditional IT projects focus on stability and efficiency, RPA projects focus on short implementation cycles, test and learn approach, agile approach, and tight cooperation with business units (Exhibit 3.2). The challenge is to have enough flexibility for quick implementation, integration, and scale up of RPA solutions within the existing IT governance framework.

Exhibit 3.2 Governance of RPA projects

Governance of RPA projects covers both IT processes and organizational aspects:

Tasks automation Needs – specifying the business need for purchased or internally developed RPA solutions;

Architecture – defining integration and standardization requirements;

Organizational architecture – RPA project and implementation will have an impact on the organizational architecture following the framework developed by Brickley et al. (1997), leading to major potential changes in the decision-making authority, the performance evaluation system (managers and employees), and the corporate reward system (incentive-compensation systems);

Infrastructure – determining technical resources/environment needed to support RPA software;

Governance structure – defining RPA Governance board to manage the demand pipeline, assessing RPA opportunities and choosing which RPA projects to invest in, defining the RPA project methodology.

On governance structure for RPA projects, there are different approaches identified in the literature review, depending on many parameters such as culture of IT governance in the organization and understanding and maturity of RPA in the business. In most cases, organizations manage to fit RPA within the existing governance structure. For a few companies, the governance of RPA may evolve toward Center of Excellence in the organization as RPA expands new business processes across the business units (Willcocks et al., 2015).

Source: Adapted from Daidj et al. (2021).

Many scholars call for the revision of established IT governance approaches (Willcocks et al., 2015; Asatiani & Penttinen, 2016; Bygstad, 2017; Bygstad & Iden 2017; Asatiani et al., 2019). Bygstad and Iden (2017) have suggested to adopt two different governance structures reflecting the two modes (bi-modal) or one governance structure (platform model) operating in two different modes. In the bi-modal model, RPA solutions are implemented in a separated process but they are aligned with IT policies and standards once set into production. In the platform model, a centralized IT governance structure encourages RPA initiatives which are, however, implemented independently.

ITG frameworks and professional practices

In parallel to academic research on the subject of IT governance, professionals have also seized the topic, and this is the focus of this section.

ITG at a glance

At a first level of understanding, IT governance can also be addressed by answering to the Five Ws (Who, What, When Where, and Why) or Five Ws and one H (How) named also the Six Ws. They represent six basic questions to ask when gathering information or solving a problem (Table 3.7).

Various international and national ITG frameworks

There are many internationally recognized IT governance frameworks that can be used. Frameworks such as ITIL®, COBIT®, ISO/IEC 38500 include in more detail the processes and mechanisms needed to develop, implement, evaluate, and improve an IT governance program (Exhibit 3.3). Other frameworks on corporate governance with developments on ITG exist but they are often dedicated to specific geographical regions or countries (e.g., the King Code of Corporate Governance was elaborated by the King Committee in response to the emergence of the South African companies in the 2000s).

In addition, many organizations have developed their own model tailored to suit their specific needs according to the business they run. It is, for example, common to mention IT project governance models such as PRINCE or Project Management Body of Knowledge (PMBoK), a subset of the project management body of knowledge, elaborated by the Project Management Institute (PMI). These frameworks are useful for companies conducting various project activities and managing the delivery of IT projects.

Table 3.7 The six Ws of IT governance

What? (What not)	IT governance is an integral part of corporate governance and analogously combines leadership, organizational structures, and processes that ensure that IT sustains and extends the organization's strategies and objectives. (Though guided by it, daily operations or operative project management, are not core part of IT governance nor can IT governance substitute for a sound business strategy). What? Strategic alignment Value delivery Risk management Resource management Performance measurement (see below)
Who?	IT governance is the responsibility of the executive board and the executive management (including IT) and supports the interaction of all the organization's parties involved with IT.
Where?	IT governance has been largely adopted by private companies as well as by public organizations (Sethibe et al., 2007; Rusu, & Viscusi, 2017; Jonathan & Rusu, 2018). Centered on the IT department in relation to other departments and/or functions.
When?	The frequency depends on organization's approach to IT governance in relation to its business needs for and reliance on IT to drive and support its main objectives (it could be every 3 to 12 months). "... it is ultimately up to the board to determine how often it requires reports on the progress of IT governance based on the criticality of IT in their organization" (Posthumus et al., 2010, p. 30).
Why?	The IT Governance Institute (a division of ISACA) breaks down IT governance into five domains (2003, 2005, and 2007). To make sure the following basic elements are in place. Strategic alignment and responsiveness: governance works hand in hand with IT portfolio management to align IT investments with strategic objectives to improve responsiveness to challenges and manage current and future IT investments (see above and Chapter 2). Value delivery: fulfilling business' expectations from IT investments while mitigating risks. Performance management and objective decision-making: governance allows leadership to actively commit to improving the management and control of IT activities Resource management: proper management of critical resources (including people, infrastructure, and applications) enables control in planning and organizing IT initiatives. Risk management: aims to ensure the protection of the enterprise's IT assets by improving risk awareness among all stakeholders.
How?	IT governance provides guidelines, establishes criteria and standards for decision-making, monitoring, measuring, and improving the performance of IT

Source: Adapted from GSE-Project Highlight in IT governance. Updated and completed by the author.

Exhibit 3.3 IT governance frameworks, models, and standards

ISO 38500 – The international IT governance standard. International Organization for Standardization (ISO)/International Electrotechnical Commission (IEC) 38500:2015, Governance of IT for the Organization, 2015 version is a framework for corporate governance of IT. It provides principles, definitions, and a framework that organizations of all types and sizes can use to better align their use of IT with organizational decisions and meet their legal, regulatory, and ethical obligations.

ITIL (The IT Infrastructure Library) was initially developed in the 1980s by the British Office of Government Commerce (OGC) as a library of best-practice processes to more effectively manage IT. It is a framework for IT service management (ITSM). ITIL gives guidance on approaches, functions, roles, and processes. Since its creation, it has been widely adopted around the world. ITIL is supported by ISO/IEC 20000:2011 – the international standard for ITSM against which organizations can achieve independent certification. Its latest iteration, ITIL 4, was launched in February 2019. While not claiming to be a governance framework for IT, ITIL presents some useful practices that can be applied to just about any organization to improve how they manage IT.

COBIT is short for Control Objectives for Information and Related Technology. It was developed by the Information Systems Audit and Control Foundation (ISACF) in 1996. ISACF, founded in 1969, later became Information Systems Audit and Control Association (ISACA). ISACA is a non-profit, independent association that advocates for professionals involved in information security, assurance, risk management, and IT governance.

In 1998, ISACA established the IT Governance Institute, ITGI, who is today responsible for COBIT. COBIT is an international IT governance control framework that helps organizations meet business challenges taking into account several dimensions such as regulatory compliance, risk management, and alignment of IT strategy with organizational goals. There have been several updates since the first version of COBIT (COBIT 1) in 1996. The latest iteration of the framework (COBIT 5) was released in November 2018. COBIT is one applicable assessment framework that could help in the compliance issue (SOX, for example). COBIT 5 includes new concepts and addresses new issues about IT governance.

Other frameworks:

The COSO (the Committee of Sponsoring Organizations) is an organization of private organizations, established in the USA, dedicated to providing a common model of guidance. It provides comprehensive risk management (fraud deterrence) to internal controls.

Val IT is a governance framework elaborated in the 2000s. Val IT is based on COBIT by providing further business and financial perspectives. It has been used to create business value from IT investments. It consists of a set of guiding principles and a number of processes and best practices that are further defined as a set of key management practices to support and help executive management and boards at a corporate level.

Calder-Moir IT Governance Framework provides structured guidance on how to approach IT governance. It helps organizations to implement ISO/IEC 38500, the first international standard to provide guidelines for corporate governance of IT. It can help benchmark the balance and effectiveness of IT governance practices within an organization.

Source: Elaborated by the author.

Risks management and compliance

A general level, risks are various impacting several dimensions (strategy, IT, management, operations, cybersecurity, etc.) and can be represented in an overall risk mapping and/or matrix. They should be reduced to an acceptable level, and controls should be adapted according to the organization's environment in terms of risk acceptance, risk response, and legal compliance. In the next chapter, we'll present audit methodologies including risks issues. In this section, we rather focus on links between ITG, risks management, and compliance. How risks have been progressively included in ITG frameworks?

Toward a life cycle of ITG and/or a virtuous circle?

One of the best-known examples of the notion of life cycle is used in marketing (product and technology life cycle) and in strategic management (organization life cycle). A company progresses through different phases and the speed at which it experiences these stages depends on the market environment of its industry. In general, there are four stages in a life cycle: beginning (introduction), growth, maturity (and saturation), and finally decline. The life cycle is also closely linked with management actions and decisions. It is common to quote the life cycle of an IT system "from development through operations and maintenance of IT systems, as well as horizontal processes such as project management" (EDPS, 2018, p. 16).

Regarding more specifically ITG, as for any key strategic component, its development follows several stages that could lead to a vicious or virtuous circle. As mentioned previously, ITG is based on five pillars closely related as follows: strategic alignment, value delivery, resources management, risk

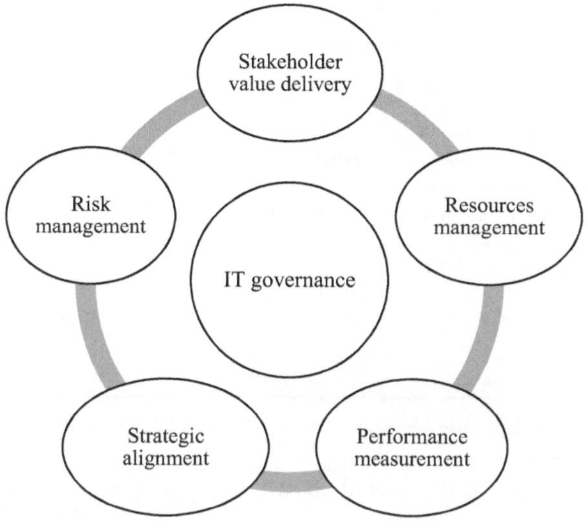

Figure 3.3 ITG five pillars
Source: Elaborated by the author.

management, and performance measurement. Stakeholder value delivery could be considered as the driver of this circle (Figure 3.3).

ITG and risks management: the evolution of the COBIT framework

In most of ITG frameworks previously, risks are mentioned in order to be identified and managed properly. To make links with the former section, we propose to comment the evolution of the COBIT framework. As a generic framework, it should be customized according to the organization needs and environment. The COBIT control objectives document is divided into four domains that describe the risks and activities within IT that needs to be managed In addition, it has evolved since its first elaboration. It was originally developed as a tool to control IT and reduce risk within IT organizations. Its scope has been progressively extended as shown in Table 3.8. COBIT 5 fosters the use of balanced scorecards (Chapter 2) and goal cascades to help IT leaders (Suer et al., 2014). COBIT 5 goals cascade is the mechanism to translate stakeholder needs into specific, actionable, and customized enterprise goals, IT-related goals and enabler goals.

COBIT 5's seven enablers (factors which influence at an individual or collective level, how governance and management over enterprise IT will work) are:

- Principles, Policies and Frameworks
- Processes
- Organizational Structures
- Culture, Ethics and Behavior
- Information

- Services, Infrastructure and Applications
- People, Skills and Competencies

Table 3.8 Governance of Enterprise IT (GEIT): the evolution of the scope

	1996	*1998*	*2000*	*2005–2007*	*2012–2019*
Evolution of scope	COBIT 1 Audit	COBIT 2 Control	COBIT 3 Management	COBIT4.0/4.1 IT governance	COBIT 5 Governance of enterprise IT

Source: Adapted from ISACA (2022).

Relevant enablers (from the seven) should be applied to the executive strategies and tactics for the company and employees. COBIT 5 defines 37 governance and management processes clustered as follows:

- One governance domain: Evaluate, Direct, and Monitor (EDM).
- Four management domains: Plan, Built, Run, and Monitor (PBRM). These four domains are in line with the responsibility areas of PBRM (an evolution of the COBIT 4.1 domains), and they provide end-to-end coverage of IT (Appendix 3.1).

As seen previously in Table 3.6, the "three lines of defense" can be used as one of the main models to define roles, responsibilities, and accountabilities for decision-making, risk, and control to achieve effective governance risk management and assurance. Operational management (including IT) represents the first line of defense and is responsible for the implementation and maintenance of processes and controls to manage risks. Compliance functions and risk management represent the second line of defense and are responsible for monitoring risks across the organization. Internal audit represents the third line of defense and is responsible for providing independent assurance that risk management and controls are operating effectively, and advise senior management and the board when deficiencies are identified.

Oyemade (2012) has proposed to combine the three lines of defense with risk IT and COBIT frameworks as shown in Table 3.9. "The adoption and implementation of the Risk IT and COBIT frameworks within the boundaries of the three lines of defense model further strengthen an enterprise's IT governance framework" (Oyemade, 2012, p. 25).

The development of compliance requirements

The compliance is defined by the IIA (2018) as "the adherence to policies, plans, procedures, laws, regulations, contracts, or other requirements" (p. 26). In addition, compliance is closely related to compliance risk (Exhibit 3.4).

Table 3.9 The three lines of defense in relation to COBIT framework

Three lines of defense		*Risk IT and COBIT frameworks*
First line of defense		
Responsibility: Business operations performs day-to-day risk management activity	→	Risk IT framework
Function: An established risk and control environment	→	COBIT framework
Second Line of defense		
Responsibility: Oversight functions such as finance, HR, quality, and risk management, define policy and provide assurance.	→	COBIT framework
Function: Strategic management, policy and procedure setting, functional oversight		
Third line of defense		
Responsibility: Independence assurance includes internal audit, external audit, and other independent assurance providers and offers independent challenges to the levels of assurance provided by business operations and oversight functions.	→	COBIT framework
Function: Provides independent challenge and assurance		

Source: Adapted from Oyemade (2012, p. 25).

Exhibit 3.4 The role of compliance

Compliance is typically described as the process of adhering to obligations derived from laws, regulations, industry and organizational standards, contractual commitments, corporate commitments (e.g., social responsibility statements, corporate filings), values, ethics, and corporate policies and procedures. Similar to the internal audit, the compliance function plays a critical role in providing information to the board and other roles across the organization that contribute to good corporate governance.

The existence of the compliance function is strongly suggested by regulatory bodies and enforcement organizations (…).

Central to the role of compliance is the management of compliance risk; the risk of legal or regulatory sanctions, material financial loss, or loss to reputation. While the role of the compliance professional varies by industry and the types of regulations that must be addressed, there is a common set of duties that is required of most compliance professionals. These can be broken down into four major categories: tracking and assessing regulations, developing and implementing policies, providing education and guidance, and monitoring, auditing, and documenting.

Source: Extract from Thomson Reuters (2012, p. 4).

We have previously mentioned that IT governance is challenged by compliance requirements, corporate governance, or public listing rules. More and more legal and regulatory obligations have been adopted since the beginning of the 2000s, such as those set out in the GDPR (General Data Protection Regulation) in 2018 or the Companies Act 2006 in the UK (up to date with

Exhibit 3.5 The GDPR (General Data Protection Regulation) – overview

The European Data Protection Regulation is applicable as of May 25th, 2018 in all member states to harmonize data privacy laws across Europe.

Personal data shall be:

"a processed lawfully, fairly and in a transparent manner in relation to individuals ('lawfulness, fairness and transparency');

b collected for specified, explicit, and legitimate purposes and not further processed in a manner that is incompatible with those purposes; further processing for archiving purposes in the public interest, scientific or historical research purposes or statistical purposes shall not be considered to be incompatible with the initial purposes ('purpose limitation');

c adequate, relevant, and limited to what is necessary in relation to the purposes for which they are processed ('data minimisation');

d accurate and, where necessary, kept up to date; every reasonable step must be taken to ensure that personal data that are inaccurate, having regard to the purposes for which they are processed, are erased or rectified without delay ('accuracy');

e kept in a form which permits identification of data subjects for no longer than is necessary for the purposes for which the personal data are processed; personal data may be stored for longer periods insofar as the personal data will be processed solely for archiving purposes in the public interest, scientific or historical research purposes or statistical purposes subject to implementation of the appropriate technical and organisational measures required by the GDPR in order to safeguard the rights and freedoms of individuals ('storage limitation');

f processed in a manner that ensures appropriate security of the personal data, including protection against unauthorised or unlawful processing and against accidental loss, destruction or damage, using appropriate technical or organisational measures ('integrity and confidentiality')."

Source: Based on Europa website (https://eur-lex.europa.eu/eli/reg/2016/679/oj).

all changes known to be in force on or before 14 March 2022). Exhibit 3.5 presents the main data protection principles according to the GDPR.

Conclusion

IT governance is a subset of corporate governance that includes all organizational assets and processes. IT governance is a broad topic that raises several questions in many areas: information technology, information system management, risk management, IT and business alignment, strategy, project management, compliance, etc. There are IT governance solutions and tools associated with most of these disciplines, but most of them are very detailed and have specific scopes (Nicho & Khan, 2017). Leung et al. (2004) have stated that "internal auditors are positive about their role in corporate governance but are less confident with respect to how to put such a role into practice" (p. 6)

At a general level, IT governance should sustain the organization objectives (Gunawardena & Ramesh, 2014). IT governance is a key strategic element because it is fundamentally concerned with goals that ensure that IT delivers value to the business in a controlled and efficient manner in order to increase business benefits (De Haes & Van Grembergen, 2004; Schwertsik et al., 2009). Leading organizations have to rely on an effective IT governance as legal, regulatory, operational, and overall business risks are more and more pregnant in the current context.

Questions for discussion

What is the impact of IT governance on business performance?

How can you ensure good IT governance?

What role do auditors play in the IT governance?

To what extent IT governance, risk management and compliance are inter-related?

How to include emerging and/or disruptive technologies in an IT governance framework?

Recommended reading

Almeida, R., Pereira, R., & Mira da Silva, M. (2013). IT governance mechanisms: A literature review. In J. Falcão e Cunha, M. Snene & H. Nóvoa (Eds.), *Proceedings of 2013 annual conference of exploring services science* (pp. 186–199). Berlin, Heidelberg: Springer. https://doi.org/10.1007/978-3-642-36356-6_14

Grembergen, W.V., Haes, S.D., & Guldentops, E. (2004). Structures, Processes, and relational mechanisms for information technology governance: Theories and practices. In W.V. Grembergen (Ed.), *Strategies for information technology* (pp. 1–36). London: Idea Group Inc.

Nicho, M., & Muamaar, S. (2016). Towards a taxonomy of challenges in an integrated IT governance framework implementation. *Journal of International Technology and Information Management*, *25*(2), 1–31.

References

AFAI-CIGREF (2005). *The place of IT governance in the enterprise governance. Balancing performance and conformance.* Retrieved February 14, 2022 from: https://cigref.typepad.fr/itgifrance/files/place_IT_governance_in_enterprise_governance.pdf

Arrow, K.J. (1974). *The limits of organization.* New York and London: W.W. Norton & Company.

Asatiani, A., Kämäräinen, T., & Penttinen, E. (2019). *Unexpected problems associated with the federated IT governance structure in Robotic Process Automation (RPA) deployment.* Aalto University, Finland: Aalto University publication series BUSINESS + ECONOMY. http://urn.fi/URN:ISBN:978-952-60-8698-9

Asatiani, A., & Penttinen, E. (2016). Turning robotic process automation into commercial success – Case OpusCapita. *Journal of Information Technology Teaching Cases, 6*(2), 67–74.

Beachboard, J., Aytes, K., & Probst, J. (2010). IT governance and IT management: Is there a difference that makes a difference? *Proceedings of Informing Science & IT Education Conference (InSITE), 10*, 77–86. https://doi.org/10.28945/1234

Beimborn, D., Schlosser, F., & Weitzel, T. (2009). Proposing a theoretical model for IT governance and IT business alignment. *Proceedings of the 42nd Annual Hawaii International Conference on System Sciences*, 1–11. https://doi.org/10.1109/HICSS.2009.358.

Berle, A., & Means, G. (1982). *The modern corporation and private property.* Buffalo, NY: Hein. Originally published by Macmillan in 1932.

Brickley, J., Smith, C., & Zimmerman, J. (1997). Management fads and organizational architecture. *Journal of Applied Corporate Finance, 10*(2), 24–39.

Brown, C.V. (1997). Examining the emergence of hybrid IS governance solutions: Evidence from a single case site. *Information Systems Research, 8*(1), 69–94.

Burtscher, C., Manwani, M., & Remenyi, D. (2009). Towards a conceptual map of IT governance: A review of current academic and practitioner thinking. *Proceedings of the UK Academy for Information Systems Conference* (15).

Bygstad, B. (2017). Generative innovation: A comparison of lightweight and heavyweight IT. *Journal of Information Technology, 32*(2), 180–193.

Bygstad, B., & Iden, J. (2017). A governance model for managing lightweight IT. *Proceedings of World Conference on Information Systems and Technologies,* 569, 384–393. Cham: Springer. https://doi.org/10.1007/978-3-319-56535-4

Calder A. (2007). *IT governance - A pocket guide.* Cambridgeshire: IT Governance Publishing.

Chabrak N., & Daidj, N. (2007). Enron: Widespread myopia. *Critical Perspectives on Accounting, 18*(5), 539–557.

Chandler, A.D. (1977). *The visible hand: The managerial revolution in American business.* Cambridge, MA: The Belknap Press of Harvard University Press.

Chaudhuri, A. (2011). Enabling effective IT governance: Leveraging ISO/IEC 38500:2008 and COBIT to achieve business–IT alignment. *EDPACS, 44*(2), 1–18. https://doi.org/10.1080/07366981.2011.599278.

Daidj, N. (2016). *Strategy, structure and corporate governance. Expressing inter-firms networks.* Aldershot: Taylor & Francis Group.

Daidj, N., Tounkara, T., & Bordeaux, C. (2021). *The evolution of IT audit.* White paper. https://www.imt-bs.eu/livre-blanc-futur-audit-it-nabyla-daidj-thierno-tounkara/

De Brouwer, G. (2003). *Macroeconomics and governance.* Treasury working paper, 2003–2004. December 3. Retrieved September 18, 2021 from: http://archive.treasury.gov.au/documents/773/PDF/ Macroeconomics%20and%20Governance.pdf

De Haes, S., Van Grembergen, W., Joshi, A., & Huygh, T. (2020). *Enterprise governance of information technology: achieving alignment and value in digital organizations*. Cham, Switzerland: Springer Nature Switzerland AG.

De Haes, S., Huygh, T., Joshi, A., & Caluve, L. (2019). National corporate governance codes and IT governance transparency in annual reports. *Journal of Global Information Management, 27*(4), 91–118. https://doi.org/10.4018/JGIM.2019100105

De Haes, S., Joshi, A., Huygh, T., & Jansen, S. (2017). Exploring how corporate governance codes address IT governance. *ISACA Journal, 4*, 1–7.

De Haes, S., & Van Grembergen, W. (2015). *Enterprise governance of information technology*. 2nd Edition. Cham: Springer.

De Haes, S., & Van Grembergen, W. (2009). An exploratory study into IT governance implementations and its impact on business/IT alignment. *Information Systems Management, 26*(2), 123–137.

De Haes, S., & Van Grembergen, W. (2008). Analysing the relationship between IT governance and business/IT alignment maturity. *Proceedings of the 41st International Conference on System Sciences*, 428–428.

De Haes, S., & Van Grembergen, W. (2005). IT governance structures, processes and relational mechanisms: Achieving IT/business alignment in a major Belgian financial group. *Proceedings of the 38th Hawaii International Conference on System Sciences*, 237b–237b. https://doi.org/10.1109/HICSS.2005.362.

De Haes, S., & Van Grembergen, W. (2004). IT governance and its mechanisms. *Information Systems Control Journal, 1*, 27–33.

Dutta, A., Roy, R., & Seetharaman, P. (2022). An assimilation maturity model for IT governance and auditing, *Information & Management, 59*(1), 103569. https://doi.org/10.1016/j.im.2021.103569

The European Confederation of Institutes of Internal Auditing (ECIIA) (2022). *What is internal auditing*? Retrieved January 12, 2022 from: https://www.eciia.eu/what-is-internal-auditing/

The European Confederation of Institutes of Internal Auditing/The Federation of European Risk Management Associations (2011). *ECIIA/FERMA guidance on the 8th EU company law directive (article 41)*. Retrieved January 12, 2022 from: https://www.iia.nl/SiteFiles/ECIIA%20FERMA%20-2.pdf

European Data Protection Supervisor (EDPS) (2018). *Guidelines on the protection of personal data in IT governance and IT management of EU institutions*. Retrieved January 12, 2022 from: https://edps.europa.eu/sites/edp/files/publication/it_governance_management_en.pdf

Fama, E.F., & Jensen, M.C. (1983). Separation of ownership and control. *Journal of Law and Economics, 26*(2), 301–325.

Freeman, R.E. (1984). *Strategic management: A stakeholder approach*. Boston, MA: Pitman Publishing Inc.

Gheorghe, M. (2010). Audit methodology for IT governance. *Informatica Economica, 14*(1), 32–42.

Gill, A. (2008). Corporate governance as social responsibility: A research agenda. *Berkeley Journal of International Law, 26(2)*, 452–478.

Gunawardena, L., & Ramesh, L. (2014). Understanding IT governance and why it often fails. https://www.architectureandgovernance.com/it-governance/understanding-governance-often-fails/

Hardy, G. (2009). The role of the IT auditor in IT governance. *Information Systems Control Journal, 4*, 1–5.

The Institute of Internal Auditors (IIA) (2013). *Position paper: The three lines of defense in effective risk management and control.* Retrieved January 15, 2022 from: https://www.iia.nl/SiteFiles/IIA_leden/ippf%20pp%20the%20three%20lines%20of%20defense%20in%20effective%20risk%20management%20and%20control[1].pdf

The Institute of Internal Auditors (IIA) - International Professional Practices Framework (2018). *Supplemental guidance. Global technology audit guide (GTAG).* Auditing IT Governance. Retrieved January 15, 2022 from: https://www.iia.nl/SiteFiles/GTAG%2017%20Auditing%20IT%20Governance.pdf

ISACA (2012). COBIT® 5. *A business framework for the governance and management of enterprise IT.* Retrieved November 11, 2022 from: https://www.oo2.fr/sites/default/files/document/pdf/cobit-5_res_eng_1012.pdf

IT Compliance Institute (2007). *IT governance and strategy. Practical guidance for managers on how to prepare for successful audits.* Retrieved November 11, 2022 from: http://download.101com.com/pub/itci/files/itci_itacl governance_0702b.pdf

IT Governance Institute (2007). *CobiT 4.1 – Framework, control objectives, management guidelines and maturity models.* Retrieved December 11, 2018 from: https://www.bauer.uh.edu/parks/cobit_4.1.pdf

IT Governance Institute (2005). *IT governance domain practices and competencies: IT alignment - Who is in charge?* Retrieved November 11, 2022 from: http://www.isaca.org/Knowledge- Center/Research/Research Deliverables/Pages/IT-Governance-Domains-Practices-and-Competencies-IT- Alignment-Who-Is-in-Charge.aspx

IT Governance Institute (2003). *Board briefing on IT governance.* 2nd Edition. Rolling Meadows, IL Retrieved December 11, 2018 from: http://www.isaca.org/knowledge-center/research/researchdeliverables/pages/board-briefing-on-it-governance-2nd-edition.aspx

Jensen, M.E., & Meckling, W.H. (1976). Theory of the firm: Managerial behavior, agency costs and ownership structure. *Journal of Financial Economics, 3*(4), 305–360.

Johnson, G., Scholes, K., & Whittington, R. (2008). *Exploring corporate strategy.* Harlow: Financial Times/Prentice Hall.

Jonathan, G.M., & Rusu, L. (2018). IT governance in public organizations: A systematic literature review. *International Journal of IT/Business Alignment and Governance (IJITBAG), 9*(2), 30–52. https://doi.org/10.4018/ijitbag.2018070103

Joshi, A., Bollen, L., & Hassink, H. (2013). An empirical assessment of IT governance transparency: Evidence from commercial banking. *Information Systems Management, 30*(2), 116–136. https://doi.org/10.1080/10580530.2013.773805.

Knight, F.H. (1921). *Risk, uncertainty and profit.* New York: Houghton Mifflin Company.

Lazonick, W., & O'Sullivan, M. (2000). Maximizing shareholder value: A new ideology for corporate governance. *Economy and Society, 29*(1), 13–35.

Leung, P., Cooper, B.J.R, & Robertson, P.T. (2004). *The role of internal audit in corporate governance & management.* Melbourne: RMIT Publishing.

Luftman, J. (1996). *Competing in the information age: Practical applications of the strategic alignment model.* New York: Oxford University Press.

Luftman, J. & Brier, T. (1999). Achieving and sustaining business-IT alignment. *California Management Review, 42*(1), 109–122. https://doi.org/10.2307/41166021

Mizruchi, M.S. (1996). What do interlocks do? An analysis, critique and assessment of research on interlocking directorates. *Annual Review of Sociology, 22*(1), 271–298.

Nicho, M., & Khan, S. (2017). IT governance measurement tools and its application in IT-business alignment. *Journal of International Technology and Information Management, 26*(1), 81–111.

Nolan, R., & McFarlane, F. (2005) Information technology and the board of directors. *Harvard Business Review 83*(10), 96–106.

OECD (2021). *Government at a glance 2021.* Paris: OECD Publishing. https://doi.org/10.1787/1c258f55-en

Oyemade, R. (2012). Effective IT governance through the three lines of defense, risk IT and COBIT. *ISACA Journal, 1*, 24–25.

Peterson, R.R. (2004). Crafting information technology governance. *Information Systems Management, 21*(4), 7–22. http://doi.org/10.1201/1078/44705.21.4.20040901/84183.2

Peterson, R.R. (2003) Information strategies and tactics for information technology governance. In W. V. Grembergen (Ed.), *Strategies for information technology governance* (pp. 37–80). Hershey, PA: Idea Group Publishing.

Peterson, R.R., O'Callaghan, R., & Ribbers, P.M.A. (2000). Information technology governance by design: Investigating hybrid configurations and integration mechanisms. *Proceedings of the 21st International Conference on Information systems*, 435–452.

Posthumus, S., Von Solms, R., & King, M. (2010). The board and IT governance: The what, who and how. *South African Journal of Business Management, 41*(3), 23–32. http://doi.org/10.4102/sajbm.v41i3.522.

Rusu, L., & Viscusi, G. (2017). *Information technology governance in public organizations.* Integrated Series in Information Systems. Cham: Springer.

Sambamurthy, V., & Zmud, R.W. (1999). Arrangements for information technology governance: A theory of multiple contingencies. *MIS Quarterly, 23*(2), 261–290. https://doi.org/10.2307/249754

Schwertsik, A., Wolf, P., & Krcmar, H. (2009). IT-controlling in federal organizations. *Proceedings of the 17th European Conference on Information Systems (ECIS)*, 2158–2169.

Sethibe, T., Campbell, J., & McDonald, C. (2007). IT governance in public and private sector organisations: Examining the differences and defining future research directions. *Proceedings of ACIS*, 118. http://aisel.aisnet.org/acis2007/118

Solomon, J., & Solomon, A. (2004). *Corporate governance and accountability.* Chichester: John Wiley & Sons.

Suer, M., Cullens, C., & Brancato, D. (2014). COBIT 5 processes from a systems management perspective. https://www.isaca.org/resources/isaca-journal/past-issues/2014/cobit-5-processes-from-a-systems-management-perspective.

Thomson Reuters (2012). *Fundamentals of GRC. The connected roles of internal audit and compliance.* White Paper. Retrieved January 11, 2022 from: https://www.iia.nl/SiteFiles/Downloads/Fundamentals_of%20GRC_Internal_Audit_and_Compliance_US.pdf

Turel, O., & Bart, C. (2014). Board-level IT governance and organizational performance. *European Journal of Information Systems 23*(2), 223–239. https://doi.org/10.1057/ejis.2012.61.

Van Grembergen, W. (2002). Introduction to the minitrack IT governance and its mechanisms. *Proceedings of the 35th Hawaii International Conference on System Sciences (HICSS)*. https://doi.org/10.1109/HICSS.2007.292

Van Grembergen, W. & De Haes, S (n.d.). *Enterprise governance of IT.* University of Antwerp Management School (UAMS). Retrieved February 9, 2022 from: https://www.aiea.it/sites/default/files/attivita/sds/van_grembergen.pdf

Van Grembergen, W., De Haes, S., & Guldentops, E. (2003). Structures, processes and relational mechanisms for information technology governance: Theories and practices. In W. Van Grembergen (Ed.), *Strategies for information technology governance* (pp. 1–36). Hershey, PA: Idea Group Publishing.

Webb, P., Pollard, C., & Ridley, G. (2006). Attempting to define IT governance: Wisdom or folly? *Proceedings of the 39th Annual Hawaii International Conference on System Sciences*, wei194a–194a.

Weill, P. (2004). Don't just lead govern: How top-performing firms govern IT. *MIS Quarterly Executive*, *3*(1), 1–17.

Weill, P., & Ross, J. W. (2004). *IT governance: How top performers manage IT decision rights for superior results.* Boston, MA: Harvard Business School Press.

Weill, P., & Woodham, R. (2002). Don't just lead, govern: Implementing effective IT governance. *MIT Sloan School of Management Research Paper Series*, Cambridge, Working Paper 4237-02, 17.

Willcocks, L., Lacity, M., & Craig, A. (2015). *The IT function and robotic process automation.* The Outsourcing Unit Working Research Paper Series (15/05). The London School of Economics and Political Science, London, UK.

Appendix 3.1

COBIT 5 Process Reference model

Evaluate, Direct and Monitor (EDM)					
EDM01	*EDM02*		*EDM03*	*EDM04*	*EDM05*
Ensure Governance Framework Setting and Maintenance	*Ensure Benefits Delivery*		*Ensure Risk Optimization*	*Ensure Resource Optimization*	*Ensure Stakeholder Transparency*
Align, Plan and Organize (APO)					Monitor, Evaluate and Assess (MEA)
APO01	APO02	APO03	APO04	APO05	MEA01
Manage the IT Framework	Manage Strategy	Manage Enterprise Architecture	Manage Innovation	Manage Portfolio	Monitor, Evaluate and Assess Performance and Conformance
APO06	APO07	APO08	APO09	APO010	
Manage Budget and Costs	Manage Human Resources	Manage Relationships	Manage Service Agreements	Manage Suppliers	
APO011	APO012	APO013			
Manage Quality	Manage Risk	Manage Security			
Build, Acquire and Implement (BAI)					
BAI01	BAI02	BAI03	BAI04	BAI05	MEA02
Manage Programs and Projects	Manage Requirement Definitions	Manage Solutions Identification and Build	Manage Availability and Capacity	Manage Organizational Change Enablement	Monitor, Evaluate, and Assess the System of Internal Control
BAI06	BAI07	BAI08	BAI09	BAI10	
Manage Changes	Manage Change Acceptance and Transitioning	Manage Knowledge	Manage Assets	Manage Configuration	

(Continued)

Evaluate, Direct and Monitor (EDM)

EDM01	*EDM02*	*EDM03*	*EDM04*	*EDM05*
Ensure Governance Framework Setting and Maintenance	*Ensure Benefits Delivery*	*Ensure Risk Optimization*	*Ensure Resource Optimization*	*Ensure Stakeholder Transparency*

Deliver, Service and Support (DSS)

DSS01 Manage Operations	DSS02 Manage Service Requests and Incidents	DSS03 Manage Problems	DSS04 Manage Continuity	DSS05 Manage Security Services	MEA03 Monitor, Evaluate and Assess Compliance with External Requirements
DSS06 Manage Business Process Controls					

Processes for Management of Enterprise IT

Source: COBIT 5. An ISACA® Framework (2012, p. 24). https://community.mis.temple.edu/mis5203sec003spring2020/files/2019/01/COBIT5-Ver2-enabling.pdf

4 The evolution of auditing methodologies

Introduction

This chapter addresses three, of particular interest, main auditing methodologies to perform information technology (IT) audit and information system (IS) audit as follows: the risk-based approach, IT governance, and agility.

Audit methodologies highlight risks that have existed for years. The growing complexity of the environment in all its dimensions (economic, legal, regulatory, digital, technological, etc.) is encouraging the development of new models for risk analysis and management strategies. Risk analysis consists of better understanding of qualitative aspects and also takes into account quantitative information (financial results, performance indicators, etc.). In this uncertain context in which strategic decision-making is made even more difficult, auditors and internal controllers once again play a fundamental role.

The audit of IS governance is a transversal approach that includes many dimensions that do not systematically appear in other methodologies. Finally, there is an urgent need to transform the internal audit function through innovation and agility.

> In today's world, disruptions are bigger, coming faster, and require responses that are quicker and more fluid. In this environment, internal audit is vulnerable — vulnerable to complacency, vulnerable to insignificance, vulnerable to being replaced (…). Transformation of internal audit is the only acceptable solution. Internal audit must transform itself to provide value to organizations in the midst of disruption. This will require agility, innovation, talent, and engagement with the board.
>
> (IIA, 2018, p. 5)

This chapter is divided into three sections. In the first section, we review the "traditional" IT audit approaches. In the second section, we discuss the issue of digital maturity in relation to internal auditing. The third section is dedicated to the evolution of IT audit methodologies driven by digital technology. Three specific approaches are presented as follows: the risk-based framework, the IT governance audit methodology, and finally the stakes of agile auditing.

DOI: 10.4324/9781003215110-5

The "traditional" IT audit approaches

Several methodologies exist to carry out an IT audit and an IS audit. We have chosen to present two of them, which favor a specific approach but which also overlap.

The multiple-level methodology

This analysis is based on several domains as follows: technical, functional, organizational, service contracts, and governance and security. Several audit and consulting groups promote this method, including ORIA (Table 4.1).

In this context, the information system is broken down into five layers that cover Support Infrastructure, Network & Telecom Infrastructure, Server & Storage Infrastructure, User Environment, and Applications & Data (Exhibit 4.1). According to ORIA, "the number of layers may vary depending on the size of the Information System to be studied and the degree of precision of the final result expected in the Audit."

The initial model integrates colors (substituted here by crosses) reflecting the risks involved and the actions to be conducted accordingly. Three situations can be identified:

- Situation under control (one cross)

Improvements may be necessary, but the policy is mature enough to ensure its contribution to the stability of the IS.

- Situation at risk (two crosses)

An active policy exists, but it is incomplete. Actions are required.

- Critical situation (three crosses)

The current policy is weak or even lacking and jeopardizes the stability of the IS in the area in question. An action plan must be initiated immediately.

The matrix clearly identifies the components for which priority action must be taken. It thus enables a first prioritized and planned approach to the action plan and operational recommendations.

Table 4.1 An example of a multi-level methodology

Technical audit	*Functional audit*	*Organizational audit*
	Contract (services) audits Governance audit* and security ⟶	

* Note: This type of audit is developed further in this chapter.
Source: Adapted from ORIA (2018).

Exhibit 4.1 Analysis of information system layers

Hardware	Level of intervention			
↓	Layer	Resource	Management	Preservation
	Infrastructure support	X	XX	XXX
	Infrastructure network & telecom	XX	X	X
Software	Infrastructure servers & storage	XXX	XX	XXX
	Users environment & data	X XX	XX XXX	X XXX

Source: Adapted from ORIA (2018).

The breakdown according to the scope of auditing mission

It is the general scope or the specificity of assignments whose main purpose is IS that is decisive here. This is the position defended by the Internal Audit Harmonization Committee in France (*Comité d'harmonisation de l'audit interne de l'État*): "IS auditing can either be a sub-area of a generalist audit (organization, processes, compliance, etc.), or it can be the main focus of the mission (application, project, security, compliance with legislation, etc.)" (2014, p. 5). These are cross-cutting approaches (Table 4.2) into which governance and security issues could be integrated.

Table 4.2 From global audit assignments to IT audits

IT audit as part of global audit	*Audit missions whose main purpose is related to the IS domain*
Organizational audits	Application audits
Process audits	IT project audits
Regularity audits	Security audits
Outsourced functions audit	Data quality audits
Non-IS project audits	Specific regularity audits

Traditional audit approaches have been successful for decades. The traditional audit approach is effective because it provides an overview of risks. However, it does not always provide an exhaustive or precise view of the risk, due to certain limitations related, in particular, to the scope of the audit, materiality thresholds, selected samples, etc.

A trend that has been growing in recent years is the implementation of 'Bottom-Up' audits: these are based on automated or semi-automated analysis of the company's data and will make it possible to detect anomalies, weak signals characteristic of anomalies, and sometimes to identify not only theoretical risks but also real risks. For example, the classic audit approach can highlight a theoretical risk of non-compliance with the separation of functions (purchase order/delivery/invoice/payment), but the 'Bottom-Up' approach will go beyond this by identifying precisely the risky operations linked to a fraud or an error and the related evaluation in euros over a given period (Daidj et al., 2021).

Digital maturity model in internal audit

The impact of the digital transformation: the emergence of digital maturity model (DMM)

As seen in Chapter 1, the digital transformation has led organizations to respond to several changes in relation to digitalization and the increasing use of digital tools more and required within the audit profession (Bierstaker et al., 2001; Dowling & Leech, 2014). In this digital context, both scholars and practitioners have elaborated digital maturity models not only to understand "what 'digital' really means?" (Dörner & Edelman, 2015) but even more importantly to provide guidelines for a clear path throughout the digital transformation journey.

From a theoretical and conceptual perspective, maturity models are an issue of growing interest in IS research (Becker et al., 2009).

There are several maturity concepts (or understandings) of maturity as Lahrmann et al. (2011) have pointed out. The dimensions of maturity can be explained through specific areas such as capability (IT capability), process, or design objects structuring the field of interest. Each dimension is further specified by a number of measures (practices, objects, or activities) at each level (Fraser et al., 2002; De Bruin et al., 2005). Digital maturity can be considered as a systematic way for an organization to transform digitally (Kane et al., 2017).

The Digital Maturity Model (DMM) is used by researchers for several purposes:

- to test the various dimensions of the DMM (customer experience, product innovation, strategy, organization, process digitization, collaboration, IT, culture and expertise, transformation management) at each stage in a digital business transformation process (Berghaus & Back, 2016). Five stages have been then considered: Stage 1 – Promote and Support; Stage 2 – Create and Build; Stage 3 – Commit to transform; Stage 4 – User-centered and elaborated processes; Stage 5 – Data-driven enterprise.
- To measure the maturity level of digital technology and determine the target maturity level to be achieved in the future accordingly. Maturity models are explored in two ways (Berghaus & Back, 2016). In their descriptive functionality, maturity models identify the dimensions that need to be designed, and in their prescriptive functionality, they allow companies to define actions to be made or capabilities needed to reach the desired stage of maturity (Pöppelbuß & Röglinger, 2011; Mullaly, 2014);

- To link with capability maturity model. In that context, a maturity level consists of related specific and generic practices for a predefined set of maturity dimensions that can improve the organization's overall maturity (Teichert, 2019).

Practitioners share the same views than scholars by defining the DMM as a framework used to determine the level of maturity and readiness of an organization or company digitally today, and to help build a roadmap for the plans and future of the organization or company. Moreover, they attempt to provide a clear, scaleable, reliable (metrics), and adaptable (various contexts) tool for organizations (Deloitte, 2018). The digital transformation journey is divided into three main actions: imagine (identify the opportunities and define vision), deliver (prioritize capabilities to enhance based on business objectives), and run (evaluate process improvement and effectiveness).

TM Forum (an alliance of more than 850 global companies working together to break down technology and cultural barriers between digital service providers, technology suppliers, consultancies, and systems integrators) has also emphasized the role of capabilities for companies in their digital transformation journey across their organization. In its framework, TM Forum (2017, 2020) has identified five maturity levels as shown in Table 4.3.

Table 4.3 The five DMM maturity levels

Increasing contribution to business value ↑	Leading	Best in class digital transformation capability, optimized for agility, is pervasively embedded within organizational culture, processes, and trusted partners ecosystems
	Advancing	Digital transformation excellence is delivering coherent organization-wide change and strategically competitive advantage in multiple areas of the business
	Performing	Effective strategic leadership is delivering a coordinated and innovative approach to a digital transformation-led simplification in multiple areas of the business
	Emerging	Isolated digital transformation initiatives aimed at specific improvements
	Initiating	Digital strategy is in early formulation. Business as usual

Source: Adopted from TM Forum (2020).

DMM and internal audit: toward continuous auditing methodology

The DMM has been applied for internal audit leading to the development of new practices in auditing called continuous auditing. The terms continuous audit and continuous auditing can be used interchangeably.

> Rooted in an internal audit methodology, the maturity model serves as a guide along the journey from traditional internal audit models toward more mature levels of continuous auditing, and through to the continuous assurance of enterprise risk management – an ultimate goal of internal audit, as well as, most enterprises and their executive management. A key first step within the maturity model is the successful integration of data analytics
>
> (KPMG, 2013, p. 2).

The first guidance on continuous auditing was published jointly by the CICA and AICPA (1999) and is often called the Red Book. They define

> the continuous audit as a methodology that enables independent auditors to provide written assurance on a subject matter, for which an entity's management is responsible, using a series of auditor's reports issued virtually simultaneously with, or a short period of time after, the occurrence of events underlying the subject matter.
>
> (CICA/AICPA, 1999)

Since 1999, this report has been updated by various professional bodies. The Institute of Internal Auditors published its GTAG 3 *Continuous Auditing: Implications for Assurance, Monitoring, and Risk Assessment* (IIA, 2005) and ISACA its *IT Audit and Assurance Guidelines, G42, Continuous Assurance* (2010). In 2010, the Australian Institute of Chartered Accountants also published its *Continuous Assurance for the Now Economy.*

Continuous auditing (CA) is "more timely, close-to-the-event" auditing (Vasarhelyi & Halper, 1990; Alles et al., 2002). Alles et al. (2006) have expanded the scope of the continuous audit by dividing it into continuous control monitoring (CCM) and continuous data assurance (CDA). Vasarhelyi et al. (2010, 2012) have also promoted the inclusion of continuous risk monitoring and assessment (CRMA) in the CA schema.

> The audit planning process provides a template for how to make the Continuous Assurance system dynamic: by formally incorporating into it a risk assessment system that encompasses assessment of auditor perceptions of risks and allocation of audit resources to risky areas of the audit.
>
> (AICPA, 2015, pp. 17–18)

The audit profession has accelerated adoption of continuous auditing and assurance mechanisms in order to take into consideration Sarbanes-Oxley (SOX) requirements and other compliance activities and to embed them into existing processes (Table 4.4).

KPMG (2016) has developed its own maturity model representing the states of maturity from the least mature state of traditional auditing through to the most mature state of continuous assurance of enterprise risk management (Table 4.5).

Table 4.4 Continuous auditing process

Criteria	
Immutability and irreversibility	Immutable record of full list of transactions Audit trail that cannot be tampered with Reduced cost for fraud detection
Sampling	Audit of entire population of transactions Less uncertainty about audit conclusions
Timing	Real-time continuous Spot trends or future risks proactively
More accurate view	More accurate and transparent picture Deeper understanding of overall business mode

Sources: AICPA (2015), Deloitte (2018), Schmitz and Leoni (2019).

Table 4.5 Audit methodology-based maturity model

Maturity level	*Least mature ⟷ Most mature*				
	Maturity level I	*Maturity level II*	*Maturity level III*	*Maturity level IV*	*Maturity level V*
Internal audit methodology	Traditional auditing	Ad Hoc integrated analytics	Continuous risk assessment and continuous auditing	Integrated continuous auditing and continuous monitoring	Continuous assurance of enterprise risk management
Strategic analysis	O	O	∅	∅	⊗
Enterprise risk assessment	O	O	∅	∅	⊗
Internal audit plan development	O	∅	∅	⊗	⊗
Execution and reporting	∅	∅	⊗	⊗	⊗
Continuous improvement	O	O	O	∅	⊗
Types of data analytics applicable	Descriptive	Descriptive, diagnostic	Descriptive, diagnostic, predictive	Descriptive, diagnostic, predictive prescriptive	Descriptive, diagnostic, predictive prescriptive

Source: Adapted from KPMG (2016) quoted by Vermeren and Cuisset (2016, p. 33).
Note added by the author
O: Data analytics are generally not used
∅: Data analytics are partially used but are sub-optimized
⊗: Data analytics are effectively and consistently used (optimized)

The evolution of IT audit methodologies driven by digital technology

They have evolved under the impetus of the digitalization of a large number of activities conducted by various actors in the value chain (clients, suppliers, partners, etc.), the digital transformation of practices, and the rise of new technologies. For example, EY (2022) mentions the development of an 'Internal Audit (IA) Disrupted by Design' approach that transforms internal audit holistically (people, processes, and technology) to build or maintain trust. "Organizations are increasingly relying on Internal Audit (IA) to provide them with insights into diverse and emerging risks and create the foundation for trust. EY IA believes in technology-enabled IA transformation with equal focus on people, process and purpose."

The risk-based methodology: several approaches

Definitions

According to the definition of the Chartered Institute of Internal Auditors (2020 p. 1), the professional association for internal auditors in the UK and Ireland, risk-based internal auditing (RBIA) is "a methodology that links internal auditing to an organisation's overall risk management framework. RBIA allows internal audit to provide assurance to the board that risk management processes are managing risks effectively, in relation to the risk appetite." It a dynamic process.

> RBIA is at the cutting edge of internal audit practice. As a result, it is an area that is evolving rapidly and where there is still little consensus about the best way to implement it. It is more difficult to manage than traditional methodologies.

The evolution of risks and related methodologies

Risk-based audit methodologies have existed for decades. Among all the risks that a company must face, the IT domain is one of the most exposed to external threats in parallel with potential internal dysfunctions that an organization can experience. Moreover, the digitalization of the company's processes is a source of risks. Several risk assessment analyses exist. The Big Four have elaborated their own internal audit risk-based methodology (Table 4.6).

The COSO (Committee of Sponsoring Organizations of the Treadway Commission) initially established by five major accounting associations and institutes in the United States in the mid-1980s has developed one of the world's most widely used risk management frameworks: "Enterprise Risk Management (ERM)-Integrated Framework." The first version of COSO ERM framework has been proposed in 2004. In an updated version issued in 2017, two new items, strategy and performance, have been added. Since, several initiatives have been taken in order to include environmental, social, and governance (ESG)-related risks into ERM. It is designed to be used by any entity facing ESG-related risks – from startups, not-for-profits, for-profit, large corporations or government entities – whether public and private.

Table 4.6 Continuous internal audit and risks-based approach

Establish a baseline Deepen understanding add strategic value				
Compliance focused	*Risk-based approach*	*Effective & detective*	*Business enhancements & efficiencies*	*Value-added observations*
Traditional approach	Internal audit function continuum			Optimized approach
"What could go wrong" approach focused on mitigating existing top enterprise risks	Compliance			"What must go right" approach focused on achieving strategic organizational objectives
Historical				Transformational
Provider of independent assessments of historical performance	Financial			Sought out as a partner that enhances the organization's ability to achieve key objectives
Promote compliance	Performance (operational)			Promote quality improvement and innovation
Historical evaluation of existing policies and controls	Information technology			Strategic evaluation of legal and regulatory requirements balanced with reputation risk appetite

Source: Adapted from RSM US LLP (2021, p. 4).

IT governance audit methodology

Several IT Governance audit frameworks exist and are applied. One of them, presented below, has been developed by three associations operating in France:

- AFAI-ISACA: *The Association Française de l'Audit et du Conseil Informatiques* (AFAI) is the ISACA's French chapter and is the association of reference for IT professionals. ISACA is a global association that provides IT professionals with knowledge, credentials, training and community in audit, governance, risk, privacy, etc. It helps enterprises thrive with performance improvement solutions and customizable IS/IT training that enable organizations to evaluate, perform, and achieve transformative outcomes and business success.
- CIGREF: it is a network of major French companies and public administrations set up in order to develop its members' ability to acquire and master digital technology.

- IFACI: The *Institut Français de l'Audit et du Contrôle Internes* (IFACI) brings together 5,500 internal audit and control professionals and, more widely, all the roles that help control risk.

They have provided in 2019 an updated version of their IT Governance Audit Guide (the first one was published in 2011), a concrete tool for auditors, inspectors and IT professionals. This guide is based on a transversal approach (IT governance audit) that includes many dimensions that do not systematically appear in other methodologies. IT governance is defined as a steering approach whose purpose is to provide the best contribution to value creation, align the digital strategy with the overall company's strategy, optimize the use of resources and control risks according to the stakes. How are companies, IS and IS governance changing in the digital age? These are the very questions that the authors of this guide seek to answer.

The guide helps structure an analysis approach, particularly for IS governance in the digital age. As explained by the authors,

> This document and the related tool (…) are the first steps before a more detailed IT audit that may require a more complete framework (COBIT). It is a tool to assess the level of mastery of best practices in moving toward continuous improvement for both the auditor and the practitioner.
>
> (AFAI-ISACA et al., 2019, p. 10)

The guide starts with the definition of the IT department and its main contributions to the digital transformation of companies. Its function can be divided into three roles and mandates (Table 4.7). The IT department now operates various solutions and technologies. In an uncertain context, agility should be more and more adopted to face significant challenges in IT integration and architecture and to react quickly to changes.

> The IT department must reconcile both of these aspects (Core and Fast) of IT development to take advantage of opportunities to innovate and control the risks of 'shadow IT' and 'shadow development'. Shadow IT puts the company in danger in terms of security and compliance, particularly concerning personal data processing.
>
> (AFAI-ISACA et al., 2019, p. 9)

Table 4.7 The IT department roles and mandates

Roles	*Main activity*	*Mandates*
Service provider	Run	Operational excellence for all services in place
Business partner	Build	Completing projects in line with the scope, budget, and deadlines
Strategist	Vision	Drafting it evolution strategy

Source: Adapted from AFAI-ISACA et al. (2019, p. 7).

A particular attention should made on the coexistence of core IT (named also legacy system) and fast IT. Core IT is IT inherited from all the changes that have occurred up to now. Fast IT represents agile computing using innovative technologies, exploiting (produced, stored, shared, analyzed) data to respond to new uses, cultures and organizations (social, collaborative, connected, etc.).

The guide breaks down the analysis of IT governance into several vectors, from the strategic alignment until the completion of business unit projects and communicating to the entire company. The 2019 guide integrates a new set of vectors to be audited which have evolved since the first version in 2011. Twelve vectors have been identified: strategy, innovation, risks, data, architecture, project portfolio, projects, human resources, providers and suppliers, services, budget and performance, marketing and communication.

In the 2019 version, there are some notable changes (Table 4.8). Two of them are worth mentioning.

The first one is linked with the fact that some vectors included in the previous 2011 edition have been merged and integrated and that two new

Table 4.8 Evolution of vectors between the 2011 and 2019 editions of the guide

Vectors	*2011*	*2019*
1	IT planning and integration into the company's strategic plan	Strategy: Integrate digital challenges into the company's strategic plan
2	Systems and corporate architecture in service of strategic stakes	Innovation: Spread digital culture and promote innovative technologies
3	Project portfolio management centered on value creation for business units	Risks: Take into account the digital risks (cyber and technological) in the strategic stakes and business processes
4	Management of IT risks according to their impacts on business units	Data: Manage, capitalize, and protect company data
5	Alignment of the IT function with business unit processes	Architecture: Align the IT architecture with strategic stakes
6	Mastery of project completion according to business stakes	Project Portfolio: Optimize the value of IT and manage its evolutions
7	Provide IT services that meet client expectations	Projects: Control project and solution implementation
8	Steer outsourced services	Human resources: Organize and manage talent and skills
9	IT management control that fosters transparency	Providers/Suppliers: Steer relationships with providers of digital solutions and services
10	Prospective management of IT skills	Services: Provide digital services that meet client expectations
11	Manage and measure IT performance	Budget and performance: Steer the IT budget and performance
12	Manage communication	Marketing and communication: Showcase services and communicate on the technological challenge

Source: Adapted from AFAI-ISACA et al. (2019, p. 11).

vectors have been added as they are two pillars in the context of the digital transformation: innovation and data management.

Insofar as innovation is at the heart of corporate strategy, but also features prominently in internal auditing (in one way or another, for example, with the growing role of new technologies), it is not surprising to find it in this context. Innovation is driven by two main aims: spread digital culture and promotion innovative technologies. There are four main stakes for the company:

- Ensure that the company has the capacity for digital innovation to support its development and competitiveness
- Communicate on innovation within the company and to decision-making committees
- Be able to identify and adapt technology opportunities within the company
- Create the most favorable conditions for developing concrete innovations: technology monitoring, benchmarks, labs, open innovation, start-ups ecosystem

The second axis is not surprisingly in relation to data management and its main objectives expressed as follows: manage, capitalize, and protect company data. Data should now be considered as a strategic asset for the company as they give the company a competitive advantage. Data could also allow the development of new projects and services. The use of collected data should be combined with the development of trust.

The second change is in relation to the redefinition of the role of strategy which is reinforced and will be strengthened by a business vision of the digital transformation and the future IS. The core principle of strategic IS alignment is reaffirmed in these terms: "Align IT's evolution with the company's strategic stakes by involving General Management and business units" (p. 12). Technology opportunities must be identified early to improve business processes and performance. As seen in Chapter 2, the challenge of strategic alignment addresses the entire chain: organization – business – IS – process – technology (Daidj, 2019).

Based on this methodology, the auditor/assessor could weigh the various best practices and vectors and can judge the overall level of mastery for each best practice and give their assessment for the entire vector. The recommendations in this guide are both operational (Exhibit 4.2) and strategic accordingly. For example, for the architecture vector, the goal is to align IT architecture with strategic stakes as follows:

- Make the IT section of the company's strategic plan a reality in business unit processes to encourage management's involvement and maximize the chances of reaching the targets set.
- Provide an architectural framework to the project portfolio to make sure it helps reach the IT target.

- Identify the trajectory and main steps to reach the strategic plan's IT target considering the resources and investments required for each of them.
- Reduce IT costs and increase its adaptability through streamlining, simplification, encouraging the reuse of features, and taking advantage of opportunities to outsource services.

The best practices related to IT architecture could be determined according to six main axes:

- Mapping of application, data, flows, and infrastructure
- IT roadmap breaking down the company's digital strategy
- Core IT and Fast IT cohabit with the integration of multiple cloud computing systems
- Communication with business units to share challenges, stakes, and impacts
- Rules and principles of architecture with application conditions
- Architectural governance based on a reference framework taking changes into account

Toward the development of agile internal and IT audit

Agility is a concept that is widely used today. It has its origin in IT projects. In 2001, the agile manifesto was launched. It was written by several US IT

Exhibit 4.2 Evaluation tool*

At the end of the guide, an evaluation tool (Excel) is provided. It is based on a matrix with best practices on the horizontal axis and criteria on the vertical axis.

Stage 1 – Evaluation of each criterion
Stage 2 – Evaluation of each practice
Stage 3 – Evaluation of the vector (overall evaluation)

Insufficient

The scale includes four colors: red (low), insufficient (yellow), satisfactory (light green), good (green), and Not applicable (N/A). The scale has been defined without an 'average' option to force an evaluation. This does not give a final score but a 'wall of colors' giving a snapshot of a certain shade creating an overall scoring.

Source: Adapted from AFAI-ISACA et al. (2019, p. 98).

*The evaluation tool is available at CIGREF site.

experts advocating agile software development "by doing it and helping others to do it" (Appendix 4.1). It is now considered as the reference definition of agile development and its underlying principles.

What is agility?

Agility is generally presented as one of the best answers to adopt by companies in an uncertain and fast-changing environment (COSO, 2022). It is about adapting to technological changes as well as to mergers, restructuring and rationalization operations, which are often coupled with downsizing and optimization of operational processes. In these agile approaches, the customer is at the center of the system: the main objective is to satisfy his needs at all levels (before, during and after the purchase) (Table 4.9).

All companies must become agile and flexible. This is the new credo. But what is agility? It is a multidimensional concept that relates to several features and levels of analysis: the technology, the techniques (Exhibit 4.3), project, the functions, and the organizational structures. Gradually, agility has spread more widely and has been applied to organization, corporate culture, and project management (Tounkara, 2019).

IT project management

Originally, agility was mostly associated with new project management methods aiming at a more efficient organization and monitoring of IT projects (IT, IS, etc.). Project management has integrated the development of agile and hybrid methods (classic V-cycle combined with agile). Agility includes a range of methodologies and agile development practices such as Scrum, Kanban, etc. (Exhibit 4.1). Companies have to choose and implement the one that is the most adapted to their organizational context.

In an agile project, each phase (planning, requirements analysis, design, coding, testing, etc.) is led by a team that can evolve according to the needs of the project itself. Continuous improvement (in connection with the notion of continuous audit as developed in this chapter) is promoted as the new operational imperative. One of the key success factors of agile practices is the support and development of an "agile state of mind" and a change in the teams' mindset (belief) and behaviors (Gibbons, 2015). This requires greater collaboration between employees, better communication, and greater transparency (Table 4.10).

Table 4.9 Agile's four values

Individuals and interactions over	Process and tools
Working software over	Comprehensive documentation
Customer collaboration over	Contract negotiation
Responding to change over	Following a plan

Source: Adapted from Jonnalagadda and Amiia (2017, p. 4).

Exhibit 4.3 An overview of agile techniques

Scrum

This common agile methodology has small cross-functional teams work on audit projects for short periods of time (usually two-week sprints). Teams track the progress of audit tasks using the following categories: backlog, to do, in progress, done, and complete. The Scrum team is self-governing and determines what to tackle within each sprint.

Sprints

Tasks are completed during time-boxed intervals, which can include:

Sprint planning: The team decides which product backlog (a prioritized features list) items to work on and plan how to complete each.
Daily Scrum: A 15-minute (often standup) meeting.
Sprint review: The team holds an informal meeting.
Sprint retrospective: The team meets to discuss how they're doing and ways to improve.

MoSCoW

> An acronym for "Must have, Should have, Could have, and Will not have." This approach helps stakeholders prioritize tasks to determine which audit activities will add the most value. It can be a challenge to use MoSCoW when auditors are set in their ways of covering everything on a specific audit.
>
> (Hussain, 2019).

Kanban

A Kanban board is often used in scrum to visualize the team's progress at various stages and to promote transparent communication. A Kanban board displays cards and columns to help teams commit to and complete tasks.

Shu Ha Ri

This is a Japanese martial art concept that describes the progression of learning. Because the "student" first starts learning and then gradually moves toward mastering a skill and letting go of old habits, it can be a good introductory method for inexperienced agile audit teams. In a highly regulated industry (e.g., financial services or healthcare), this method also means minimal to no changes in auditing methodology.

Source: Adapted from Galvanize (2020, p. 13).

Table 4.10 Comparison between agile and traditional project management

Project phase	*Traditional*	*Agile*
Initiation	Formalized project Capability Quality Foreseeable, evolution requirements Formal communication policies High assurance and stability approach	Prioritized Informal stories Test cases Unforeseeable rapid change Informal, face-to-face communication Radical change and rapid value approach
Planning	Documented Explicit documented knowledge Formal plan Comprehensive approach Well-defined scope Slow change in scope (approved) Predictability Optimization Plan-driven resource allocation Low risk because of plans Inflexible plan and scope Extensive use of quality control and tools Plan- and business-driven project Plan-driven schedule	Less-documented driven flexible plan Tacit interpersonal knowledge Iterative plan Requirements-driven approach Changing scope Frequent, radical changes Unpredictable Requirements-based, flexible Need-based resource allocation High risk, unpredictable Flexible plan and scope No quality tools usage due to scope changes Business- and need-driven project Time-driven schedule
Execution	Extensive design Longer increments Detailed execution plan Comprehensive scope change control Contractual and scope-based procurement Integration during integration Large teams for execution	Simple design Short increments Iterative and reactive execution plan Easy refactoring Requirement-based procurement Continuous integration Small teams for execution
Monitoring and Controlling	Quantitative control Documented-test plans and procedures Earned value for tracking project costs Weekly and monthly	Qualitative control Executable test cases define testing Frequently changing baseline Simple graphic tools for reporting
Closeout	Systematic approach to contract closeout Easy to capture lessons learned Explicit and tacit-based lessons learned	Lack of guidelines (terms and conditions) Difficult to capture lessons learned Tacit-knowledge intensive lessons learned

Source: Anantatmula and Anantatmula (2008).

The agile organization

New organizational forms, based on the principle of agility, have emerged. The agile enterprise is characterized by a specific organization with the development of new functions, methods, and processes that allow it to react and adapt quickly to changing external conditions (market).

The agile organization can be defined as an organizational model that not only accelerates reaction time, but is also flexible, and even more so, is able to anticipate and innovate continuously because of partnerships between all stakeholders (internal and external). Methods to improve application development and IT solution delivery are being implemented through a new DevOps function that performs these development and operations tasks. The DevOps is a cross-functional combination of the terms and concepts for development and operations. It is defined as a software engineering methodology which aims to integrate the work of software development, IT teams, and software operations teams by allowing a culture of collaboration and shared responsibility.

In the continuity of project-based organizational structures, there is also an increasing reference to so-called "agile" structures based on various team organization types: squads, tribes (larger units), chapters, and guilds.

Agility and internal & IT audit

Although the audit environment has traditionally been considered as, relatively stable, technological disruptions are making the future of audit more uncertain. The adaptation to external changes (market, technology, law, and compliance) is becoming more imperative accordingly (PWC, 2009). These new challenges and opportunities will significantly affect the audit process (Alles, 2015). New methodology such as agile has been then expanded in the field of audit. The agile approach is now being leveraged across most of business functions, including internal audit, to improve performance (KPMG, 2021).

Main insights from the literature review

From a theoretical perspective, several scholars have studied the development of agile audit in case of IT projects. The application of the agile methodology to internal and IT audit is limited so far.

At a general level, Newmark et al. (2018) have highlighted that the audit process as currently structured could benefit from more agility in various situations including the following:

1 Engagements are consistently over budget.
2 Engagements are easily disrupted by unexpected client-related issues or delays in client readiness.
3 Individual audit areas are rarely finalized until the very end of the audit.
4 A lack of innovation and new ideas.

Several guidelines are provided by the authors based on the adoption of Scrum, an agile project management approach, considered as a possible way to bring agility into the audit process (Table 4.11). Ken Schwaber and Jeff Sutherland, the creators of Scrum in 1995, have defined it as "a framework within which people can address complex adaptive problems, while productively and creatively delivering products of the highest possible value. Scrum is: lightweight, simple to understand and difficult to master" (2017, p. 3).

Mkoba and Marnewick (2020) have examined three conceptual agile methodology audit models for agile IT projects developed by Kim et al. (2013), Newmark et al. (2018), and Guerrero et al. (2019) before presenting their own framework for auditing agile projects. In addition, the two authors contribute knowledge to the agile project management curriculum of the education and training institutions. The main conceptual findings are summarized in Table 4.11.

Agile audit practice: being agile in internal auditing

At a general level and as mentioned previously, agile methodology is based on a sprint cycle repeated several times depending on the release plan involving small cross-functional teams working. The agile manifesto has been adapted in

Table 4.11 Comparison of agile audit frameworks

Authors	*Context framework/model*	*Audit check items*	*Key findings/ Recommendations*
Kim et al. (2013)	Comparative analysis between a large IT organization's Agile methodology and the current audit model. Agile methodology audit model	Requirement definition Release plan Architecture/ Construction (Sprint launch; analysis /design; development; test; sprint review)	IS audit should understand the character of agile and review the comprehensive development process.
Newmark et al. (2018)	As the audit process evolves due to technological progress, the structure of an audit engagement will likely need to adapt as well by adopting agile approach. Scrum framework	Internal audit environment including: Scrum processes and structure Scrum culture (Transparency across all participants. Inspection to ensure high quality. Adaptation to environmental changes and adjusting ineffective processes). Scrum mindset or values Scrum skills	The use of Scrum for auditing teams offers a new paradigm that moves from a more rigid and reactive planned auditing focus to a new emphasis on iterative identification of auditing tasks in response to changing conditions

Guerrero et al. (2019)	There are a wide number of potential team practices (TP) that could improve the team productivity and quality that are not measured or visualized automatically. Finally, they rely in the skills or efforts of the project manager in a learning context. Eagle: A team practices audit framework for agile software development	Number of stories (smallest units of work in an agile framework) Degree and frequency of practice (team) adherence	The Eagle tool represents a first attempt to create a framework to audit the agile software development teams by providing a means to express, monitor, and visualize their Team practices. Organizations will be able to define their best practices to follow and track the adherence of their teams and members.
Mkoba and Marnewik (2020)	The lack of an audit framework for auditing agile projects to ensure IT project success. A conceptual framework for auditing agile projects	Product vision audit Product backlog audit Release backlog audit Sprint backlog audit Product audit Steering committee (+ Adherence to agile values and guiding principles)	A tool on how to audit agile projects using scrum methodology. The project management practitioners from both public and private sector including auditors can use the framework to audit agile projects to improve success rates of agile projects.

Source: Developed by the author, based on the articles cited.

an auditing context by Nykolyshyn (2019) as shown in Appendix 4.2. Today, it is widely acknowledged that agile auditing with strategic vision and risk assessment are a few of the capabilities, processes and practices auditors should adopt on a daily basis. The agile audit shortens the audit cycle with iterative periods (sprints) and emphasizes frequent communication and incremental value (Table 4.12).

As most of the stakeholders are demanding more efficient assurance, accurate advice on processes and controls, and higher anticipation of risks, the Big

Table 4.12 Agility and traditional methods

Internal audit LC	Scoping →	Planning →	Fieldwork →	Reporting
	Scoping documents	planning document	draft observations	final report
Waterfall SDLC	Requirements →	Design →	Build →	Test
	Requirements documents	design documents	unverified code	software
Agile SDLC	Design build test (requirements)	Design build test (requirements)	Design build test (requirements)	Design build test (requirements)
	Potentially shippable product	Potentially shippable product	Potentially shippable product	Potentially shippable product
	Software	Software	Software	Software
	Continuous integration Test driven development Fair programming Story driven development Shared workspace Collective code ownership			

Source: Adapted from Jonnalagadda and Amiia (2017, p. 5).

Four share converging views on the adoption of agility in auditing in order to achieve greater efficiency (Table 4.13). Two of them propose even a revised and adapted version of the Agile Manifesto to internal auditing.

Most audit functions need to improve their acquisition and development of next-generation auditing skills such as agility. This is the outcome of several analyses. Protividi (2020) has conducted its annual survey on "Internal Audit Capabilities and Needs" showing that internal audit requires more and more agile methodologies supported by a more in-depth understanding of risks. Respondents were asked to assess, on a scale of 1 to 5, their competency in different areas of next generation methodology, with "1" being the lowest level of competency and "5" being the highest. For each area, they were then asked to indicate whether they believe their level of knowledge is adequate or requires improvement, taking into account the circumstances of their organization and industry (Table 4.14).

In addition, Protividi (2018) has elaborated a next-generation internal audit model divided into three main categories: governance, methodology, and enabling technology (Table 4.15).

Other practitioners such as MetricStream (2022), a global SaaS leader of Integrated Risk Management (IRM) and Governance, Risk, and Compliance (GRC) solutions), have identified the five key success factors of agile internal audit technology (management software) raising several questions as follows:

Table 4.13 The scope and the drivers of agile internal audit (IA) activities

	Definition *What is agile internal audit?*	*Revised internal audit agile manifesto*	*The journey to agility*
Deloitte	It is the mindset an Internal Audit function will adopt to focus on stakeholder needs, accelerate audit cycles, drive timely insights, reduce wasted effort, and generate less documentation. Agile prompts internal auditors and stakeholders to determine, upfront, the value to be delivered by an audit or project. What level of assurance is needed? What risks are most concerning? Then the audit or project aims to produce that value. Agile also prioritizes audits and projects based on both importance and urgency as well as readiness to undertake the work. Finally, reporting doesn't focus on documenting the work but on providing insight.	Nine elements 1 Outcome-driven – value-driven 2 Just-in-time – proactive approach to the "right projects at the right depth/focus" 3 One size does not fit all – customized project focused on value and risk 4 Collaborative approach – take the journey with our clients 5 Mix it up a little bit, break some eggs – challenge "that's the way we've always done it" 6 Decisioning "as you go" with transparency and alignment 7 Continuous communication with all stakeholders 8 Be quick and iterative versus confined to a plan 9 Impact over thoroughness – "-good enough" (80/20 rule)	By aligning mindset and process, Agile Internal Audit frameworks direct time and effort toward the issues, challenges, and risks that most affect the organization's ability to implement strategy and achieve goals.
EY	Don't confuse the word "agile" with the project management methodology.		With an agile approach, IA functions can even become change agents.

(*Continued*)

Table 4.13 Continued

	Definition What is agile internal audit?	*Revised internal audit agile manifesto*	*The journey to agility*
	Adding agile into internal audit projects may add complexity and unnecessary project management to an audit process that should already be agile in nature and generally executed and reported in under a month.		One way to approach this is to deploy a Flexible Audit Response Model (FARM). It offers multiple options beyond traditional audits for IA to respond to the risks highlighted in risk monitoring, ranging from a quick analytics review to a full audit, if needed. The key is that FARM enables IA's response to identified risks to be swift, efficient, responsive, and enabled by technology.
KPMG	Agile internal audit is a mindset and method IA professionals use for evolving the profession, adapting to disruption, and managing change. Applying the Agile method empowers IA teams to focus on the needs of stakeholders, improve the audit plan, accelerate audit delivery cycles, and provide timely and impactful insights.	KPMG IA manifesto empowered teams over hierarchical attitudes. IA departments that apply an Agile approach are collections of proactive and collaborative thinkers, not just individuals focused on their discrete tasks and responsibilities. Nimble, heads-up collaboration over rigid, heads-down processes. Timely insights over checking the box. Agile requires engaging regularly with stakeholders, allowing IA to identify adjustments to the audit based on stakeholder and team feedback.	Agile translates to IA activities and what benefits these Agile concepts can deliver across the audit lifecycle.

Table 4.13 Continued

	Definition What is agile internal audit?	Revised internal audit agile manifesto	The journey to agility
		Succinct, impactful reporting over lengthy, fruitless reports. Driving change over communicating observations.	
PWC	'Agile' is often contrasted with 'Waterfall' – a method of working which tends to be more structured, with defined stages which are completed in a linear fashion. Whereas most internal audit functions recognize they operate in a waterfall fashion, many are seeing the value of moving to a more collaborative and iterative approach to audit planning, scoping and delivery.		'Agile' can be used to improve the speed at which internal audit performs compliance-based audits, but its real value tends to arise in audit areas where there are high levels of uncertainty or the audit subject is moving at pace, e.g., a program that is using an iterative approach to solution design.

Source: Based on information presented on the Big Four web sites (2021/2022).
Source: Adapted from Protividi (2020).

Table 4.14 Next-generation methodology competencies

Need to improve (rank)	*Areas evaluated by respondents*	*Competency level (5-pt.scale)*
Overall results		
1	Agile audit approach	2.7
2	Dynamic risk assessment	2.8
3	High-impact reporting	2.8
4	Continuous monitoring	3.1
CAE results		
1	Agile audit approach	2.8
2	Dynamic risk assessment	2.9
3	High-impact reporting	2.8
4	Continuous monitoring	3.1

Note added by the author. Online survey conducted in the fourth quarter of 2019 based on 777 respondents all around the world including Chief Audit Executive (CAE), Director of Auditing, IT Audit Director, Audit Manager, IT Audit Manager, etc. The full methodology is presented in their report.

- Scalability. Can the system scale up with the organization, supporting complex internal audit operations across different lines of business and geographies?
- Integration. Can the system be integrated with other risk and compliance applications? Does it support cross-functional communication? Does it provide common libraries of risk and controls that can be leveraged by multiple assurance functions?
- Mobility. Does the system support mobile auditing? How does it enable data input and upload in remote field sites with no connectivity to the corporate network?
- Ease of use. Does the system have sufficient depth, analytics, and other capabilities to support internal audit? Is it engaging enough to be used by the front lines to capture data on risks and issues?
- Cost. How long will the system take to implement? Is the total cost of ownership low? Is it easily configurable or will it require extensive customization?

In a recent report on internal auditing, KPMG (2019b) has developed similar arguments, also emphasizing the differences between "traditional" internal auditing and agile internal auditing, which is based on five principles:

- Flexibility (adaptation of teams)
- Collaboration (frequent meetings between teams)
- Work sprints (audit projects are composed of several sprints. Expectations are reviewed at the beginning of each sprint, and findings from one sprint are addressed before the next sprint begins)
- Sliced reporting (rather than a single report at the end of the engagement)
- Flexible approach linked to resources (depending on the needs of the mission, even if it means using outsourced skills)

More precisely, KPMG (2019b) proposes its own methodology within the framework of the Scaled Agile Framework (SAFe) based on several general lean agile requirements (i.e., alignment, collaboration, transparency, and delivery for large numbers of teams) and specific principles:

1. Take an economic view
2. Apply systems thinking
3. Assume variability; preserve options
4. Build incrementally with fast, integrated learning cycles
5. Base milestones on objective evaluation of working systems
6. Visualize and limit work in progress (WIP), reduce batch sizes, and manage queue lengths
7. Apply cadence, synchronize with cross-domain planning
8. Unlock the intrinsic motivation of knowledge workers
9. Decentralize decision-making

In brief, their agile internal audit methodology is based on the IIA framework, the SAFe, and their best practices. The main drivers of the approach are as follows:

Table 4.15 Next-generation internal audit model

	Governance	*Methodology*	*Enabling technology*
Context	Next-generation governance covers the internal audit function's strategy, structure and skills (including how those skills are developed and sourced).	Good governance depends on the internal audit organization's ability to increase audit and reporting quality through more insightful and actionable reporting, continuous monitoring, real-time risk view and assessment, and more streamlined and flexible audits. Agile and advanced data management and analysis approaches represent key enablers of real-time view.	The same technologies driving the need for change are being deployed by internal audit organizations to help them rise to the challenge. Extensive reliance on automation, data analysis and a variety of advanced technology applications is a defining feature of next-generation internal audit function. (see Chapter 5)
Key features	Internal audit Strategic vision (see Chapter 2)	Dynamic risk assessment (identify risk trends in real time, prioritize risks using risk-based principles and optimize assurance coverage)	Advanced analytics and ubiquitous data analyses (full samples, data-driven flow charting, risk thresholds, etc.)
	Organizational structure	Agile audit approach (agile, analytics-driven and scalable execution)	Automated processes
	Resources and talent management	High-impact reporting (and simplified)	Process mining
	Aligned enterprise assurance	Continuous monitoring	Artificial intelligence and machine learning (enable internal audit groups to increase the effectiveness and efficiency of complex testing and help move complex analysis to more real-time).

Source: Based on Protividi (2018) and Lehmann & Thor (2020) and adapted by the author.

- Organizational risk register: list of risks and auditable areas for the organization
- Project backlog: list of risks related to a specific audit project
- Sprint backlog: list of control objectives related to the sprint

These backlogs are updated and refined during planning. Gathering input should be a continuous activity performed by internal audit throughout the year.

KPMG (2019a) has also underlined in a white paper on working agile within internal audit functions agile application for the entire organization in line with the three lines of defense (described in Chapter 3):

10 Agile within the first Line of Defense (LOD)
11 Agile within the second LOD (a.o. risk, compliance)
12 Agile internal audit. In the future, a large number of internal audit functions will apply agile auditing with varying degrees. Agile internal audit is the mindset and method that an internal audit function uses to focus on the needs of stakeholders; accelerate the audit cycles, providing timely insight and reduce the waste of resources. By applying an agile method, the productivity and added value can be increased and the lead time of an audit can be reduced.

Conclusion

Risk-based audit methodologies have existed for years. However, the increasing complexity of the environment in all its dimensions (economic, legal, regulatory, digital, technological, etc.) favors the development of new analysis models and risk management strategies. Risk analysis consists of a better understanding of qualitative aspects and also of quantitative information (financial results, performance indicators, etc.). In this uncertain context, in which strategic decision-making is made even more difficult, internal auditors and controllers once again play a fundamental role.

The digital transformation forces organizations to place flexibility and time-to-market at the core of their business. Many companies are in a state of transition and attempt to experiment agility that requires balance between technology and organization. Internal audit functions have to face the same challenges and internal audit departments could benefit from an agile approach.

Questions for discussion

Who is at the origin of the development of digital maturity models – practitioner or academic?

What are the most common dimensions used in internal audit methodologies?

What are the main differences between an agile audit approach and a non-agile audit methodology?

How to define the next generation of internal audit methodology?

In times of crisis (like the COVID-19 crisis), how could agility improve efficiency of internal auditors?

Recommended reading

AFAI-ISACA, CIGREF, & IFACI (2919). *IT governance: Audit guide for companies in the digital era*, 2nd edition. Paris, France: CIGREF. Retrieved October 22, 2020 from: https://www.cigref.fr/it-governance-audit-guide-for-companies-digital-era-2019

AICPA (2015). *Audit analytics and continuous audit: Looking toward the future.* Retrieved April 3, 2021 from: https://us.aicpa.org/content/dam/aicpa/interestareas/frc/assuranceadvisoryservices/downloadabledocuments/auditanalytics_lookingtowardfuture.pdf

Deloitte (2017). *Becoming agile. A guide to elevating internal audit's performance and value Part 1: Understanding agile internal audit.* Retrieved November 30, 2021 from: https://www2.deloitte.com/content/dam/Deloitte/global/Documents/Finance/gx-fa-agile-internal-audit-introduction-elevating-performance.pdf

References

Alles, M. (2015). Drivers of the use and facilitators and obstacles of the evolution of Big Data by the audit profession. *Accounting Horizons, 29*(2), 439–449.

Alles, M., Brennan, G., Kogan, A., & Vasarhelyi, M.A. (2006). Continuous monitoring of business process controls: A pilot implementation of a continuous auditing system at Siemens. *International Journal of Accounting Information Systems*, 7(2), 137–161. https://doi.org/10.1016/j.accinf.2005.10.004

Alles, M.G., A. Kogan, A., & Vasarhelyi. M.A. (2002). Feasibility and economics of continuous assurance. *Auditing: A Journal of Practice & Theory, 21*(1), 125–138. https://doi.org/10.2308/aud.2002.21.1.125

Anantatmula, V.S., & Anantatmula, M. (2008). Use of agile methodology for IT consulting projects. Paper presented at *PMI® Research Conference: Defining the Future of Project Management*, Warsaw, Poland. Newtown Square, PA: Project Management Institute.

Becker, J., Knacksted, R., & Pöppelbuss, J. (2009). Development of maturity models for IT-management. *Business Information & Systems Engineering, 1*(3), 213–222.

Berghaus, S., & Back, A. (2016). Stages in digital business transformation: Results of an empirical maturity study. In *Proceedings of the Tenth Mediterranean Conference on Information Systems (MCIS). 22*. Paphos, Cyprus, St. Gallen: University of St. Gallen. http://aisel.aisnet.org/mcis2016/22

Bierstaker, J.L., Burnaby, P., & Thibodeau, J. (2001). The impact of information technology on the audit process: An assessment of the state of the art and implications for the future. *Managerial Auditing Journal, 16*(3), 159–164. https://doi.org/10.1108/02686900110385489

Canadian Institute of Chartered Accountants/American Institute of Certified Public Accountants (CICA/AICPA) (1999). *Continuous auditing.* Research Report. Toronto: The Canadian Institute of Chartered Accountants.

Chartered Institute of Internal Auditors (2020). *Risk based internal auditing.* Retrieved December 18, 2021 from: https://www.iia.org.uk/resources/risk-management/risk-based-internal-auditing%3FdownloadPdf%3Dtrue+&cd=2&hl=fr&ct=clnk&gl=fr

COSO (2022). *Enabling organizational agility in an age of speed and disruption.* Retrieved March 10, 2022 from: https://www.coso.org/Documents/Enabling-Organizational-Agility-in-an-Age-of-Speed-and-Disruption.pdf

Daidj, N. (2019). Strategic and business-IT alignment under digitalization: Towards new insights? In K. Mezghani & W. Aloulou (Eds.), *Business transformations in the era of digitalization* (pp. 93–105). Hershey: IGI Global.

Daidj, N., Tounkara, T., & Bordeaux, C. (2021). *The evolution of internal audit*. White paper (in French). Retrieved December 18, 2021 from: https://www.imt-bs.eu/livre-blanc-futur-audit-it-nabyla-daidj-thierno-tounkara/

De Bruin, T., Rosemann, M., Freeze, R., & Kaulkarni, U. (2005). Understanding the main phases of developing a maturity assessment model. In D. Bunker, B. Campbell, & J. Underwood (Eds.), *Australasian* conference on information systems (ACIS) (pp. 8–19). Sydney: Australasian Chapter of the Association for Information Systems.

Deloitte (2018). *Digital maturity model. Achieving digital maturity to drive growth.* Retrieved March 5, 2022 from: https://www2.deloitte.com/content/dam/Deloitte/global/Documents/Technology-Media-Telecommunications/deloitte-digital-maturity-model.pdf

Dörner, K., & Edelman, D. (2015). *What 'digital' really means.* Retrieved January 13, 2022 from: https://www.mckinsey.com/~/media/McKinsey/Industries/Technology%20Media%20and%20Telecommunications/High%20Tech/Our%20Insights/What%20digital%20really%20means/What_digital_really_means.pdf

Dowling, C., & Leech, S.A. (2014). A Big 4 firm's use of information technology to control the audit process: How an audit support system is changing auditor behavior. *Contemporary Accounting Research*, *31*(1), 230–252. https://doi.org/10.1111/1911-3846.12010

EY (2022). *Internal audit.* https://www.ey.com/en_gl/consulting/internal-audit

Fraser, P., Moultrie, J., & Gregory, M.J. (2002). The use of maturity models/grids as a tool in assessing product development capability. *IEEE International Engineering Management Conference (IEMC 2002), Managing Technology for the New Economy* (pp. 244–249). Proceedings – IEEE Engineering Management Society. Cambridge, UK: IEEE.

Galvanize (2020). *Sprinting ahead with agile auditing.* Retrieved December 18, 2021 from: https://iiabelgium.org/wp-content/uploads/2020/08/eBook-sprinting-ahead-with-agile-auditing-002.pdf

Gibbons, P. (2015). *The science of successful organizational change: How leaders set strategy, change behavior, and create an agile culture.* Upper Saddle River, NJ: Pearson Education LTD.

Guerrero, A., Fresno, R.A., Ju, A., Fox, A., Fernandez, P., Müller, C., & Ruiz-Cortés, A. (2019). Eagle: A team practices audit framework for agile software development. ESEC/FSE 2019: *Proceedings of the 27th ACM Joint Meeting on European Software Engineering Conference and Symposium on the Foundations of Software Engineering* (pp. 1139–1143). https://doi.org/10.1145/3338906.3341181

Hussain, I. (2019). *Applying agile principles to internal audit.* MIS Training Institute. Retrieved April 11, 2022 from: https://www.misti.a2hosted.com/internal-audit-insights/applying-agile-principles-to-internal-audit

The Institute of Internal Auditors (IIA) (2005). *Global technology audit guide (GTAG) 3: Continuous auditing: Implications for assurance, monitoring, and risk assessment.* Retrieved November 9, 2021 from: https://www.iia.nl/SiteFiles/IIA_leden/Praktijkgidsen/GTAG3.pdf

Jonnalagadda, G., & Amiia, R.F. (2017). *Session 6 "Auditing on the Run" – Developing agility and resilience in the audit function*. Retrieved February 12, 2020 from: https://iia.org.au/sf_docs/default-source/conferences/sa-conference-2017/presentation---session-6---auditing-on-the-run---g-jonnalagadda-r-fantin.pdf?sfvrsn=2

Kane, G., Palmer, D., Philips, A., et al. 2017. *Achieving digital maturity*. Research Report Summer 2017. MIT Sloan Management Review & Deloitte University Press. Retrieved June 3, 2020 from: https://www2.deloitte.com/content/dam/Deloitte/za/Documents/technology/za_DUP_Achieving-digital-maturity.pdf

Kim, D.H., Kim, D.S., Koh, C., & Kim, H.W. (2013). An information system audit model for project quality improvement by the agile methodology. *International Journal of Information and Education Technology, 3*(3), 295–299. https://doi.org/10.7763/IJIET.2013.V3.284

KPMG (2021). *Adapting agile to internal audit. A deeper dive into the agile framework for internal audit*. Retrieved February 17, 2022 from: https://advisory.kpmg.us/content/dam/advisory/en/pdfs/2021/adapting-agile-internal-audit.pdf

KPMG (2019a). *Agile internal audit. White paper on working agile within internal audit functions. Part I: Introducing working agile*. Retrieved November 30, 2021 from: https://assets.kpmg/content/dam/kpmg/sg/pdf/2019/09/agile-internal-audit.pdf

KPMG (2019b). *Agile internal audit. Matching the pace of change*. Retrieved November 30, 2021 from https://assets.kpmg/content/dam/kpmg/ca/pdf/2019/06/kpmg-in-canada-agile-ia-en.pdf

KPMG (2016). *Technology-enabled internal audit*. Retrieved February 12, 2022 from: https://www.compact.nl/en/articles/technology-enabled-internal-audit/

KPMG (2013). *Transforming internal audit: A maturity model from data analytics to continuous assurance*. Retrieved November 30, 2021 from: https://www.kpmg.com/US/en/services/Advisory/risk-and-compliance/internal-audit-risk-and-regulatory compliance/Documents/transforming-internal-audit.pdf

Lahrmann, G., Marx, F., Winter, R., & Wortmann, F. (2011). Business intelligence maturity: Development and evaluation of a theoretical model. *Proceedings of the 44th Hawaii International Conference on System Sciences* (pp. 1–10).

Lehmann, D., & Thor, M. (2020). The next generation of internal audit. Harnessing value from innovation and transformation. *The CPA Journal, 90*(1), 60–61.

MetricStream (2022). *4 key differentiators of an agile internal audit function*. Retrieved March 28, 2022 from: https://www.metricstream.com/insights/4-key-differentiators-of-an-agile-internal-audit.htm

Mkoba, E.S., & Marnewick, C. (2020). Conceptual framework for auditing agile projects. *IEEE Access, 8*, 126460–126476.

Mullaly, M. (2014). If maturity is the answer, then exactly what was the question? *International Journal of Managing Projects in Business,* 7(2), 169–185.

Newmark, R.I., Dickey, G., & Wilcox, W. (2018). Agility in audit: Could scrum improve the audit process? *Current Issues in Auditing, 12*(1), A18– A28. https://doi.org/10.2308/ciia-52148

Nykolyshyn, L. (2019). Our triumphs and challenges using agile auditing principles. AuditCon. A higher education summit. The Association of College and University Auditors (ACUA). September 15–19, 2019, Baltimore, MA. Retrieved December 16, 2021 from: https://acua.org/ACUA/media/About_ACUA/images/-8A-Our-Triumphs-Challenges-Using-Agile-Auditing-Auditing-Principles-Nykolyshyn.pdf

ORIA (2018). *Information system audit*. Retrieved December 2, 2021 from: https://www.oria.fr/2018/03/audit-audit-des-systemes-dinformation/

Pöppelbuß, J., & Röglinger, M. (2011). What makes a useful maturity model? A framework of general design principles for maturity and its demonstration in business process management. Proceedings of the 19th European Conference on Information Systems (ECIS). 28. AIS.

Protividi (2020). *Exploring the next generation of internal auditing. It's time for internal audit leaders to stand up and ride their own wave of transformation and innovation.* Retrieved December 16, 2021 from: https://www.protiviti.com/sites/default/files/2020-ia-capabilities-needs-survey-protiviti-global.pdf

Protividi (2018). *The next generation of internal auditing – Are you ready? Catch the innovation wave.* Retrieved December 16, 2021 from: https://www.protiviti.com/sites/default/files/united_states/insights/next-generation-internal-audit-protiviti.pdf

PWC (2009). *Maximizing internal audit. A 10-step imperative for thriving in a challenging economy.* Retrieved December 16, 2021 from: https://www.utsystem.edu/sites/default/files/offices/system-audit/PWC%20maximizing-internal-audit.pdf

RSM (2021). *Internal audit – proposed internal audit plan.* Calendar Year ending December 31, 2021. Retrieved March 31, 2022 from: https://www.pwcva.gov/assets/202104/PWC%20CY%202021%20Proposed%20IA%20Plan%20ACCEPTED%201.19.21.pdf

Schmitz, J., & Leoni, G. (2019). Accounting and auditing at the time of block chain technology: A research agenda. *Australian Accounting Review, 29* (2), 331–342. https://doi.org/10.1111/auar.12286

Schwaber, K., & Sutherland, J. (2017). *The scrum guide.* Retrieved December 16, 2021 from: https://scrumguides.org/docs/scrumguide/v2017/2017-Scrum-Guide-US.pdf

Teichert, R. (2019). Digital transformation maturity: A systematic review of literature. *Acta Universitatis Agriculturae et Silviculturae Mendelianae Brunensis, 67*(6), 1673–1687. https://doi.org/10.11118/actaun201967061673

TM Forum (2020). Get started with the 10 telco transformation journeys. https://inform.tmforum.org/digital-transformation-and-maturity/2020/09/get-started-with-the-10-telco-transformation-journeys

TM Forum (2017). *Digital Maturity Model (DMM): A blueprint for digital transformation.* Retrieved March 25, 2022 from: https://www.tmforum.org/wp-content/uploads/2017/05/DMM-WP-2017-Web.pdf

Tounkara, T. (2019). MindScrum: A serious gaming method for teaching agility in project management courses. *3rd International Conference on Game Evolution: Management & Pedagogy.* May 2019. Créteil, France.

Vasarhelyi, M.A., Alles, M., Kuenkaikaew, S., & Littley, J. (2012). The acceptance and adoption of continuous auditing by internal auditors: A micro analysis. *International Journal of Accounting Information Systems, 13*(3), 267–281. https://doi.org/10.1016/j.accinf.2012.06.011

Vasarhelyi, M.A., Alles, M., & Williams, K.T. (2010). *Continuous assurance for the now economy.* A Thought Leadership Paper for the Institute of Chartered Accountants in Australia.

Vasarhelyi, M.A., & Halper, F.B. (1990).The continuous audit of online systems. *Auditing: A Journal of Practice and Theory, 10*(1), 110–125.

Vermeren Y., & Cuisset G. (2016). Etat des lieux de l'utilisation de l'analyse de données au sein de l'audit interne. *Audit, Risques & Contrôle, 8*, 32–35.

Appendix 4.1

Exhibit – The agile manifesto (extracts)

We are uncovering better ways of developing software by doing it and helping others do it.

Through this work we have come to value:
Individuals and interactions over processes and tools
Working software over comprehensive documentation
Customer collaboration over contract negotiation
Responding to change over following a plan

That is, while there is value in the items on the right, we value the items on the left more.

Principles behind the Agile Manifesto

We follow these principles:

Our highest priority is to satisfy the customer
through early and continuous delivery
of valuable software.

Welcome changing requirements, even late in
development. Agile processes harness change for
the customer's competitive advantage.

Deliver working software frequently, from a couple of weeks to a couple of months, with a preference to the shorter timescale.

Business people and developers must work together daily throughout the project.

Build projects around motivated individuals. Give them the environment and support they need, and trust them to get the job done.

The most efficient and effective method of conveying information to and within a development team is face-to-face conversation.

Working software is the primary measure of progress.

Agile processes promote sustainable development. The sponsors, developers, and users should be able to maintain a constant pace indefinitely.

Continuous attention to technical excellence and good design enhances agility.

Simplicity – the art of maximizing the amount of work not done – is essential.

The best architectures, requirements, and designs emerge from self-organizing teams.

At regular intervals, the team reflects on how to become more effective, then tunes and adjusts its behavior accordingly.

Source: https://agilemanifesto.org/

Appendix 4.2

The agile manifesto adapted for auditing activities

12 Agile PM principles

I Individuals and Interactions

1 Build audit projects around motivated individuals; give them the environment and support they need and trust them to get the job done.
2 Recognize that the best work emerges from self-organizing teams.
3 The most efficient and effective method of conveying information within an audit team is face-to-face conversation.

II Audit Insights

4 Relevant and timely audit insights are the primary measure of progress.
5 Deliver audit insights frequently, ideally a couple of weeks to a couple of months, with preference for the shorter timescale.
6 Satisfy parties through early and continuous delivery of audit insights.

III Stakeholder Collaboration

7 The Audit team and University staff must work together on a regular basis throughout the project.
8 Agile processes promote sustainable project completion. The sponsors, auditors and stakeholders should be able to maintain a constant pace indefinitely.

IV Responding to Change

9 Welcome changing risk and scope, even late in an audit project.
10 Simplicity – the art of maximizing the amount of work not done – is essential.
11 Continuous attention to technical excellence and pragmatism enhances agility.
12 Having the team reflect at regular intervals on how to become more effective, then tuning and adjusting behavior accordingly

Source: Nykolyshyn (2019).

5 The evolution of IT/IS audit activities in the digital era

The impact of technology-enabled internal audit

Introduction

Several scholars have analyzed the acceptance and usage level of IT by internal or external auditors, as well as the perceived importance of IT usage. They have used traditional models dedicated to information technology usage, including the Technology Acceptance Model (TAM), the unified theory of acceptance and use of technology (UTAUT), the theory of planned behavior (TPB), the diffusion of innovation (DOI), and the technology organization environment (TOE) framework. Some of these models have been applied to the adoption and the diffusion of computer-assisted audit techniques (CAATs) and generalized audit software (GAS) in auditing activities (Section "Introduction").

Over a couple of decades, there has been a tremendous shift toward emerging technologies such as blockchain, data analytics, robotics, machine learning, and artificial intelligence (AI). Like every innovation, these technologies can be interpreted as both an opportunity and a threat. This chapter analyses how the digital revolution raises several challenges to the auditing framework. Emerging technologies such as artificial intelligence, machine learning, data analytics, and robotic process automation (RPA) have and will have a very significant impact on the way internal audits are conducted and will contribute, in particular, to speeding up and improving the data processing process (KPMG, 2016, 2018a).

The internal audit function should adequately identify and respond to emerging risks and not just assessing the well-known controls. One of the identified current and future missions for internal audits is to use more technology, data, and analytics in their audit approach and methodology (Lamboglia et al., 2021). Auditors should consider two main issues closely related regarding the technology challenges in the evolution of internal auditing activities. Performing technology-based auditing could include one or both of the two following distinct but complementary components:

1 Auditing with new technology to improve internal audit and risk processes (Section "Technology adoption models in auditing").

DOI: 10.4324/9781003215110-6

2 Audit of new technology applications and related uses in the organization (Section "Beyond traditional audit techniques: auditing with new technologies").

Technology adoption models in auditing

The concepts, applications, and development of technology adoption models and theories presented briefly in this section are based on the literature review that encompasses different views and interpretations. They can provide interesting insights for auditing activities that are directly impacted by information system and technology adoption. Before describing the main technology acceptance frameworks, some basic principles of information systems are provided.

The key role of information system

The usage of information systems (IS) is of most importance to pursue an adequate monitorization by auditing. Before focusing on the collection and processing of data, we must consider the first level of review, which is the information system itself as explained by Cascarino (2017, p. 111),

> from an analytical perspective, the bulk of information and the evidence utilized by the auditors is derived directly from information systems. (...) in order to conduct [such] data analysis, it is critical that the auditor satisfy himself or herself that the controls within the computer systems themselves are of a standard that allows reliance to be placed upon the integrity, accuracy, and completeness of data extracted for analysis.

The so-called continuous audit involves information systems to automate the audit process.

The IS handles the company's information resources. Several layers must be considered:

- Infrastructure:
  Access devices: PC, mobile devices (tablets, smartphone), etc.
  High-performance servers: they host the IS applications.
  Networks: they ensure the link between the workstations and the servers.
- Applications:
  Business applications: each company needs a very small number of business-specific applications that support its core business and are only valuable for its business.
  Support applications: Universal applications (necessary to implement the business applications and/or to complete them), not specific to the company's business, such as office automation tools and software (IP telephony,

fixed-mobile convergence, video conferencing, collaborative tools, instant messaging, etc.).

- Services: each of them describes a functionality that the IS must provide to allow a user to meet his informational needs in the context of conducting his activity. A service is designed for a specific user according to the profile and needs of this type of actor. Each of these services combines the following basic actions: collect information, store information, process/produce information, disseminate/communicate information.
- Data: the set of information resources needed in the context, i.e., to meet the various information needs.

As explained in previous chapters, an IT audit will include all controls on the IT infrastructure (in-house IT facility) and the functioning of system software related to services, applications and data. In addition,

> application controls involve those controls, both manual and computerized, operating within the business area to ensure that transactions are processed completely and accurately. The controls in this area are normally specific to the business function, resulting in an audit program that will typically involve a certain degree of standard audit tests and analysis.
> (Cascarino, 2017, p. 112)

The emergence and development of technology adoption models

Since the beginning of the 2000s, with the ever-increasing development of technology and, in particular, of information technology, several technology adoption models have been elaborated, primarily developed from theories in psychology and sociology before being extended to management of innovation and information systems (Surendran, 2012). Technology adoption theories and models are various. These include, but are not restricted to, the theory of planned behavior (TPB), the technology acceptance model (TAM), the Unified Theory of Acceptance and Use of Technology (UTAUT), the theory of reasoned action (TRA or ToRA), the theory of planned behavior (TPB), the theory of diffusion of innovation (DOI), the technology-organization-environment (TOE) framework, the motivational model, the theory of task-technology fit, the social cognitive theory, etc.

Two main types of models are generally identified. The first category refers to IT adoption at the individual level (TAM, UTAUT and TPB). The second one is based on the study of IT adoption at the organizational level (DOI, TOE).

Most of the models quoted above aim to explain the past, current, and future application of technology adoption and how users come to accept and use (or on the contrary reject) a technology or information system as show in Exhibit 5.1.

Some of these models have been regularly updated and have given rise to various subsequent versions such as with the TAM dedicated to IS contexts,

Exhibit 5.1 Basic concept underlying acceptance models

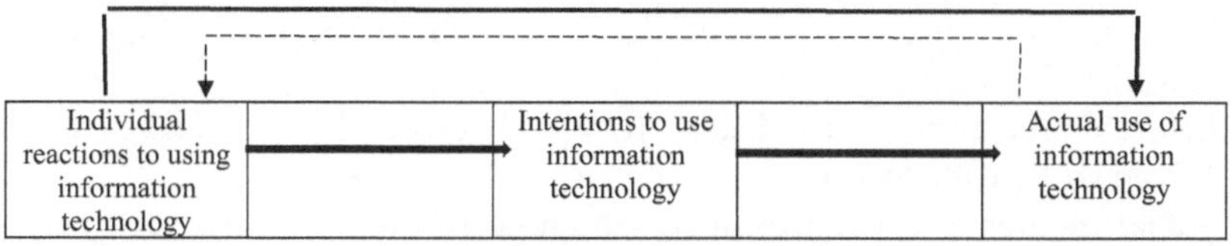

Source: Adapted from Venkatesh et al. (2003, p. 427).

Table 5.1 Technology acceptance model (TAM)

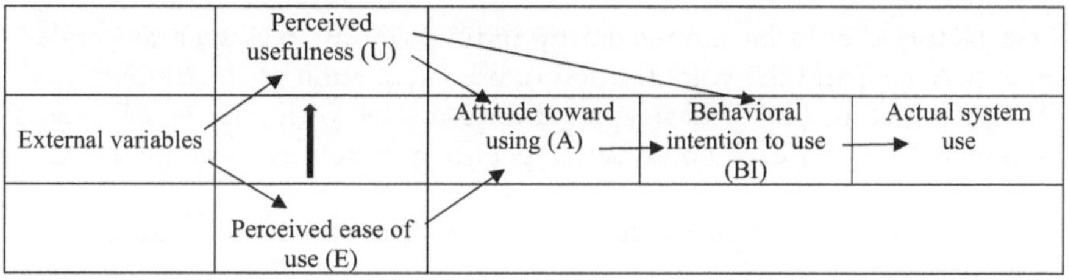

Source: Adapted from Davis et al. (1989, p. 985).

and designed to predict information technology acceptance and usage on the job (Venkatesh et al., 2003).

The original model was proposed by Davis (1989) before being extended in 1996 by Venkatesh and Davis (Table 5.1). In 2000, Venkatesh and Davis (2000) proposed a new version named TAM 2. Finally, in 2008, Venkatesh and Bala (2008) provided a further version TAM 3 based on the individual differences, system characteristics, social influence, and facilitating conditions, which are determinants of perceived usefulness and perceived ease of use. The perceived usefulness can be defined as "the degree to which a person believes that using a particular system would enhance his or her job performance" (Davis, 1989, p. 320). The perceived ease of use is "the degree to which a person believes that using a particular system would be free of effort" (Davis 1989, p. 320). In this model, the perceived ease of use to perceived usefulness, IT anxiety to perceived ease of use, and perceived ease of use to behavioral intention could be moderated by experience.

The UTAUT model, considered as one of the most comprehensive technology acceptance models, has been also proposed in two versions: UTAUT 1 (Venkatesh et al., 2003) and UTAUT 2 (Venkatesh et al., 2012). UTAUT 1 has been elaborated in order to understand the use of various technologies within an organization. UTAUT 2 is rather dedicated to the use of various technologies within the consumer market. Only UTAUT 1 is presented below as the topic of UTAUT 2 is less directly related and relevant to the topic and the discussion of this chapter.

UTAUT 1 has four constructs that influence intention to use (technology) or usage behavior as follows (Table 5.2):

- Performance expectancy is the degree to which the technology is perceived to be useful.
- Effort expectancy is the degree to which using the technology is perceived to be easy to use.
- Social influence is the extent to which consumers perceive that important others (e.g., family and friends) believe they should use a particular technology.
- Facilitating conditions is the degree to which the individual believes to be in possession of the resources to use the technology.

These factors should be moderated by individual variables such as gender, age, experience, and the voluntariness of use (Venkatesh et al., 2003).

Venkatesh et al. (2003) have applied their model to the use of a Personal Computer (PC). For each construct, a specific question has been be posed.

1. Expectation of performance: What use does a PC generate for the employees?
2. Expectation of effort: How much effort do employees have to contribute to use a PC?
3. Social influence: What do the colleagues and superiors of the employees say about using a PC?
4. Facilitating conditions: Do the employees know how to use a PC?

Finally, their research has concluded that the first three constructs are direct determinants of the intention to use new technology. Facilitating conditions is a direct determinant of the intention to use a new technology and user behavior. Gender, age, experience, and voluntariness of use moderate the impact of the four key constructs.

Table 5.2 The constructs of the UTAUT model

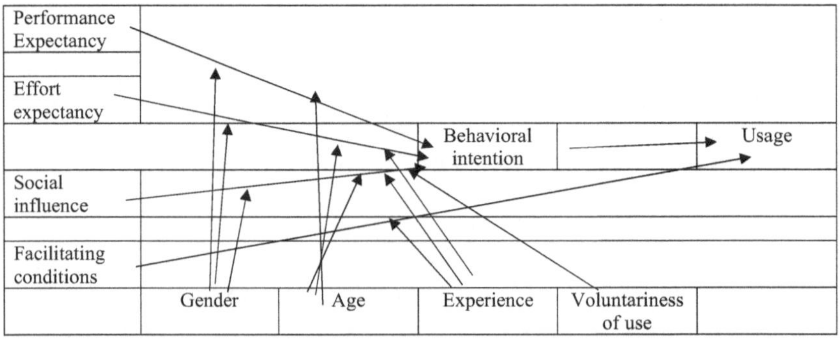

Source: Adapted from Venkatesh et al. (2003).

UTAUT is not only a theoretical model but has also very concrete applications according to Venkatesh et al. (2003). UTAUT

> provides a useful tool for managers needing to assess the likelihood of success for new technology introductions and helps them understand the drivers of acceptance in order to proactively design interventions (including training, marketing, etc.) targeted at populations of users that may be less inclined to adopt and use new systems.
>
> (pp. 425–426)

Auditing activities in an increasingly IT environment

This topic has been studied in-depth by several scholars. The objective here is not to present a comprehensive review of the literature but to highlight the main issues raised by various authors that could also be of interest to practitioners. At a general level, several scholars have focused their research on two main issues:

- The impact of specific IT applications and/or software
- The influence of IT on the audit profession

The main specific IT applications and/or software

Technology-based audit tools are defined in internal auditing standards as "any automated audit tool, such as generalized audit software (GAS), test data generators, computerized audit programs, specialized audit utilities, and CAATs" (IIA, 2017, p. 24). These techniques internal (and external) auditors can use to reach more efficiently their audit objectives.

CAATTs are split into five categories: test data, integrated test facility, parallel simulation, embedded audit module, and generalized audit software (Braun & Davis, 2003). The "(broad) definition would include automated working papers and traditional word processing applications" (Braun & Davis, 2003, p. 726), or can be stated as "the use of certain software that can be used by the auditor to perform audits and to achieve the goals of auditing" (Sayana, 2003, p. 1).

The term "computer-assisted audit techniques" (CAATs) has be found for the first time in 1974 (AICPA, 1979). Auditing Practice Regulation 1009 "Computer-Assisted Audit Techniques" has been developed based on the International Auditing Practice Regulation IASP – "Computer- Assisted Audit Techniques") approved by the International Federation of Accountants (IFAC) in the 2001 edition. The classical manual audit techniques have been then progressively replaced with modern techniques such as computer-aided audit tools (CAATs), sometimes be known also as CAATTs (Computer Assisted Audit Tools and Techniques) or BEASTs (Beneficial Electronic Audit Support Tools). CAATs tools and software have been used for many years to automate the IT audit process and to improve it. Specifically, it refers to software for extracting and analyzing data used for fraud detection and prevention and risk management (Audit Command Language (ACL), containing spreadsheets (e.g., Excel), databases (e.g., Access), statistical analysis (e.g., SAS), etc.

Generalized audit software (GAS) is considered as one of the most common computer-assisted audit tool (CAAT) used in recent years. GAS makes easier for the internal auditor data extraction from various sources (i.e., databases and files) from an organization's integrated systems in order to conduct detailed analyses of this data (Lin & Wang, 2011). GAS enables the internal auditor to test an entire population, compared to the traditional sampling approach. In addition, audit work can be done more quickly and internal auditors can test more data to find errors or fraud.

Embedding specific IT applications in technology acceptance models

As mentioned previously, there are various technology adoption models. Several scholars have attempted to investigate further the adoption of specific automated audit tools such as CAATs in view of these theories and to examine technology implementation (CAATs) in an auditing setting (Table 5.3).

Following up this general overview of the main factors affecting the adoption of audit technology, in general, the more specific impact of the new technologies on auditing activities and processes is presented in the next section. Before proceeding with the next developments, the interesting point to note at this stage is that the technology adoption models have also been applied more recently to the integration of new technologies such as data analytics in auditing (Table 5.4).

Beyond traditional audit techniques: auditing with new technologies

Since the mid-2010s, new and disruptive technologies have emerged at a rapid pace. At the same time, internal audits and more specifically IT audits have evolved as the size and complexity of systems implemented within organizations have grown.

Adding value with technology

"In order for organizations to survive in this complex and rapidly changing environment, it is critical that the systems deployed are controlled and dependable" (Cascarino, 2017, p. 111). New technologies such as cloud computing, artificial intelligence, data analytics, Robotic Process Automation (RPA), blockchain have had a fundamental impact on the nature of business (Table 5.5). All the players in the market share this vision and insist that new

Table 5.3 The adoption of more specific IT applications (CAATs, GAS) and technology acceptance frameworks

Authors	*Technology acceptance models and related assumptions*	*Main findings*
CAATs use by external auditors		
Curtis and Payne (2008) / Curtis and Payne (2014)	UTAUT/TAM Effort Expectancy Social Influence is positively associated with intention to use	Examination of CAATS utilization decisions by external auditors. Senior auditors' behavioral intention to use CAATs. Performance expectancy, effort expectancy, and facilitating conditions are positively related to the intention to adopt a software for substantive testing. Auditors are more likely to implement new technology when they are aware that the managing partner/CEO is encouraging implementation within the firm and when the firms have longer-term budgets and evaluation periods.
Janvrin et al. (2008)	Perceived importance of IT use refers to the degree of importance that auditors attach to the use of IT during the audit process. Audit IT use refers to the extent auditors employ or use IT throughout the audit process.	Auditors accepted the CAATs. IT use and perceived importance varies by firm size. In general, auditors employed by Big 4 firms are more likely to use audit applications and rate their importance higher than auditors from non-Big 4 firms for several applications. The Big 4 firms have "deep pockets" that enable them to (1) purchase and implement superior IT, and (2) use IT specialists to a greater extent than non-Big 4 firms. Big 4 firms' use of IT may also be a reflection of having clients with correspondingly greater IT complexity.
Janvrin et al. (2009)	Use of IT. Intention to use CAATs. Agreement of the users to the intention to use. Facilitating conditions.	Computer-related audit procedure use varies by audit firm size and by audit phase. In the substantive testing phase, auditors used a mix of procedures, despite potential advantages of using computer-related procedures (i.e., continuous auditing). Auditors are more likely to use computer-related audit procedures when they rely on internal controls. However, results vary as to which computer related procedures were significantly related to internal control reliance.
CAATs use by internal auditors		
Mahzan and Lymer (2009, 2014)	UTAUT	Examination of the motivation for CAATTs adoption by internal auditors.

(*Continued*)

Authors	*Technology acceptance models and related assumptions*	*Main findings*
CAATs use by internal auditors		
		Results suggest that two constructs from UTAUT (performance expectancy and facilitating conditions) appear to be particularly important factors influencing successful adoptions of GAS in this domain. The constructs of social influence and effort expectancy are not found by this study to be as important in this specific IT adoption domain. UTAUT also proposes four moderating factors that influence the constructs. Two of them – experience and voluntariness – are keys to the constructs application to this domain.
Pedrosa et al. (2015) / Pedrosa et al. (2020)	UTAUT/TAM Technology adoption at an individual level (auditor)/ Understanding the adoption of technology based on auditors' attitudes.	The perceived usefulness of CAATs, the effort expectancy, the facilitating conditions, and the number of auditors are the main drivers of the adoption and use of CAATs.
Dias and Marques (2018)	Use of IT	Internal auditors mostly use generic rather than specific tools in their audit work. In Portugal, most of internal auditors are using basic audit analytics techniques (e.g., excel) to support the audit procedures. The use of specific computer tools to support auditing is influenced by the size of the workplace, more specifically by the size of the audit department. Other factors that also influence the use of these computerized techniques are the experience in auditing and the existence of a certified internal auditor in the workplace.
Rosli et al. (2012)	Individual-Technology-Organization-Environment (I-TOE) Providing a better understanding on relationship of both organizational and individual factors in foreseeing CAATTs adoption and investment.	Investigation of the acceptance of CAATTs in audit firms Factors influencing at the organizational level, the acceptance and use of technology by the audit profession. New variables of technology risk, technology task fit, organization readiness, and top management commitment have been added accordingly.

Source: Developed by the author, based on the articles cited.

Table 5.4 Technology acceptance frameworks and the use of data analytics in auditing

Authors	*Technology acceptance models and related assumptions*	*Main findings*
Data analytics in external audits		
Krieger et al. (2021)	TOE Examination of the process by which audit firms adopt advanced data analytics (ADA)	Importance of technological capabilities of audit firms for the adoption of advanced data analytics; technological capabilities within audit teams can be leveraged to support both the ideation of possible use cases for advanced data analytics, as well as the diffusion of solutions into practice. Auditors with technological affinity can support the ideation phase, which in turn can improve the acceptance of solutions by other auditors, as they are involved in the development process. Involving auditors in the ideation phase can help to align the solution's design with the auditors' mindset in order to ensure usability.
Data analytics in internal audits		
Al-Ateeq et al. (2022)	TAM Analysis of the impacts of using two dimensions of the TAM, perceived usefulness and perceived ease of use, on the adoption of big data analytics in auditing, and the subsequent impact on audit quality.	Perceived usefulness and perceived ease of use have a direct effect on audit quality, without mediating the actual use of data analytics. However, the use of big data analytics is shown to moderate the relationship between perceived usefulness and audit quality, but not between the perceived ease of use and audit quality.
Li et al. (2018)	TOE Examination of organizational factors that have an impact on audit analytics post-adoption usage at both the application-level (referring to the extent to which audit analytics software is used by auditors) and the feature-level (based on specific audit analytics techniques, feature of software, and the frequency of their usage).	Both application-level and feature-level audit analytics usage improve the performance of the internal audit process. Application-level audit analytics usage by internal auditors is driven by their perceived level of importance and technological capability. Encouragement by management and regulators are the most important factors in shaping how internal auditors use audit analytics. Factors that relate to firm's characteristics, such as IT complexity and firm size, do not have significant influence.

(*Continued*)

Authors	*Technology acceptance models and related assumptions*	*Main findings*
Data analytics in internal audits		
		Feature-level audit analytics usage is influenced by professional help, technological competence, and application-level audit analytics usage. It supports the argument that advanced audit analytics tools require expertise in statistics and technology, which can be acquired by frequently using audit analytics throughout the audit process, or by enhancing technological competence and seeking assistance from vendors.

Source: Developed by the author, based on the articles cited.

Table 5.5 The digitization spectrum

Degree of automation			
Foundation	*Analytics*	*Robotics*	*Cognitive intelligence*
Related technologies			
Data integration Integrated data to provide a consistent information foundation (e.g., compliance risk and regulatory data warehouse)	Predictive analytics Software solutions using predictive models (e.g., compliance risk models)	Robotic process automation Rules-based systems that mimic human behavior to automate parts of repeatable processes	Natural Language generation (NLG) Applications that accept structured data inputs (Excel-like rows/columns) to generate seemingly unstructured narratives)
	Data visualization software placing data in a visual context (e.g., GRC dashboards)		Natural language processing (NLP) Applications that process unstructured data (e.g., text) and allow querying and generation of structured data Machine learning (ML) Applications that are able to improve predictability and operation based on data they receive over time Artificial intelligence (AI) Applications able to mimic human behavior, such as visual perception, speech recognition, decision-making, and translation between languages

Source: Adapted from Deloitte (2018a, p. 3).

technologies will be increasingly used in auditing tasks and activities (Asif Qureshi, 2020).

In December 2019, the IAASB provided an updated version of the ISA 315 "Identifying and Assessing the Risks of Material Misstatement," which highlights the importance of technology (Brown et al., 2019; IAASB, 2019). The standard refers to "Automated Tools and Techniques," which auditors can refer to when performing audit procedures (IAASB, 2019). The definition of this term is broad, as it includes emerging technologies, such as AI and RPA, in addition to data analytics (IAASB, 2016).

Toward data-driven internal audits

Most definitions of big data focus on the 7Vs: volume, variety, velocity, variability, visualization, veracity, and value. In a big data environment with its many sources of information, and large data-based organizations, data formatting, quantity and quality of data (structured and unstructured data), storage modes, backup, and security modes could be heterogeneous. One of the major challenges of internal auditing is then processing a huge amount of data, identifying possible anomalies and visualizing the data. Several data analytics technologies and tools can help to address this effectively (Table 5.6).

The challenges of data analytics in auditing activities

As seen in the previous section, CAATs can improve the effectiveness and efficiency of auditing procedures in internal audit.

Table 5.6 An overview of emerging and advanced technologies in auditing activities

	Artificial intelligence		
	Machine learning		
		Deep learning	
No artificial intelligence	Artificial intelligence	Artificial intelligence including machine learning	Artificial intelligence including deep learning
Basic data analytics (descriptive & diagnostic)	Cognitive process automation (with AI)	Data analytics (predictive & prescriptive)	Algorithms using large complicated neural networks
Automation		Algorithms using neural networks	Cognitive technologies
Robotic Process automation		Natural Language Processing	Computer vision
Basic algorithms			

Source: Adapted from AICPA (2019, p. 5).

> Early in the development of IT auditing, some audit leaders believed all auditors would become IT auditors because the computer was so pervasive. Instead, as IT complexities continued to increase and other audit priorities developed, IT auditing developed into a department within internal audit, or as a prime area for outsourcing. Expanding on the initial use of CAATs, one of the biggest advances in the use of IT in internal audit has been the increased use of data mining, continuous auditing, and analytics for auditing data.
>
> (Cangemi, 2015, p. 5)

Data analytics should make substantive contributions to auditing (Earley, 2015; Tang & Karim, 2017).

One of the major challenges of internal auditing is the processing of a considerable amount of data (Alles & Gray, 2014). Data analytics techniques can replace sampling audit techniques (insufficient in case of low level of assurance) by testing the correct functioning of a process or a series of controls on a whole population. A process can be composed of several activities across different organizational units (Krieger et al., 2021). Textual data is the most common type of big data in auditing.

In recent years, the use of data analytics has been progressively spreading as shown in Figure 5.1. The internal audit environment is increasingly using analytics (Alles et al. 2006; Vasarhelyi et al. 2015). Data analytics allows the automation of routine procedures and can greatly expand the breadth and scope of audit coverage. Analytics is crucial to identify potential anomalies, to visualize data, to anticipate potential risks, to detect potential fraud, and finally to seek for fraud evidence. More specifically, with data visualization, auditors can identify more easily patterns and errors in figures, question management's assertions and react more cautiously to audit evidence (Dilla et al. 2010; Rose et al. 2017; Anderson et al., 2020; Holt & Loraas, 2021).

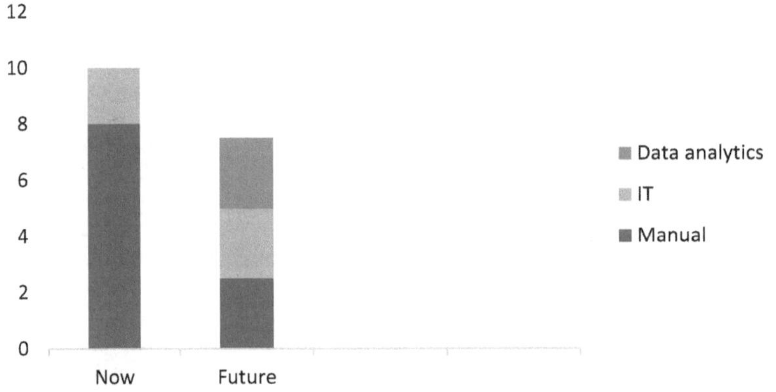

Figure 5.1 The increased weight of analytics in the audit process
Source: Adapted from KPMG and Randstad quoted by Maes and Chuah (2016, p. 37).

> Internal audit functions that have successfully implemented sustainable analytics activities have not only been able to clearly visualize and articulate the value analytics can deliver to their functions and the broader business, but also have started to realize that value in enhanced efficiency, effectiveness, and risk awareness.
>
> (Braun et al., 2017, p. 41)

Several technologies and data analysis tools can help to meet this challenge effectively.

The audit process analytics driven includes continuous auditing, dynamic audit planning, audit scoping and planning, and audit execution and reporting. Data analytics has also a great impact on audit quality as its use on larger sets of audit relevant data is much broader than traditional analytical methods (Figure 5.2).

Data analytics and artificial intelligence (AI)

Using *analytics* and automation (see below) is a first step for auditors in their digital journey toward an AI-enabled audit (Issa et al., 2016). "Artificial Intelligence (AI) based natural language processing can work like human auditors and identify patterns in structured or unstructured data for risks, fraud or control issues" (Jones et al., 2021, p. 9).

AI is already being used to reinforce the reliability of auditing processes. The audit of the future is likely to reduce human-to-human interaction related to highly repetitive and rules-based tasks and to allow auditors to devote more time to higher value-added activities. The Chartered Professional Accountants of Canada – AICPA (2020), in their report dedicated to the data-driven audit, have explored how data analytics, automation, and AI will transform the audit in its various phases as defined below. To achieve this aim, these next-generation technologies should be widely adopted.

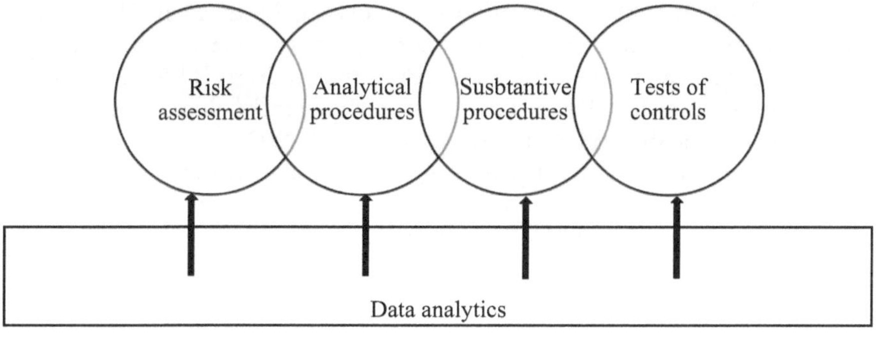

Figure 5.2 Audit procedures to obtain audit evidence

Source: Adapted from the International Auditing and Assurance Standards Board's Data Analytics Working Group (2016, p. 7).

Phase 1- Pre-Engagement

Phase 2- Audit planning (client acceptance and continuance, audit scope, risk assessment, understanding the entity, materiality assessment)

Phase 3- Audit fieldwork (test of controls if applicable, substantive audit procedures, including test of details or substantive analytical procedures, evidence gathering, review of deficiencies and determining whether the auditor needs additional audit evidence)

Phase 4- Forming an opinion and reporting (in case of specific financial audits, it could be review of financial statements and disclosures, review of material misstatements, conclude on the audit and prepare audit report)

In addition, challenges and considerations for the auditor are described for each phase. For example, for phase 4, the auditor will have to take into consideration regulatory and legal rules and the way a specific AI tool could incorporate these requirements.

The strategic move to automation: the development of RPA

Converging definitions of RPA from both practitioners and scholars

A literature review on auditing and RPA has been conducted based on papers published between 2010 and 2022. The main findings are reported in Appendix 5.1 (Table A5.1).

According to ACCA, Chartered Accountants (CA) ANZ, and KPMG (2018), "RPA is software that can be easily programmed or instructed by end users to perform high-volume, repeatable, rules-based tasks in today's world where multiple loosely integrated systems are commonplace." (ACCA et al., 2018, p. 10). Gartner, based on its glossary, highlights the fact that RPA is "a productivity tool that allows a user to configure one or more scripts (which some vendors refer to as "bots") to activate specific keystrokes in an automated fashion. The result is that the bots can be used to mimic or emulate selected tasks (transaction steps) within an overall business or IT process. These may include manipulating data, passing data to and from different applications, triggering responses, or executing transactions. RPA uses a combination of user interface interaction and descriptor technologies. The scripts can overlay on one or more software applications." (2022).

Hartley and Sawaya (2019) propose a broader definition using the expression of "umbrella" dedicated to "tools that operate on the user interface of other computer systems in the way a human would do. RPA aims to replace people by automation done in an 'outside-in' manner. This differs from the classical 'inside-out' approach to improve information systems." (p. 709).

There are several levels in automation from basic one to cognitive automation combining the worlds of automation, AI and cognitive computing

Table 5.7 What is RPA?

Basic automation	*Robotic process automation*		*Cognitive automation*
Scripting Tasks Linear Standard Repeatable	Orchestration Activities Orchestrated Standard Complex Multi-scripted	Autonomics Process Dynamic Non standard Contextual Inference	Cognitive System Self-Aware Predictive Self-learning Self-healing

Source: Adapted from AICPA (2019, p. 17) quoting the Institute for Robotic Process Automation and Artificial Intelligence.

(Table 5.7). Cognitive automation (referring to AI techniques), creates more capabilities and handles the more complex processes. It uses technologies that mimic human thought and action. It can be considered as the higher end of the intelligent automation spectrum.

RPA: a bridge *between legacy* and modern cloud applications

RPA is considered as a lightweight IT (Bygstad & Iden, 2017) used to describe front-end software that is generally adopted outside of the IT department (Willcocks & Lacity, 2016). RPA is relatively easier and cheaper to implement, configure and maintain, compared to traditional IT systems or other forms of automation (Bygstad & Iden, 2017). RPA robot is generally considered as a software that can be installed on a computer, interacting with other IT systems on the front-end, while other traditional software are integrated via the back-end (Asatiani & Penttinen, 2016). RPA does not require changing the existing IT systems. "RPA is system agnostic. It sits "on top of" existing applications and replicates the actions of a human user at the user interface level. This means there is no need to change, replace or compromise existing enterprise applications for the software to work" (ACCA et al., 2018, p. 10).

However, if badly implemented outside proper controls by the IT function, a high risk pointed out by scholars is to lose control of architecture (Osmundsen et al., 2019), security applications and to have damaging consequences. In addition, in this case, RPA implementation often suffers from limited scalability (Bygstad & Iden, 2017).

The use of RPA in auditing: the end of the *swivel chair work*?

Two types of automation are generally identified:

- Attended automation leading to automate repetitive, manual, front-office activities and mimics actions performed by auditors on their desktop.

- Unattended automation does not require a person to be at their computer. Unattended bots do the work by themselves instead of humans recording and playing back actions.

RPA is often linked with images of robot-like machines assembling computers or cars. But RPA goes far beyond this common vision. It can reduce if not eliminate all repetitive and rules-based tasks in an environment where there are multiple integrated systems, and there is an increasing use of cloud-based systems and a standardization of processes (KPMG, 2018b). For internal audit, RPA brings both opportunity (collaboration with other entities) and responsibility (understanding of risks introduced by RPA and ensuring that firm's controls are well designed) as mentioned by PWC (2017a, 2017b). "Where data cannot move seamlessly between systems, the use of robotic process automation (RPA) can remove the need for manual intervention to cover the 'last mile'" (ACCA & CA ANZ, 2019, p. 7). RPA-based new practices will speed up audit processes and reduce the risk of errors. "The 'swivel chair' automation product, so called because it replicates the actions of a human accessing multiple systems, cuts across the IT legacy landscape, and helps connect the flow of data. It automates the logical transfer of data within processes quickly and accurately, freeing up valuable resources from mundane tasks. RPA 'user-interface' technology utilizes the same application interfaces as a human would, i.e., USERIDs, for integrity and audit trail purposes" (ACCA et al. 2018, p. 10). Auditors will be able to focus on higher value-added missions (Eulerich et al., 2022). The example in table shows how RPA can be applied to a process of chargeback is provided in Table 5.8.

The impact of blockchain technology (BT) on auditing

The final technology to be presented in this general overview is blockchain. Blockchain technology's main pillars include decentralization, transparency & traceability, immutability & neutrality, security & data protection and automation. Smart *contracts-code*-based are directly linked with BT leading to the well-known expression "Code is Law."

BT can be defined as a digital (decentralized) ledger of transactions that is duplicated and distributed across the network of computer systems on the blockchain. The decentralized database managed by multiple participants is known as Distributed Ledger Technology (DLT). Applications for blockchain technology are numerous (financial services, insurance, real estate, life sciences and healthcare, supply chain, government and the public sector, digital identity, etc.).

Table 5.8 Application of RPA in the record to report process

	Seven manual processes *Time to perform: 240 hours/month* *Accuracy: 90%*						
Before	Payment completed on behalf of different legal entity	Receive request for payment and register document via email	Approve invoice via expense memo	Initiate payment	Confirm no duplicate payments/ manual review	Manually create journal entries	Approve and post
	Two manual processes *Time to perform: 20 hours/month* *Accuracy: 100%* *Five RPA processes (in bold)*						
After	Payment completed on behalf of different legal entity	**Receive request for payment and register document**	**Approve invoice via expense memo**	**Initiate payment**	**Confirm no duplicate payments**	**Create journal entries**	Approve and post

Source: ACCA, CA ANZ, KPMG (2018, p. 18).

What are the connections between blockchain and auditing? Since the beginning of the 2010s, both scholars and practitioners have discussed the current and future use of blockchain in auditing and its main implications (KPMG, 2018c).

For the academic part, even though many of these articles are dedicated to external auditing, we will summarize the main points to take into account. Several scholars have studied this topic (Liu et al., 2019; Rozario & Thomas, 2019; Schmitz & Leoni, 2019; Elommal & Manita, 2022). Rozario and Thomas (2019) have shown that blockchain, by automating data flows, would transform the audit process and improve its efficiency. Schmitz and Leoni (2019) consider that the perspectives of scholars and practitioners are various and neither group seems to be explicitly favorable or unfavorable toward blockchain development for external audit. "Blockchain is a promising technology for increasing trust between different stakeholders, the benefits it can give to the profession and its ability to detect fraudulent transactions remain limited" (Schmitz & Leoni, 2019, p. 338).

In the literature, as pointed out by Elommal and Manita (2022), two main types of blockchain exist: public and private or "permissioned and permissionless" blockchain. They explore the impact of BT on six dimensions. Blockchain will allow an auditor to (1) save time and improve the efficiency of their audit, (2) favor an audit covering the whole population instead of an audit based on sampling techniques, (3) focus the audit on testing controls rather than testing transactions, (4) set up a continuous audit process, (5) play a more strategic audit role, and (6) develop new advisory services. The two authors finally underline the need for the establishment of a clear and coherent legislative system and new audit standards, allowing auditors to embed this technology and enhance audit practices.

Liu et al. (2019) have also explored the possible opportunities and challenges presented by the two types of blockchain (permissionless and permissioned) for internal and external auditors (Table 5.9). Their study concludes with a series of recommendations to practitioners to adapt to this technology and develop their activities.

Practitioners have highlighted the fact that blockchain technology is already mobilized in the framework of external audit missions for accounting reporting processes as well as for the financial audit of companies. Its use for internal auditing, in particular, is still limited so far. Deloitte (2017) has pointed out the fact that BT could be at the core of the continuous audit: "instead of assessments at year end (or interim), audit firms will be in a position to perform continuous on-line assessments throughout the period under audit" (p. 3).

We could not conclude this section without addressing briefly the potential implications of the nascent technology named metaverse for auditing (Davis, 2022). According to Mystakidis (2022), the metaverse can be defined as "the post-reality universe, a perpetual and persistent multiuser environment merging physical reality with digital virtuality. It is based

Table 5.9 The use of blockchain: opportunities and challenges to auditors

	Opportunities	*Challenges*
Permissionless blockchain	Examine transaction record on blockchain; Develop novel audit process on blockchain transactions; Verify the consistency between items on blockchain and in the physical world	
Permissioned blockchain	Develop guidelines for blockchain implementation; Leverage industry knowledge and experience to offer advice for best practices for blockchain consensus protocols; Leverage business networks to form permissioned blockchain based on market demand; Act as planner and coordinator of potential participants of a blockchain; Leverage their expertise on IT auditing to audit internal control of blockchain, including data integrity and security; Offer independent rating services to a specific blockchain; Act as administrator of blockchain	No reversal of erroneous transactions; No centralized authority to verify the existence, ownership, and measurement of items recorded on blockchain; Data retrieval due to clients' loss of private key; No centralized authority to report cyberattack. Need to be proficient in various blockchain technologies; Difficult to reach consensus rules among all participants, when acting as an organizational agent; Audit transaction linked to a side agreement that is "off-chain"; Tackle the situation when central authority has power to override information on blockchain; Cope with change of consensus protocol in a blockchain.

Source: Adapted from Liu et al. (2019, p. A26).

on the convergence of technologies that enable multisensory interactions with virtual environments, digital objects and people such as virtual reality (VR) and augmented reality (AR)". Several experts in auditing have already stressed the fact that the metaverse has the potential to shape organizations and therefore the internal audit activity. Davis (2022) outlines the potential benefits to be derived from this technology in the medium term, for example, in remote audit reviews. Metaverse could provide an enabling environment and platform to achieve a thorough remote audit by offering a one-on-one engagement/interview with the auditees. Obviously, this technology is not completely risk-free. "The risk inherent in the usage may include identity theft and a lack of proper tools in place to verify and authenticate the personality behind the avatar in use. Over time, these and other concerns will gradually be addressed" states the author in his comments.

Auditing of new (or emerging) technologies

While there is no debate that internal auditing is benefiting from the contribution of new technologies to its own missions as shown in the previous section, how will auditors audit automation, robotization, and artificial intelligence solutions? That is one question Deloitte addresses in a blog posted on its website in March 2020 (https://blog.deloitte.fr/audit-interne-les-cles-d-une-necessaire-evolution). For Yoan Chazal, Benjamin Brecy, and Dylan Bergounhe, the three authors of this blog, internal auditing must imperatively evolve to meet three major objectives as follows:

- Strengthen the prospective vision
- Integrate new technologies into the internal audit methodology (see previous section)
- Audit RPA and artificial intelligence solutions

We will focus more specifically here on the third issue by analyzing data analytics, RPA, and blockchain technology.

Auditing algorithmic decision-making and artificial intelligence (AI) solutions

Statista (2021) expects AI software revenue to grow rapidly from US$ 10.1 billion in 2018 to US$ 126 billion by 2025. The overall AI market includes a wide array of applications such as natural language processing, robotic process automation, and machine learning (ML). The use of algorithms (defined as automated routine processes for analyzing data, solving problems, and performing tasks) offers organizations a multitude of potential benefits but at the same time increases the risks companies have to face. Algorithms are becoming more and more prevalent and complex as shown in the previous section. Their increasingly use raises crucial questions and regulators require organizations to explain their algorithmic decisions.

As explained by Guszcza et al. (2018), auditors must address a number of questions when conducting an audit of algorithms:

> Is the algorithm suitably transparent to end-users? Is it likely to be used in a socially acceptable way? Might it produce undesirable psychological effects or inadvertently exploit natural human frailties? Is the algorithm being used for a deceptive purpose? Is there evidence of internal bias or incompetence in its design? Is it adequately reporting how it arrives at its

recommendations and indicating its level of confidence? Even if thoughtfully performed, algorithm auditing will still raise difficult questions that only society — through their elected representatives and regulators — can answer.

As there are several potential challenges for IT auditors involved in AI audit missions, several guidelines could be provided (Table 5. 10).

RPA: auditing a bot environment

As defined previously, RPA refers to a set of modular software programs also called "bots" that perform structured, repeatable, and logic-based tasks by mimicking the human actions. Several factors must be taken into consideration or required during missions of audit bots:

- General conditions about the development of bots within organizations. "Security by design" is often demanded in the development of framework.
- The auditors must track and record data for all the processes and BOTs and need code/workflows and all the information provided by the BOT and used by it in control. "A key question that arises is: to what extent (software) robots and artificial intelligence at the client side impact the audit approach? In the case of clients using software robots in key processes, the auditors will have to gain a certain level of comfort over the

Table 5.10 Challenges and solutions for AI auditing

Challenges for the auditor of AI	*Keys to the successful auditing of AI*
Immature auditing frameworks or regulations specific to AI	Adopt and adapt existing frameworks and regulations
Limited precedents for AI use cases	Explain and communicate proactively about AI with stakeholders
Uncertain definitions and taxonomies of AI	Explain and communicate proactively about AI with stakeholders
Wide variance among AI systems and solutions	Become informed about AI design and architecture to set proper scope
Emerging nature of AI technology	Become informed about AI design and architecture to set proper scope
Lack of explicit AI auditing guidance	Focus on transparency through an iterative process. Focus on controls and governance, not algorithms
Lack of strategic starting points	Involve all stakeholders
Possibly steep learning curve for the AI auditor	Become informed about AI design and engage specialists as needed
Supplier risk created by AI outsourcing to third parties	Document architectural practices for cross-team transparency

Source: ISACA (2018, p. 8).

reliability of the data processing carried out by the robot. This means that the auditors will need to boost their technology understanding in order to assess the reliability of *robot software*. The profession may be supported by the same digital trend, what if the programming code of the robot can be analyzed by an 'audit-bot'?" (KPMG, 2018a, p. 2).

- Most common use cases in audit/compliance: Quarterly User Access Reviews (UAR); data/evidence gathering; system configuration testing; rules-based workpaper automation; orchestration of audit automation tools and scripts; user provisioning and deprovisioning controls; master data management compliance; application change management compliance; continuous monitoring; reporting automation (ISACA-RSM, 2020).

In its report dedicated to Auditing the RPA environment, Deloitte (2018b) has identified the specific risks emerging from of an automated setup that must be taken in consideration by auditors. The following table illustrates the various phases of audit and the issues to address at each of these phases (Table 5.11).

Table 5.11 The different phases of audit when auditing a BOT environment

Phases of audit		*Considerations*
Planning	Detailed understanding of the areas where RPA is implemented audit plans	Audit plans and risk assessment for RPA Update to control matrices for automation through RPA Upfront involvement of IS Auditor/BOT Specialist
Walkthrough	Understanding of the process & IT Identification of risks Identification of control	New IS/IT risks and scoped in systems Changes to automated controls, IPE/IUC, audit logs and interfaces More IS Risks and therefore enhanced ITGCC control
Design evaluation	Evaluation of the design of controls exception handling process Identification of gaps	Substantial work by IS Auditor to test controls from Design (Configuration controls, logs, Cyber risks) Testing for IPE/IUC
Operating effectiveness	Controls testing substantive testing	Increased controls testing and minimal substantive testing Process governance and roles
Reporting	Gaps reporting recommendations	Logs and audit trails Changes to control design, RCM, SOPs, roles, etc., Technology recommendations

* Note (added by the author): Information "Produced or Provided" by the Entity (IPE) is evidence for the audit that is generated by the entity and used by the auditors to test a control. Information Used by the "Company or Entity" (IUC) is evidence that is used by the Company/Entity, in order to perform or execute their internal controls (https://linfordco.com/blog/iuc-ipe-audit-procedures-for-soc-audits/). SOP is the Standard Operating Procedure.

Source: Deloitte (2018b, p. 2).

Auditing blockchain technology (and its applications)

Since the end of the 2010s, auditors (and, in particular, IT auditors) are likely to audit more and more blockchain technology and its applications as new blockchain-based techniques and procedures will emerge in the future. As processes move to blockchain technology, both internal and external auditors will be involved in the reflection of how this technology will change the audit process.

Blockchain technology will be implemented at client sites and in their business applications in various sectors. As blockchain allows an unchangeable and accurate record of transactions, both financial and operational, auditors should get access to it.

In a white paper entitled "Auditing blockchain solutions," KPMG (2018c) has underlined that the auditors entrusted with the task of validating and reviewing solutions built on blockchain might need to adopt a customized audit framework for blockchain. To reduce a number of specific risks derived from blockchain, the audit firm provides a grid centered on seven items, related key success factors as follows:

- Key ownership and management. Secure storage, maintenance, review and governance of cryptographic private keys used for authentication and validation by nodes.
- Interoperability and integration. Consistent communication between multiple blockchain platforms and integration with organizations' enterprise and legacy systems.
- Consensus mechanism. Blocks in the chain are validated by nodes to maintain a single version of the truth to keep adversaries from derailing the system and forking the chain.
- Heterogeneous regulatory compliance. Compliance with laws and regulations across various country and state legislations that will govern information and transactions processed.
- Access and permissions management. Permissions configured for defined roles for access, validation and authorization of blockchain transactions by internal and external participants.
- Infrastructure and application management. Secure software development practices and testing of blockchain applications, platform, infrastructure, and communication interfaces.
- Network and nodes governance. Monitoring of network for information compliance and node reputation checks to handle and resolve disputes.

Toward augmented auditors: **the emergence of auditors 4.0.**

The impact of changes in technology for auditing on the auditor's roles, skills and competences is already noticeable (PWC, 2015, 2019). It will be even more significant for the auditing profession in the upcoming years. The new technologies described previously can improve the work of internal auditors. However, at the same time, the auditors will need to understand more and more these new technologies (PWC, 2018). There is a new need of IT-skills (Ghasemi et al., 2011; Brender & Gauthier, 2018).The profession of the auditor is currently being transformed and will continue to be so under the impetus of new technologies in order to become an augmented auditor (auditor 4.0.).

In addition to the qualities traditionally associated with the auditor (rigor, analytical skills, ability to synthesize, critical thinking, business acumen, industry expertise, ethics, etc.) other skills and knowledge should be obtained and/or improved. Several trends are clearly seen accordingly and can be summarized as follows:

- Technology skills. The survey conducted in 2017 by KPMG and Forbes, has shown that the top three skills clients look for in an auditor are in the areas of technology, communication and critical thinking.

  > Clients expect their auditors to be current with new technology and looking ahead as technology evolves. They rightly believe that technology has improved the quality of audit and will continue to do so. But clients are also looking for other benefits from technology, including tracking trends and alerting organizations to emerging issues. Again, this means auditors must take a more holistic and forward-looking view when gathering and analyzing data. Better, more comprehensive audits are expected by clients, but they are also looking for value-added observations and insights.
  >
  > (p. 11)

  This opinion is shared by a large number of professional bodies and audit firms (PWC, 2015, 2019).
- The key and enhanced role of the IT auditor

In more sophisticated and complex IT environments, the level of engagement and interaction between auditors and IT auditors should increase. The composition of audit teams will change toward the hiring of IT auditors and other specialists ((i.e., compliance, tax, data analytics, data visualization, blockchain). As accuracy and completeness of several operations would be guaranteed by the technology itself, the auditor's role would be to perform an in-depth source code (in case of use of blockchain) and parameters review. As such, auditors would primarily be "IT engineer auditor."

Conclusion

As seen in the previous chapters, the auditing profession is exposed to major challenges (technology, compliance and legal requirements, risks, etc.). In addition, internal and IT auditors will use more and more new technologies in auditing assignments. These advancements in technology confirm that the internal auditor should play a greater strategic role within the organization.

The dynamic environment will push technology information auditing profession in front of a major challenge for the development of tools and methods to continue to provide high-quality service (Chambers, 2019). There is a need for further research to analyze to what extent new technologies (AI, RPA, blockchain, etc.) will change business operations (Deloitte, 2022). These developments would probably open up new opportunities for the audit process itself by expanding the breadth and scope of audit coverage.

Questions for discussion

How is innovation driven in auditing activities?

Which processes should be automated, and which should be performed by humans in auditing activities?

What tasks will internal auditors have to perform in the future and which tasks may disappear?

How will IT auditors work alongside blockchain in the future?

What are the future competencies needed by internal and IT auditors?

Recommended reading

Cangemi, M.P. (2015). *Staying a step ahead internal audit's use of technology. The IIA Research Foundation. The global internal audit common body of knowledge.* Retrieved 13 January 2022 from: http://contentz.mkt5790.com/lp/2842/191428/2015-1403_CBOK_Staying_A_Step_Ahead.pdf

Krieger, F., Drews, P., & Velte, P. (2021). Explaining the (non-) adoption of advanced data analytics in auditing: A process theory. *International Journal of Accounting Information Systems, 41*, 100511. https://doi.org/10.1016/j.accinf.2021.100511

References

ACCA, Chartered Accountants (CA) ANZ (2019). *Audit and technology.* Retrieved January 9, 2022 from: https://www.accaglobal.com/content/dam/ACCA_Global/professional-insights/audit-and-tech/pi-audit-and-technology.pdf

ACCA, Chartered Accountants (CA) ANZ, KPMG (2018). *Embracing robotic automation during the evolution of finance.* Retrieved January 15, 2022 from: https://www.accaglobal.com/content/dam/ACCA_Global/professional-insights/embracing-robotics/Embracing%20 robotic%20automation.pdf

AICPA (2019). *A CPA's introduction to AI: From algorithms to deep learning, what you need to know.* Retrieved 13 January 2022 from: https://us.aicpa.org/content/dam/aicpa/interestareas/frc/assuranceadvisoryservices/downloadabledocuments/cpas-introduction-to-ai-from-algorithms.pdf

AICPA (1979). *Audit and accounting. Guide : Computer assisted audit techniques.* New York: AICPA.

Al-Ateeq, B., Sawan, N., Al-Hajaya, K., Altarawneh, M., & Al-Makhadmeh, A. (2022). Big data analytics in auditing and the consequences for audit quality: A study using the technology acceptance model (TAM). *Corporate Governance and Organizational Behavior Review, 6*(1), 64–78. https://doi.org/10.22495/cgobrv6i1p5

Alles, M., Brennan, G., Kogan, A., & Vasarhelyi, M.A. (2006). Continuous monitoring of business process controls: A pilot implementation of a continuous auditing system at Siemens. *International Journal of Accounting Information Systems, 7*(2), 137–161.

Alles, M., & Gray, G. (2014). *A framework for analyzing the potential role of big data in auditing: A synthesis of the literature.* Working Paper. Rutgers, NJ: Rutgers University.

Anderson, S.B., Hobson, J.L., & Peecher, M.E. (2020). *The joint effects of rich data visualization and audit procedure categorization on auditor judgment.* Retrieved July 8, 2021 from: https://ssrn.com/abstract=3737234 or http://dx.doi.org/10.2139/ssrn.3737234

Asatiani, A., & Penttinen, E. (2016). Turning robotic process automation into commercial success – Case OpusCapita. *Journal of Information Technology Teaching Cases, 6*(2), 67–74.

Asif Qureshi, M. (2020). Auditing emerging technologies: Facing new-age challenges. Retrieved July 8, 2021 from: https://www.isaca.org/resources/isaca-journal/issues/2020/volume-2/auditing-emerging-technologies

Braun, R.L., & Davis, H.E. (2003). Computer-assisted audit tools and techniques: Analysis and perspectives. *Managerial Auditing Journal, 18*(9), 725–731.

Braun, G., Struthers-Kennedy, A., & Wishna, G. (2017). Building a data analytics program: Six strategies can facilitate progress when starting or furthering an analytics program. *Internal Auditor, 74*(4), 41–46.

Brender, N., & Gauthier, M. (2018). Impacts of blockchain on the auditing profession. *ISACA Journal, 5*, 27–32. https://www.isaca.org/-/media/files/isacadp/project/isaca/articles/journal/2018/volume-5/impacts-of-blockchain-on-the-auditing-profession_joa_eng_0918.pdf

Brown, V.L., Coram, P.J., Dennis, S.A., Dickins, D., Earley, C.E., Higgs, J.L., Schaefer, T.J., & Tatum, K.W. (2019). Comments of the auditing standards committee of the auditing section of the American accounting association on international auditing and assurance standards board exposure draft, proposed international standard on auditing 315 (Revised): Identifying and current issues. *Auditing, 13*(1), C1–C9. https://doi.org/10.2308/ciia-52338

Bygstad, B., & Iden, J., (2017). A governance model for managing lightweight IT. In Á. Rocha, A.M. Correia, H. Adeli, L.P. Reis, & S. Costanzo (Eds.), *Recent advances in information systems and technologies* (pp. 384–393). Cham: Springer International Publishing.

Cascarino, R.E. (2017). *Data analytics for internal auditors.* New York: Taylor & Francis Group.

Chambers, R. (2019). The road ahead for internal audit: 5 bold predictions for the 2020s. AuditBeacon. https://www.richardchambers.com/the-road-ahead-for-internal-audit-5-bold-predictions-for-the-2020s/

The Chartered Professional Accountants of Canada – AICPA (2020). *The data-driven audit: How automation and AI are changing the audit and the role of the auditor.* Retrieved October 20, 2021 from: https://us.aicpa.org/content/dam/aicpa/interestareas/frc/assuranceadvisoryservices/downloadabledocuments/the-data-driven-audit.pdf

Curtis, M.B., & Payne, E.A. (2014). Modeling voluntary CAAT utilization decisions in auditing. *Managerial Auditing Journal, 29*(4), 304–326. https://doi.org/10.1108/MAJ-07-2013-0903

Curtis, M.B., & Payne, E.A. (2008). An examination of contextual factors and individual characteristics affecting technology implementation decisions in auditing. *International Journal of Accounting Information Systems, 9*(2), 104–121. https://doi.org/10.1016/j.accinf.2007.10.002

Daidj, N., & Tounkara, T. (2020). RPA issues in organizations: A review of the literature. *Proceedings of the 25th AIM Conference (Association Information & Management).* Paris: AIM. https://aim.asso.fr/fr/publications/actes-conferences?titre=Tounkara&titre-submit=Rechercher

Davis, W. (2022). Auditing in a Virtual Universe. https://www.isaca.org/resources/news-and-trends/isaca-now-blog/2022/auditing-in-a-virtual-universe

Davis, F.D. (1989). Perceived usefulness, perceived ease of use, and user acceptance of information technology. *MIS Quarterly, 13*(3), 319–340. https://doi.org/10.2307/249008

Davis, F., Bagozzi, R.P., & Warshaw, P.R. (1989). User acceptance of computer technology: A comparison of two theoretical models. *Management Science, 35*(8), 982–1003. https://doi.org/10.1287/mnsc.35.8.982

Deloitte (2022). Robots strengthen the digital workforce. Robot process automation: Audit with RPA and audit of RPA. https://www2.deloitte.com/ch/en/pages/audit/articles/robots-strengthen-the-digital-workforce.html

Deloitte (2018a). Auditing the risks of disruptive technologies internal audit in the age of digitalization. Retrieved September 17, 2021 from: https://www2.deloitte.com/content/dam/Deloitte/us/Documents/finance/us-rfa-auditing-the-risks-of-disruptive-technologies.pdf

Deloitte (2018b). Auditing the RPA environment our approach towards addressing risks in a BOT environment. Retrieved September 17, 2021 from: https://www2.deloitte.com/content/dam/Deloitte/in/Documents/risk/in-ra-auditing-the-rpa-environment-noexp.pdf

Deloitte (2017). Blockchain: A game changer for audit processes? Retrieved September 17, 2021 from: https://www2.deloitte.com/content/dam/Deloitte/mt/Documents/audit/dt_mt_article_blockchain_gamechanger-for-audit-sandro-psaila.pdf

Dias, C., & Marques, R.P. (2018). The use of computer-assisted audit tools and techniques by Portuguese internal auditors. *Proceedings of the 3th Iberian Conference on Information Systems and Technologies (CISTI)* (pp. 1–7).

Dilla, W., Janvrin, D.J., & Raschke, R. (2010). Interactive data visualization: New directions for accounting information systems research. *Journal of Information Systems, 24*(2), 1–37.

Earley, C. (2015). Data analytics in auditing: Opportunities and challenges. *Business Horizons, 58*(5), 493–500. https://doi.org/10.1016/j.bushor.2015.05.002

Elommal, N., & Manita, R. (2022). How blockchain innovation could affect the audit profession: A qualitative study. *Journal of Innovation Economics & Management, 1*(37), 37–63. https://doi.org/10.3917/jie.037.0037

Eulerich, M., Pawlowski, J., Waddoups, N., & Wood, D.A. (2022). A framework for using robotic process automation for audit tasks. *Contemporary Accounting Research, 39*(1), 691–720. https://doi.org/10.1111/1911-3846.12723

Gartner (2022). Robotic Process Automation (RPA). Glossary. https://www.gartner.com/en/information-technology/glossary/robotic-process-automation-rpa

Ghasemi, M., Shafeiepour, V., Aslani, M., & Barvayeh, E. (2011). The impact of Information Technology (IT) on modern accounting systems. *Procedia - Social and Behavioral Sciences, 28*, 112–116. https://doi.org/10.1016/j.sbspro.2011.11.023

Guszcza, J., Rahwan, I., Bible, W., Cebrian, M., & Katyal, V. (2018). Why we need to audit algorithms. *Harvard Business Review.* Published on HBR.org. November 28, 2018. https://hbr.org/2018/11/why-we-need-to-audit-algorithms

Hartley, J., & Sawaya, W. (2019). Tortoise, not the hare: Digital transformation of supply chain business processes, *Business Horizons, 62*(6), 707–715.

Holt, T., & Loraas, T.M. (2021). A potential unintended consequence of Big Data: Does information structure lead to suboptimal auditor judgment and decision-making? *Accounting Horizons, 35*(3), 161–186. https://doi.org/10.2308/HORIZONS-19-123

IAASB (2019). *International standard on auditing 315 (revised 2019): Identifying and assessing the risks of material misstatement.* Retrieved May 25, 2021 from: https://www.iaasb.org/publications/isa-315-revised-2019-identifying-and-assessing-risks-material-misstatement

IAASB (2016). *Exploring the use of technology in the audit, with a focus on data analytics.* Data Analytics Working Group. Retrieved May 25, 2021 from: https://www.ifac.org/system/files/publications/files/IAASB- Data-Analytics-WG-Publication-Aug-25–2016-for-comms-9.1.16.pdf

The Institute of Internal Auditors (IIA) (2017). *International standards for the professional practice of internal auditing (standards).* https://na.theiia.org/standardsguidance/Public%20Documents/IPPF-Standards-2017.pdf.https://www.iia.org.au/sf_docs/default-source/quality/presentation-internal-audit-standards.pdf?sfvrsn=4

ISACA (2018). *Audit and assurance. Auditing artificial intelligence.* Retrieved January 8, 2022 from: https://ec.europa.eu/futurium/en/system/files/ged/auditing-artificial-intelligence.pdf

ISACA-RSM (2020). *Robotic Process Automation (RPA) and the auditor.* Retrieved January 8, 2022 from: https://higherlogicdownload.s3.amazonaws.com/ISACA/-a085a583-e841-4dbe-a215-60cf6d98e036/UploadedImages/RPA_and_the_Auditor_ISACA_SFL_-_Final-09302020__2_.pdf

Issa, H., Sun, T., & Vasarhelyi, M.A. (2016). Research ideas for artificial intelligence in auditing: The formalization of audit and workforce supplementation. *Journal of Emerging Technologies in Accounting, 13*(2), 1–20. https:// doi.org/10.2308/jeta-10511

Janvrin, D., Bierstaker, J., & Lowe, D.J. (2009). An investigation of factors influencing the use of computer-related audit procedures. *Journal of Information Systems, 23*(1), 97–118.

Janvrin, D., Bierstaker, J., & Lowe, D.J. (2008). An examination of audit information technology use and perceived importance, *Accounting Horizons, 22*(1), 1–21.

Jones, P., Krynauw, S., Zergenyi, R., & Ziliani, C. (2021). *Guidance on unlocking the value of internal audit functions by implementing data analytics / science.* Retrieved January 29, 2022 from: https://www.eciia.eu/2021/06/guidance-on-unlocking-the-value-of-internal-audit-functions-by-implementing-data-analytics-science/

KPMG (2018a). Impact of new technologies on audit and assurance. Retrieved October 6, 2021 from: https://assets.kpmg/content/dam/kpmg/ng/pdf/advisory/Impact-of- New-Tech-on-Audit-and-Assurance.pdf

KPMG (2018b). *Intelligent automation and internal audit. Adding value through governance, risk management, and controls.* Retrieved October 6, 2021 from: https://assets.kpmg/content/dam/kpmg/ch/pdf/intelligent-automation-and-internal-audit.pdf

KPMG (2018c). *Auditing blockchain solutions.* Retrieved October 6, 2021 from: https://assets.kpmg/content/dam/kpmg/in/pdf/2018/10/Auditing_Blockchain_Solutions.pdf

KPMG (2016). Technology-enabled internal audit. Retrieved February 12, 2022 from: https://www.compact.nl/en/articles/technology-enabled-internal-audit/

KPMG-FORBES (2017). *Audit 2025. The future is now.* Retrieved February 12, 2022 from: https://assets.kpmg/content/dam/kpmg/us/pdf/2017/03/us-audit-2025-final-report.pdf

Krieger, F., Drews, P., & Velte, P. (2021). Explaining the (non-) adoption of advanced data analytics in auditing: A process theory. *International Journal of Accounting Information Systems, 41,* [100511]. https://doi.org/10.1016/j.accinf.2021.100511

Lamboglia, R., Lavorato, D., Scornavacca, E., & Za, S. (2021). Exploring the relationship between audit and technology. A bibliometric analysis. *Meditari Accountancy Research, 29*(5), 1233–1260. https://doi.org/10.1108/MEDAR-03-2020-0836

Li, H., Dai, J., Gershberg, T. & Vasarhelyi, M.A. (2018). Understanding usage and value of audit analytics for internal auditors: An organizational approach. *International Journal of Accounting Information Systems, 28*, 59–76.

Lin, W., & Wang, C. (2011). A selection model for auditing software. *Industrial Management & Data Systems, 111*(5), 776–790. https://doi.org/10.1108/02635571111137304

Liu, M., Wu, K., & Xu J.J. (2019). How will blockchain technology impact auditing and accounting: Permissionless versus permissioned blockchain. *Current Issues in Auditing, 13*(2), A19-A29. https://doi-org.devinci.idm.oclc.org/10.2308/ciia-52540

Maes, T., & Chuah, H. (2016). Technology-enabled internal audit. *Compact, 4*, 35–39. Retrieved November 18, 2021 from: https://www.compact.nl/en/articles/technology-enabled-internal-audit/

Mahzan, N., & Lymer, A. (2014). Examining the adoption of computer-assisted audit tools and techniques: Cases of generalized audit software use by internal auditors. *Managerial Auditing Journal, 29*(4), 327–349.

Mahzan, N., & Lymer, A. (2009). Examining adoption of computer assisted audit tools and techniques (CAATTs) by internal auditors: Cases of UK internal auditors. Proceedings of 12th International Business Information Management Association (IBIMA) Conference (pp. 1–46). Kuala Lumpur, Malaysia.

Mystakidis, S. (2022). Metaverse. *Encyclopedia 2*, 486–497. https://doi.org/10.3390/encyclopedia2010031

Osmundsen, K., Iden, J., & Bygstad, B. (2019). Organizing robotic process automation: Balancing loose and tight coupling. *Proceedings of the 52nd Hawaii International Conference on System Sciences (HICSS-52)* (pp. 6918–6926). AIS. https://aisel.aisnet.org/cgi/viewcontent.cgi?article=1830&context=hicss-52

Pedrosa, I., Costa, C.J., & Aparicio, M. (2020). Determinants adoption of computer-assisted auditing tools (CAATs). *Cognition, Technology & Work, 22*(3), 565–583. https://doi.org/10.1007/s10111-019-00581-4

Pedrosa, I., Costa, C.J., & Laureano, R.M. (2015). Motivations and limitations on the use of information technology on statutory auditors' work: an exploratory study. *Proceedings of the 10th Iberian Conference on Information Systems and Technologies (CISTI).*

PWC (2019). *Elevating internal audit's role: The digitally fit function. 2019 State of the Internal Audit Profession Study.* Retrieved November 23, 2021 from: https://www.pwc.ru/en/publications/internal-audit-transformation-study.html

PWC (2018). Internal audit. Expected more. Managing your risk, creating value: The role of internal audit and emerging technologies. Retrieved November 23, 2021 from: https://app.glueup.com/resources/protected/organization/726/event/7813/719263a3-99c6-468d-a74f-c22be7db2ca9.pdf

PWC (2017a). *Confidence in the future: Human and machine collaboration in the audit.* Retrieved November 23, 2021 from: https://www.pwc.com/gx/en/about/assets/Confidence%20in%20the%20future.pdf>, accessed 2 June 2019

PWC (2017b). *Robotic process automation: A primer for internal audit professionals.* Retrieved December 2, 2021 from: https://www.pwc.com/us/en/risk-assurance/publications/assets/pwc-robotics-process-automation-a-primer-for-internal-audit-professionals-october-2017.pdf

PWC (2015). *Data driven: What students need to succeed in a rapidly changing business world.* Retrieved November 23, 2021 from: https://cpb-us-w2.wpmucdn.com/sites.gsu.edu/dist/1/1670/files/2015/08/pwc-data-driven-paper-1wdb00u.pdf

Rose, A. M., Rose, J.M., Sanderson, K.A., & Thibodeau, J-C. (2017). When should audit firms introduce analyses of big data into the audit process? *Journal of Information Systems, 31*(3), 81–99.

Rosli, K., Yeow, P.H., & Siew, E.G. (2012). Factors influencing audit technology acceptance by audit firms: A new I-TOE adoption framework. *Journal of Accounting and Auditing: Research & Practice*, 2012, 1–11. https://doi.org/10.5171/2012.876814

Rozario, A.M., & Thomas, C. (2019). Reengineering the audit with blockchain and smart contracts. *Journal of Emerging Technologies in Accounting, 16*(1), 21–35.

Sayana, S. A. (2003). Using CAATs to support IS audit. *Information Systems Control Journal, 1,* 1–3.

Schmitz, J. & Leoni, G. (2019). Accounting and auditing at the time of blockchain technology: A research agenda. *Australian Accounting Review, 29*(2), 331–342. https://doi.org/10.1111/auar.12286

Statista (2021). Artificial intelligence software market revenue worldwide 2018–2025. https://www.statista.com/statistics/607716/worldwide-artificial-intelligence-market-revenues/

Surendran, P. (2012). Technology acceptance model: A survey of literature. *International Journal of Business and Social Research, 2*(4), 175–178.

Tang, J., & Karim, K.E. (2017). Big data in business analytics: Implications for the audit profession. *The CPA Journal, 87*(6), 34–39.

Vasarhelyi, M.A., Kogan, A., & Tuttle, B.M. (2015). Big data in accounting: An overview. *Accounting Horizons, 29* (2), 381–396.

Venkatesh, V., & Bala, H. (2008). Technology acceptance model 3 and a research agenda on interventions. *Decision Sciences, 39*(2), 273–315. http://dx.doi.org/10.1111/j.1540-5915.2008.00192.x

Venkatesh, V., & Davis, F.D. (2000). A theoretical extension of the technology acceptance model: four longitudinal field studies. *Management Science, 46*(2), 186–204.

Venkatesh, V., & Davis, F.D. (1996). A model of antecedents of perceived ease of use: Development and test. *Decision Sciences, 27*(3), 451–481.

Venkatesh, V., Morris, M.G., Davis, G.B., & Davis, F.D. (2003). User acceptance of information technology: toward a unified view. *MIS Quarterly, 27*(3), 425–478.

Venkatesh, V., Thong J.Y.L., & Xu, X. (2012). Consumer acceptance and use of information technology: Extending the unified theory of acceptance and use of technology. *MIS Quarterly, 36*(1), 157–178.

Willcocks, P.L., & Lacity, M.C. (2016). *Service automation - Robots and the future of work* (1st ed.). Ashford: Steve Brookes Publishing.

Appendix 5.1

Emerging academic research on RPA

We have conducted a research on academic papers on audit and RPA published since 2010 in the main management academic journals (Daidj & Tounkara, 2020). The list of these main articles published is provided in the following table.

Several basic comments can be made at a general level:

- To date, the articles on this matter are scarce, as are the attempts to tackle theoretical and conceptual aspects;
- Main papers quoted in table have been published in the area of accounting/auditing, finance, production & operations management and finally management information systems;
- These articles raise various questions but the main idea is related to the key role of RPA in terms of impact on productivity, efficiency, and accuracy on the business processes industry in several sectors. In some papers, concern is more focused on the dramatic transformation of HR, supply chain, production functions through RPA.
- Available information from field studies is more developed but still insufficient. The number of business case studies and user cases is limited.
- Regarding more specifically linkages between RPA and accounting/auditing practices, the number of papers is higher for accounting issues than auditing concern. In addition, most of publications dedicated to auditing activities focus on external audit.

Table A5.1 Main RPA issue articles in the field of management 2010–2022

Author (year)	*Title (paper)*	*Journal*
Accounting and auditing		
Lauren Cooper, Kip Holderness, Trevor Sorensen & David Wood (2019)	Robotic process automation in public accounting, *33*(4), 15–35.	*Accounting Horizons*

(*Continued*)

Author (year)	*Title (paper)*	*Journal*
Accounting and auditing		
Julia Kokina, Shay Blanchette (2019)	Early evidence of digital labor in accounting: Innovation with robotic process automation, *35*.	*International Journal of Accounting Information Systems*
Dahlia Fernandez & Aini Aman (2018)	Impacts of robotic process automation on global accounting services, *9*, 123–131.	*Asian Journal of Accounting & Governance*
Kaya Can Tansel, Turkyimaz Mete & Burcu Birol (2019)	Impact of RPA technologies on accounting systems, *82*, 235–249.	*Journal of Accounting & Finance*
Michael Rose, Ethan Rojhani & Vivek Rodrigues (2018)	The RISE of automation: Emerging technologies such as AI present a host of risks, and opportunities, for auditors to consider, *75*(6), 36–41.	*Internal Auditor*
Andrea Rozario, Miklos Vasarhelyi (2018)	How robotic process automation is transforming accounting and auditing, *88*(6), 46–49.	*CPA Journal*
Kevin Moffitt, Andrea Rozario, Miklos Vasarhelyi (2018)	Robotic process automation for auditing, *15*(1), 1–10.	*Journal of Emerging Technologies in Accounting*
Kokina, Julia and Davenport, Thomas (2017)	The emergence of artificial intelligence: How automation is changing auditing?	*Journal of Emerging Technologies in Accounting*
Hradecká, M. (2019)	Robotic internal audit – Control methods in the selected company.	*AGRIS On-Line Papers in Economics and Informatics*
Feiqi Huang & Miklos Vasarhelyi (2019)	Applying robotic process automation (RPA) in auditing: A framework	*International Journal of Accounting Information Systems*
Management information systems		
Ben Kehoe & Pieter Abbeel (2014)	A survey of research on cloud robotics and automation, 1–9.	*IEEE Transactions on Automation Science and Engineering*
W.M. P. van der Aalst, Martin Bichler & Armin Heinzl (2018)	Robotic process automation, *60*(4), 269–272	*Business and Information Systems Engineering*
Bygstad (2017)	Generative innovation: A comparison of lightweight and heavyweight IT, *32*(2), 180–193.	*Journal of Information Technology*

Aleksandre Asatiani & Esko Penttinen (2016)	Turning robotic process automation into commercial success – Case OpusCapita, *6*(2), 67–74.	*Journal of Information Technology Teaching Cases*
Petri Hallikainen, Riitta Bekkhus & L. Pan Shan (2018)	How OpusCapita used internal RPA capabilities to offer services to clients, *17*(1), 41–52.	*MIS Quarterly Executive*
Mary Lacity, Leslie Willcocks (2016)	Robotic process automation at telefónica O2, *15*(1), 21–35.	*MIS Quarterly Executive*
Somayya Madakam, Rajesh Holmukhe, Durgesh Kumar Jaiswa (2019)	The future digital work force: robotic process automation, *16*, 1–18.	*Journal of Information Systems and Technology Management*
Zhao, Xia; Xue, Ling; Whinston, Andrew B. (2013)	Managing interdependent information security risks: Cyberinsurance, managed security services, and risk pooling arrangements, *30*(1), 123–152.	*Journal of Management Information Systems*

6 The impact of the COVID-19 crisis on internal audit function and related activities

Introduction

In this last chapter, a special attention is devoted to risk, uncertainty, and crisis issues that are viewed within a broader scope of consequences. Beyond the internal audit and IT issues described in previous developments, this chapter includes a cross and transverse view of risks and changes. It is an attempt to offer a vision that enables companies to look beyond a narrow or a lack of vision (that reflects in some cases its own internal organizational silos structure) as there is a need, today more than in the past, for a cross-business view.

All companies, whatever the sector of activity and the place where they operate (local, regional, national, and international) have to face numerous and varied challenges but also slowdowns, turbulences, and increased economic and political uncertainty. The last two years marked by the COVID-19 pandemic and more recently by the war in Ukraine will probably be recorded in history textbooks for many years as their outcomes and impact remain uncertain at this point.

The first section is dedicated to the description of the several levels of risk analysis including macro (economic, political, financial, etc.) and idiosyncratic risks. The COVID-19 pandemic has led to several and global shocks in the economy and the society. The new expression (in this context) of resilience throughout the economy has been used. It has given rise to new debates and reflections on the long term and the sudden and brutal emergence of crises. Are forecasting models still of interest in such a context? Could foresight help to better anticipate not only crises but also profound changes in the economy and society? How could companies appropriate these foresight tools to better respond to new market and environmental constraints (in the broadest sense)? What role should management play in this renewed and more and more risky context?

The second section focuses on the effects of COVID-19 on business and auditing activities. The COVID-19 crisis has been a major event of 2020, the effects of which will continue in 2022 with lasting repercussions on the entire economy. This is not the first pandemic facing humanity. Following this event, most of audit and consulting groups (Big Four and others) have published on their websites analyses of the post-COVID crisis, highlighting their

DOI: 10.4324/9781003215110-7

own vision of the crisis and, above all, the acceleration of the transformation of the internal audit function in order to better meet business requirements in an increasingly uncertain and risky environment. What are the priorities for the internal audit functions today?

The multidimensional impact of crisis

An analytical framework for crisis analysis

The term crisis is a broad notion that could affect several levels (world, country, region, company, etc.) and could have multiple dimensions (geopolitical, political, economic, commercial, financial, societal, health, etc.) and multiple major or minor consequences (Table 6.1). To address crisis responses, it is essential to develop an understanding of several factors as follows:

Table 6.1 The different levels of crisis analysis

	Macro	*Meso*	*Micro*
Level of analysis	Country (including regions, territories)	Market – sector	Company
Scope	Government policies, general economy	Industry structure and related markets (Agriculture, manufacturing and services sectors)	Corporate strategy
Concepts	Comparative advantage Budget, monetary, fiscal and tax, trade policy, etc. Regulations Growth *versus* recession	Competitiveness Concentration (horizontal) Vertical integration Degree of market power Competition/coopetition Technology Entry and exit barriers Network industries Two-sided markets Platforms	Competitive advantage Corporate and business strategies Governance (corporate and IT) Organization & culture Innovation Adoption of advanced technology Compliance
Performance indicators	Economic growth, Gross Domestic Product (GDP), inflation rate, employment, trade, etc.	KPIs* by sector	KPIs by entity, function, project, etc.

* Key Performance Indicators (KPIs) vary according to the type of business, the nature of the activity and the level of control required.
Source: Elaborated by the author.

- Country: macroeconomic conditions (broad environmental factors) including monetary and fiscal policy, the state of the global economy, unemployment levels, productivity, exchange rates, inflation rate. Economic conditions change over time in line with the economic and business cycle, as an economy goes through expansion and contraction. There is no doubt that macroeconomic measures that are necessary for competitive and economic reasons, in many cases also have effects on company competitive advantage.
- Region (or local territories): there are regional differences in growth that can be accounted by various factors (natural resources availability, cheap resources of skilled workers, technology, infrastructure, business environment, etc.). Foreign investors are often very aware of such regional factors when they choose to set up in a country. Political and regulatory considerations play also a dominant role in FDI attractiveness in this region. They are also linked with the "location advantage."
- Market (sector or industry): market structure (concerning organizations producing the same products or services). The market structure and the degree of competition play an important role. There are several factors that determine the market structure of a particular industry: buyers and sellers (number, interactions between them, bargaining power), prices, production and selling processes, product differentiation. Market structures can evolve over the years from monopoly to oligopoly. The two other basic types of market structure include perfect competition (theoretical model) and monopsony.
- Company level: corporate, business and to a lesser extent operational (or functional) strategies. Corporate level is about the overall scope of an organization (its portfolio of businesses), the nature of competitive advantage, the decision to enter a new market or to exit from an activity, etc. Business strategy refers to the ways a firm competes and achieves its objectives within a particular market (or a strategic business unit). Operational strategy is related to the resources and competencies of an organization and how they are used efficiently in doing business.

The identification of country and sector risks

In the context of what has been stated above, how to develop an efficient method to better understand the risks in their global and complex aspects? There are several methodologies that address this issue. One of them has been elaborated by COFACE (stands for *Compagnie Française* d'Assurance *pour le Commerce Extérieur).* COFACE was the export credit agency for France for decades since its foundation in 1946 until the end of December 2016 date at which the French agency transferred its export credit activities to the French public investment bank Bpifrance SA. COFACE is also known for its business information services and its tools for identifying, assessing, and monitoring the risks businesses are facing. They provide, in particular, in-depth analysis of country (for 161 countries) and sector (for 13 sectors) risk. The methodology they have developed is very relevant and accurate as it takes into account three levels as follows: country, sector, and business climate (Table 6.2).

Based on various criteria mentioned in the previous table, the country risk assessment covers 161 countries on an eight-step scale: A1, A2, A3, A4, B, C, D, E, in order of increasing risk. COFACE reviews the assessments of 13 sectors in 28 countries (representing approximately 88% of global GDP) in six major regions of the world.

The components included in the table raise several questions and comments:

- It is a transversal view of risks which is provided. Country and sector risk assessments are closely related. Country risk assessments have an impact on the risk assessment of a given sector in a particular country. In addition, business climate assessment is also included (based on the availability and reliability of company reports and related data). This assessment, which complements the country assessment, measures the quality of the country's business environment: overall reliability of company accounts, legal system, institutional and regulatory environment. It is integrated in the country assessment that covers 161 countries on an eight-step scale: A1, A2, A3, A4, B, C, D, E, in order of decreasing business climate quality.
- Two additional expressions are used in this risk analysis: "forecasted changes" and "prospective elements." This is noteworthy because they refer to old but still valid notions as we will see in the next section.

"Country Risk" indicates the average risk presented

Prospective and strategic foresight

To understand current changes, to assess risks and to explore possible futures, we propose to review briefly the basics of foresight (prospective) and forecast.

Foresight versus *forecasting*

Foresight does not predict the future, but rather explores the range of plausible futures that may emerge. Foresight is based on a range of tools and methodologies, such as scanning the horizon for emerging and early disruptive changes (weak signals), analyzing structural trends and developing several scenarios, to reveal and discuss a range of developments that need to be taken into account about the future. Foresight could be considered as a vision. "Strategic foresight doesn't help us figure out *what* to think about the future. It helps us figure out *how* to think about it." (Scoblic, 2020).

Forecasting is the process of making predictions about the future, based on past and present data and the analysis of trends with varying degrees of

Table 6.2 The methodology: risk identification and assessment

*Criteria category**	*Sector***	*Country****
1	Regional sector risk assessment	Country risk assessment Average risk presented by firms in a country as part of their short-term commercial transactions.
2	Analysis of strengths/weaknesses	Population, GDP, and Local Currency
3	Risk analysis synthesis (economic and financial development in the markets and the main risks in the sector in terms of global trends)	Exports and imports Distribution of exports (or imports) by country of destination (or origin). The sources used are IMF and UNCTAD statistics.
4	Sector economic insights (in-depth analysis of the sector global trends including the outlook for supply and demand for the coming year)	Analysis of strengths/weaknesses A summary of the country's strengths and weaknesses
5	Data visualization – charts (highlighting one or more key aspects of developments in the sector)	Sector risk assessment This assessment indicates the level of short-term risk for 13 sectors of the country's economy (see sector column)
6		Economic indicators The major macroeconomic aggregates essential to understanding the economic environment in a country as well as forecasted changes.
7		Risk assessment Macroeconomic and microeconomic analysis of the country and the most important prospective elements for the current year.
8		Payment and collection practices Information on the payment and debt collection practices in use in the country.
9		Business insolvencies Total number of business insolvencies and its yearly growth rate.

Source: Adapted from COFACE (2022).

* COFACE uses more and more quantitative data and key multifactorial criteria (evolution of commodity price forecasts, risks linked to structural changes that may occur in a sector, etc.).

** Sectors as follows: Agri-food; Automotive; Chemical; Construction; Energy; ICT (Information and Communication Technology); Metals; Paper; Pharmaceutical; Retail; Textile-Clothing; Transport; Wood.

*** Country risk analysis on the basis of 161 countries (the list is included in the report on page 13).

uncertainty. This process involves the use of mathematical models for forecasting natural hazards, the weather, etc. It can help in decision-making and is related to means of (major) risk assessment.

The origins of the "French prospective"

The approaches of foresight were born in France and the United States after the Second World War. Founded by Gaston Berger (1896–1960) in the 1950s, the prospective aimed at not only thinking about the future, but also preparing for it. The prospective has been was mainly applied to regional planning. The names of Jacques Monod and Pierre Massé are often associated with this first phase.

In France, it is usual to refer to foresight as prospective. Other experts, notably Bertrand de Jouvenel, who preferred to use the term "conjecture" rather than "foresight" with the creation of a committee called Futuribles, which was very much oriented toward politics and social forecasting in 1961. Since the beginning of the 1990s, Futuribles International has evolved into a place of debate and reflection. The center is today dedicated to foresight thinking and studies which aim to effectively integrate a sense of the long-term into decision-making and action. Futuribles has played a leading role in the development of foresight studies in France and throughout the world (Futuribles, 2022).

In parallel, the creation of a High Commission for Planning (*Haut Commissariat au Plan*) in 1946 responsible for "animating and coordinating foresight" within the State is another example of the French tradition of foresight. This national institution has been replaced in 2013 by France Stratégie, an independent institution reporting to the Prime Minister, whose mission is to shed light on current and future issues, develop relevant proposals and produce public policy assessments.

Pierre Wack (1985a, 1985b) was the first to recommend the method of strategic scenarios (see below) for companies insofar as they operate in turbulent and uncertain environments:

> by presenting other ways of seeing the world, decision scenarios allow managers to break out of a one-eyed view. Scenarios give managers something very precious; the ability to reperceive reality. In a turbulent business environment, there is more to see than managers normally perceive. Highly relevant information goes unnoticed because, being locked into one way of looking, managers fail to see its significance.
>
> (1985a, p. 150)

The current context of digital transformation is particularly favorable to the use of such approaches.

Strategic foresight

Several strategic foresight tools such as scenarios (including in-depth analysis) have been used in order to simplify complexity. The scenario method is still relevant and has been promoted, in particular, by PWC during the first weeks of the COVID-19 crisis in this way:

> Use scenario analysis. With uncertainty rife, and COVID-19 holding the potential to impact every part of a business for months, scenario planning is a critical tool to test preparedness. What are the best- and worst-case scenarios, and is the business equipped to cope? What could be the impact in the longer term, for example, on working capital or bank covenants, or even rents for shops and restaurants if public places are closed? Ask searching questions of your finance team to highlight critical sensitivities. Organizations in some sectors could see a significant rise in demand if more of the population is spending more time at home rather than at work — are they prepared for this?
>
> (PWC, 2020b)

What does future mean? In the follow-up of research done by Hancock and Bezold (1994) and Voros (2003, 2017) has elaborated and updated the futures cone combining several scenarios and a range of various alternative potential futures. The original figure is summarized and is presented in Table 6.3.

Post-COVID lessons: an historical event with unknown consequences

How to foresight and forecast crisis?

The first lesson that can be drawn from the COVID-19 pandemic crisis is that it was not at all anticipated in any of the models presented above. Even though some scientists had alerted to the potential risks at that time, the same

Table 6.3 The potential futures

Time			
Now	Potential (everything beyond the present moment)	Preposterous! "Impossible"	Won't ever happen
		Possible (future knowledge)	Might happen
		Plausible (current knowledge)	Could happen
		The "projected future"	Business as usual future
		The default extrapolated baseline	
		Probable	Likely to happen
		Current trends	
		Preferable	Want to happen
		Value judgments	Should happen

Source: Adapted from Hancock and Bezold (1994) and Voros (2017).

observation can be made the same for former respiratory viral infections such as SARS (severe acute respiratory syndrome) and with the 2009 pandemic H1N1 influenza virus. With hindsight, it is now necessary to discuss potential scenarios that include a global pandemic. This factor is equally important that the major risks related to climate change and extreme weather events, cyber-attacks, nuclear, chemical, and biological warfare.

Since the end of 2020, a large number of prospective studies and other initiatives have been undertaken in the wake of the pandemic crisis. Several researches have been conducted on this matter accordingly, highlighting the need for foresight or at least for a better anticipation (Böhme & Toptsidou, 2020; Liu et al., 2020) even if most of publications focus on post-COVID 19.

International organizations are also working to develop a culture of foresight. OECD (2020), for example, promotes strategic foresight in order to explore and prepare for a diversity of possible developments, to future-proof strategies, identify new potential opportunities and challenges, and design innovative ways of improving well-being under rapidly evolving circumstances.

In addition, several initiatives have been taken at the European level to strengthen foresight debates. The European Commission now has a commissioner (Maroš Šefčovič) dedicated to foresight. The *2020 Strategic Foresight Report* by the Commission has been published and the first meeting of EU "Ministers for the Future" has launched Foresight Network in May 2021.

The impact of the pandemic crisis

Post COVID-19 – an unequal recovery at a macro level?

International organizations (IMF, OECD, World Bank) as well as national economic forecasting institutes in developed countries have all economic growth forecasts revised upwards for 2022 (although the figures may differ from one source to another) and this on a global scale (Table 6.4). According to IMF, World Economic Outlook Update released in January 2022,

> global growth is expected to moderate from 5.9 in 2021 to 4.4 percent in 2022—half a percentage point lower for 2022 than in the October World Economic Outlook (WEO), largely reflecting forecast markdowns in the two largest economies. A revised assumption removing the Build Back Better fiscal policy package from the baseline, earlier withdrawal of monetary accommodation, and continued supply shortages produced a downward 1.2 percentage-points revision for the United States. In China, pandemic-induced disruptions related to the zero-tolerance COVID-19 policy and protracted financial stress among property developers have induced a 0.8 percentage-point downgrade. Global growth is expected to slow to 3.8 percent in 2023.
>
> (IMF, 2022a)

The results are also contrasted between developed countries (Table 6.4).

Since the beginning of March 2022, because of the intensifying Russian war in Ukraine and its spillover effects, IMF will likely lower its global growth projection. In addition, in the next months, inflation is expected to rise. As explained by Kristalina Georgieva (IMF Managing Director) during a roundtable on Ukraine in March 2022:

> the surging prices for energy and other commodities—wheat, corn, metals, inputs for fertilizers, semiconductors—they are coming in many countries on top of already high inflation and are causing great concern in so many places around the world. It's especially dangerous for families that are living in poverty, for whom food and fuel are the higher proportion of their expenses. When we look at the real economy, clearly we see contraction in trade, but also, a dent on consumer confidence and purchasing power. And that takes me to the third and also quite significant channel, financial conditions and business confidence. Financial conditions have been already tightening in many countries with this pressure from especially oil and gas prices.
>
> (IMF, 2022b)

Table 6.4 Latest world economic outlook growth projections

	Estimate		*Projections*		*Difference from October 2021 WEO projections* *	
(Real GDP, annual percent change)	2020	2021	2022	2023	2022	2023
World output	−3,1	5,9	4,4	3,8	−0,5	0,2
Advanced economies	−4,5	5,0	3,9	2,6	−0,6	0,4
United States	−3,4	5,6	4,0	2,6	−1,2	0,4
Euro area	−6,4	5,2	3,9	2,5	−0,4	0,5
Germany	−4,6	2,7	3,8	2,5	−0,8	0,9
France	−8,0	6,7	3,5	1,8	−0,4	0,0
Italy	−8,9	6,2	3,8	2,2	−0,4	0,6
Spain	−10,8	4,9	5,8	3,8	−0,6	1,2
Japan	−4,5	1,6	3,3	1,8	0,1	0,4
United Kingdom	−9,4	7,2	4,7	2,3	−0,3	0,4
Canada	−5,2	4,7	4,1	2,8	−0,8	0,2
Other advanced economies**	−1,9	4,7	3,6	2,9	−0,1	0,0

Source: IMF (2022a).

* Difference based on rounded figures for the current and October 2021 WEO forecasts. Countries whose forecasts have been updated relative to October 2021 WEO forecasts account for approximately 90% of world GDP measured at purchasing-power-parity weights.

** Excludes the Group of Seven (Canada, France, Germany, Italy, Japan, United Kingdom, and United States) and Euro area countries.

Toward various potential scenarios?

Since 2020, several economic alternative scenarios (economy recovery and recessions post-COVID 19) have been provided by economists. They are depicted in the form of a curve and designated by capital letters to project the economy's recovery or recession (Table 6.5). The shape is dependent on macroeconomic variables. Each letter describes a different scenario for GDP evolution. K, L, U, V, and W, are the most common letters used to

Table 6.5 The ABCs of the economic recovery scenarios post COVID-19

Alphabet letter	*Main features of scenario*	*Shape*	
K	The K-shaped scenario is a new one elaborated by economists to describe what is happening with the Covid-19 pandemic. It is broken down into "winners" and "losers" in terms of recovery. This model can be applied to both countries and companies	K	The upper line of the diagonal Represents the "winners" The lower line of the diagonal represents the "losers"
L	The L-Scenario (the worst case scenario) The extensive production stop caused by the corona crisis lasts for many months. There is no economic recovery, and GDP remains at a very low level.	L	
R	The reverse radical scenario Sharp decline, sharp partial rebound and slow recovery	R	
S	The S-Scenario Sharp decline and slow recovery		
T	The Tick-scenario (also described as the 'Nike Swoosh' recovery) A sharp decline is followed by a small partial bounce and then a long gradual recovery. The result is a deeper and longer-lasting U-shaped recovery.		
U	The U-Scenario It takes longer for the economy to recover from the massive slump in growth.	U	
V	The V-Scenario (the best-case scenario) A sharp decline in GDP is followed by a quick economic recovery. The real economic problems are only temporary.	V	
W	The W-Scenario Repeated phases of ups and downs.	W	
Z	The Z-Scenario The economy suffers a downturn but then bounces back up above the level it would have been in a pre-pandemic baseline.	Z	

Source: Elaborated by the author.

characterize all various recovery paths. A few publications mention also the letters R and S.

The World Economic Forum (WEF), for example, has suggested to fight the K-shaped curve via a tech-led strategy:

> The importance of using technology as a lever of adaptation and survival is going to become increasingly important as covid-19 instigates changes in consumer preferences and increases their use of digital platforms. If before technology was seen quasi-exclusively as the panacea of all troubles, it may be time just now to collectively design it toward solutions of which we are in dire need.
>
> (2020a)

A changing environment: the pandemic impact on sectors and organizations

At a sectoral level, COFACE has provided insights for several sectors (Table 6.6) including the ICT (based on several segments: telecommunications, electronics, media, computers, software, and IT equipment). At a general level, this sector has remained one of the most resilient sectors overall in the context of this crisis. Even more interesting in COFACE study is the increasing importance of new technologies in many sectors of activity. For example, "the adoption of new technologies, such as Artificial Intelligence (AI) and robotics, is expected to accelerate following the COVID-19 crisis, due to the need to promote remote working." In the construction sector, "innovations include AI-controlled robotic systems for sorting, collecting and processing demolition debris for recycling" (p. 23).

Beale (2020) has provided a stage-analysis based on the identification of four main phases and the related actions taken by organizations during each phase. These actions will be different for each organization depending on its size, sector, geographic footprint, business model, and other specific factors (Table 6.6).

The COVID-19 pandemic outbreak and the ensuing health and economic crisis have led companies to accelerate their transformation by making greater use of technological solutions, expanding their use of remote work and automating certain tasks.

The World Economic Forum (WEF) stressed the need for reskilling and upskilling to prepare people for the future of work. By 2025, time spent on routine work tasks will be equally divided between people and machines.

> Automation, in tandem with the COVID-19 recession, is creating a 'double-disruption' scenario for workers. In addition to the current disruption from the pandemic-induced lockdowns and economic contraction, technological adoption by companies will transform tasks, jobs and skills by 2025. Forty three percent of businesses surveyed indicate that they are set to reduce their workforce due to technology integration,

Table 6.6 Pandemic response stages

Stage 1		*Stage 2*		*Stage 3*	*Stage 4*
Response (<2 months)		Recovery (2–4 months)		Renewal (4+ months)	Catch up and acceleration (>12 months)
Pandemic preparedness	Emergency response	Remote enterprise	Preservation & return	Reinvent business	Reinvent the future
Pandemic response	Crisis emergency governance	Effective remote working	Project prioritization	"Re-imagine the new normal"	New inspiration and vision
Business continuity plans	Continuity of operations	Redesign service delivery and security impacts	Revised employee policies and procedures	Redeploy capital toward new opportunities	Resilience (organizational and strategic)
Remote working preparedness	Communications strategies	Supply and demand chains	Back to the office plan	Strategic and digital transformation	
	Employee and client safety	Employee guidance and support	Culture change		Mindset transformation
Pandemic management plans	Current available cash	Changes in customer demand		Impact on business model	Redefinition and reconfiguration of global value chains
	Emergency procurement	Conserving cash overall		Value optimization plan	Development of scalable and sustainable business models
	Low-risk level to improve cash position	Cost optimization strategy			
		Review investments plans			Sustainable competitive advantage
		Design back to office environment			

Source: Adapted from Beale (2020, p. 263). The stage 4 has been added by the author.

> 41% plan to expand their use of contractors for task-specialized work, and 34% plan to expand their workforce due to technology integration.
> (WEF, 2020b, p. 5)

The world thereafter... and the new normal

The pandemic crisis finally raises the question of how to integrate and to manage the various risks associated with an increasingly uncertain and complex environment (FERMA, 2020).

The evolution of the risk landscape for auditors

IFACI (2021) has analyzed risks in relation to auditing activities in a context of Post COVID-19. Their report is based on a quantitative survey sent in the first half of 2021 to the Chief Audit Executives (CAE) members of 12 Institutes of Internal Auditors in Austria, Belgium, France, Germany, Greece, Italy, Luxembourg, the Netherlands, Spain, Sweden, Switzerland, and the UK & Ireland. In parallel, a qualitative research has been conducted based on 50 in-depth interviews.

Five risks have been identified as the most important risks organizations are currently facing:

- Cybersecurity and data security
- Changes in laws and regulations
- Digital disruption, new technology, and AI
- Human capital, diversity, and talent management
- Business continuity, crisis management, and disasters response

The same questions have been asked in a more long-term perspective with a ranking by 2025. The priority given to certain risks is expected to change as follows:

- Cybersecurity and data security
- Digital disruption, new technology, and AI
- Human capital, diversity, and talent management
- Changes in laws and regulations
- Climate change and environmental sustainability

A key factor has appeared in this risk ranking, climate change and environmental sustainability which is considered by auditors as a major issue in the mid-term. Not surprisingly, cybersecurity remains a major concern today and in the near future.

In this survey, a third question has been posed about the top five risks the auditors interviewed are expected internal audit to spend the most time and effort by 2025.

- Financial, liquidity, and insolvency risks
- Business continuity, crisis management, and disasters response
- Changes in laws and regulations
- Organizational governance and corporate reporting
- Cybersecurity and data security

Finally, it can be noticed that there is a gap between the above mentioned responses regarding the priority given to some risks and time spending auditing according risk considered. The authors of the survey have explained this gap by making several assumptions.

> There are numerous reasons why these differentials may exist and a direct correlation between risk priority and time spent auditing should not necessarily be expected. However, any gaps could be cause for concern, potentially indicating a lack of assurance maturity or that internal audit is not pointed in the right directions. For instance, as has been observed in previous years, Organisational governance and corporate reporting sees much of internal audit's attention and yet is not viewed as high risk. Conversely, macroeconomic and geopolitical uncertainty and Climate change and environmental sustainability are viewed as significant risks to the business and yet see limited attention from internal audit. This is a major problem.
>
> (IFACI, 2021, p. 12)

The Big Four accounting firms' and other technology-IT services companies' vision

During the successive lockdowns due to the covid-19 pandemic in 2020–2021 (and other containment measures such quarantines and curfews) all around the World, The Big Four (Deloitte, EY, KPMG and PWC) and other global leaders in consulting, technology services and digital transformation (e.g., Accenture, Cap Gemini) communicated widely on their sites, discussing the impact of COVID-19 on their future operations in blogs or webinars as well.

Texts on web sites of varying length took different shapes: testimony, classic analysis, "words of the day," points of attention, etc. These statements went beyond simple communication operations to all their internal and external stakeholders. They also reflected the stance of these organizations regarding crisis management and how they viewed the lessons to draw from the COVID-19 crisis while it was just the beginning of the crisis without any vaccines at that time. Some new expressions such "resilience" are used. Some of these texts even address the issue of the evolution of capitalism. The headings of these publications are particularly meaningful. Some short extracts are presented in Exhibit 6.1.

Exhibit 6.1 The post-COVID 19 perspectives

Cap Gemini

Trust, the foundation of the "world thereafter" (April 30, 2020)

> For tomorrow's leaders, the ability to restore trust with the population is decisive.
>
> It's for the long-term, and it will require new trends to be integrated into processes and organisations. One can list of instance: relocation of value chains, valuation back of proximity, reconsideration of front line jobs, thoughtful management of digital interfaces thanks to which citizens have acquired a newly-found autonomy and – in part – overcome the economic and social consequences of the crisis. More widely, this large project of trust will require new cultural reflexes – sincerity, humility, alignment between words and actions, a cooperative spirit and reflection on a new form of democracy that brings stakeholders together around these matters and breed common good.
>
> (https://www.capgemini.com/2020/04/trust-the-foundation-of-the-world-thereafter)

KPMG

COVID-19 Clues: What to watch

To answer 'what now,' companies are asking 'what next' (April 20, 2020)

> And rightly so. COVID-19 has already spurred companies to embrace their future far quicker than they would have organically – from agile working and digitalisation, to automation and investment in renewables. If you know where you are going, actions to respond to the crisis today can set you up for the years ahead.
>
> Of course, answering 'what's next' for your business means knowing what's next for the world; what may have been right for your business BC (Before-COVID) may not be right in the 'new reality' that we will soon face. Crystal-balling a post COVID-19 world requires divination of two key questions: when will it happen; and what will it look like?
>
> (https://home.kpmg/dp/en/home/insights/2020/05/covid-19-clues-what-to-watch.html)

KPMG

The COVID-19 evolution of capitalism. COVID-19 highlights the importance of delivering societal impact beyond financial returns.

"Significant momentum has been building over the past year toward the shift to stakeholder capitalism. COVID-19 demonstrates the importance of defining a 'new normal' for investing, and highlighting the importance of delivering societal impact beyond financial returns. Welcome to the era of enlightened capital. (...)

COVID-19 exemplifies the interdependent relationship a company has with the community it serves, and highlights the prominent role that impact and key environmental, social, and governance (ESG) factors have in contributing to the resilience of a business. As we continue to navigate the uncharted waters presented by the pandemic, there are important lessons fueling the momentum for impact and ESG as the new normal in investing.

Investors drive change

Investors play a critical role in driving the shift to stakeholder capitalism. Indeed, there are now a growing number of retail and institutional investors actively scrutinizing companies based on the way they manage ESG risks and opportunities related to their operations."

(https://home.kpmg/xx/en/home/insights/2020/05/the-post-covid-19-evolution-of-capitalism.html)

Deloitte (March 2020)

Management checklist for the COVID-19 crisis

The road to resilience against COVID-19.

Focus on three key dimensions for operating during the pandemic. To support your people and operations, think about three deeply interconnected dimensions, work (what are your key activities), workforce (who performs the key activities) and workplace (from where each key activity should be performed).

Adopt agile business methods (...)

Protect your reputation (...)

Rethink your risks and potential points of failure (...)

Prepare for cash flow constraints and carefully assess your investments (...)

Incorporate security mechanisms (...)

Assess legal and tax implications (...)

Monitor and assess your business continuity plan (...)

Clearly define roles and priorities (...)

Start planning for recovery (...)

Maintain a long-term view (...)

https://www2.deloitte.com/content/dam/Deloitte/gr/Documents/about-deloitte/gr_COVID_19_%20crisis_management_checklist_noexp.pdf

All audit firms have published post-COVID analyses on their websites highlighting their own view of the crisis, the need for greater risk management and especially the acceleration of the transformation of the internal audit function.

The impact of the COVID-19 pandemic: what are the future trends of internal auditing?

Richard Chambers (the former president and CEO of the Institute of Internal Auditors (IIA) and AuditBoard have conducted a survey in 2021 to know what chief audit executives (CAE) think about the long-term impacts of COVID on their operations and the profession at large. Most respondents consider that the pandemic should transform the profession in the long-run. At the end, five key trends have been identified:

- the use of technology to conduct audits,
- employing innovative means of gathering and analyzing evidence,
- greater reliance on technology for basic communication,
- a continuous approach to assessing risks, and
- the hybrid workplace model.

We propose here to review each of these insights and to question them.

The use of technology to conduct audits

Not surprisingly, the use of technology will be crucial in conducting future internal audits (Chapter 5).

> Thanks to the sophistication of existing technologies at the time quarantines began, audit, risk, and compliance professionals overcame the remote setback by deploying and exhibiting a greater reliance on a collective array of these solutions to help employees continue achieving their day-to-day objectives from home. In particular, cloud-based platforms that were designed to not only facilitate remote collaboration, but also automate department processes — e.g. end-to-end project management — were successful in streamlining and facilitating the actions of multiple stakeholders to reach common, intersecting goals.
>
> (Chambers, 2021, p. 2)

At a general level, the Big Four firms have already invested heavily in new technology aimed at reducing the lower-value audit tasks along with human errors and to free auditors to focus on more complex aspects of the work.

Employing innovative means of gathering and analyzing evidence

When an organization is undergoing an audit, it must provide audit evidence (statements, documents, records, etc.) to ensure, in particular, an audit quality (efficiency, effectiveness, and quality of documentation). Evidence must always be sufficient, reliable, relevant, and useful in affording internal auditors a basis for conclusion. As explained by Chambers (2021),

> Among the innovative uses of technology that have proven effective in the past year has been the use of drones, reliance on pre-positioned security camera video feeds, and video documentation by smart phones and other devices. While the potential of these technologies by internal auditors has been recognized for years, physical limitations imposed by the pandemic accelerated their use. Chief audit executives have reported that the use of drones to document the physical existence of assets or control effectiveness has provided sufficient evidence more efficiently than even traditional means.
>
> (p. 2)

As Appelbaum and Nehmer (2017) have highlighted, it seems that there is no mention to date regarding the use of drones in the audit academic literature. In their paper, they have developed a framework for designing and implementing audit drone automation in internal and external audit environments. They have explored how drones fit into audits for some functions through their abilities to gather evidence to support specific assertions made by management and evaluated by auditors during the audit. Uses of drones in the audit are linked to the audit procedures used to collect evidence in support of specific assertions.

> Drones are not "generalists" in that they may be useful in a limited but not restrictive number of audit procedures. Drones are "specialists" in that they may be implemented in a targeted fashion to certain audit tasks that have yet to be automated and that are typically costly, difficult, and sometimes dangerous to complete.
>
> (p. 111)

In a more recent research, Christ et al. (2021) have also examined whether using drones and automated counting software can improve audit quality especially in inventory. Their results suggest that technology-enabled inventory audits can improve audit quality and further regulatory guidance on using such technologies would enhance adoption.

Future research should focus on the value of drone usage in auditing. Regarding practitioner reports or white papers on this topic, EY (2017) has assessed the use of drones to assist with inventory observations and the integration of inventory observations with drones and mobile applications. PWC (2019) has also undertaken a stock count audit using a drone, as part of a wider drive to harness emerging technologies to enhance audit quality and efficiency and transform the audit process.

Greater reliance on technology for basic communication

Most face-to-face meetings will be replaced with virtual meetings using video streaming technology.

> By all accounts, audit, risk, and compliance professionals have embraced video platforms not only for meetings between members of the internal audit staff, but also for meetings and other face-to-face interaction throughout the audit process and communications with key stakeholder.
> (Chambers, 2021, p. 2)

This reflects the widespread adoption of this technology across all industries and professions. Market forecasts are very high. According to Reportlinker (2022),

> the global video conferencing market is expected to grow from \$6.03 billion in 2021 to \$6.61 billion in 2022 at a compound annual growth rate (CAGR) of 9.5%. The change in growth trend is mainly due to the companies stabilizing their output after catering to the demand that grew exponentially during the COVID-19 pandemic in 2021. The market is expected to reach \$9.43 billion in 2026 at a CAGR of 9.3%.

A continuous approach to assessing risks

As we have already mentioned it previously (see former section), the identification of emerging risks and the assessment of existing risks (potential and real impact of various risks) are at the center of internal auditing activities.

> The COVID experience compels us to be more determined in the timeliness and precision with which we assess risks. To the extent that they were still in practice, periodic risk assessments are now obsolete. There must be a continuous component to assessing risks, not only in performing risk assessments with greater frequency, but in the methodologies and technologies we rely on to create to maintain a continuous perspective on risks.
> (Chambers, 2021, p. 3)

The hybrid workplace mode

New ways of work have emerged and accelerated since the beginning of the COVID-19 crisis. Kniffin et al. (2020) have used two expressions to describe changes in work practices: Work From Home (WFH) and related behaviors (virtual teamwork, virtual leadership, and management). These are not really new practices but they have been widely spread with the pandemic.

This change had a dramatic effect on internal auditors who could no longer perform planned audits using their traditional, face-to-face methodologies.

Affected internal audit functions (IAFs) shifted to performing remote audits, which means performing audit procedures from a different location than the auditee's using "information and communication technology with data analytics to assess and report on the accuracy of financial data and internal controls, gather electronic evidence, and interact with the auditee" (Teeter et al., 2010, p. 74).

> After the pandemic, businesses will be more flexible about where people are based when hiring. Based on the survey responses, it would appear that a strong majority of CAEs will embrace flexible workplace arrangements in the future. This may prove particularly true in markets where internal audit talent (especially expertise in specialized risks) is in short supply.
>
> (Chambers, 2021, p. 3)

Martinelli et al. (2020) have expressed the fact that due to the nature of their work, many internal auditors were already experienced at working remotely and able to adapt quickly to the new working environment.

> Internal audit's unique skills in risk assessment can be applied to the complexities of working remotely. Strategically, internal audit will also need to develop new relationship management skills within an organization—not just for conducting interviews or issuing reports, but also for monitoring events effectively.
>
> (p. 63)

Finally, the future of internal audit is not just about remote audits, it is about transforming traditional audit underlying processes using technology. One of these pillars is to accelerate the transition from traditional to continuous auditing (Eulerich et al., 2021).

Information systems and technologies for auditing have been a research topic in IS since the 1970s. Changes in internal auditing and IT auditing started long before the pandemic crisis. As it has been described in-depth in Chapter 5, the development and the adoption of new technologies (RPA, AI, etc.) since the mid-2010s is accelerating the transformation of internal auditing missions and activities (working methods, tools and methodology used, auditors' skills, etc.).

Since the early 2000s, several authors have highlighted the development of new practices combined with new software or tools (Chapter 5). They have discussed, in particular, the issues in relation to the collection of audit evidence in an IT environment (characterized by the ease of information access, the speed of processing, a huge capacity of storage, no paper based trails, alternative ways of information processing, etc.). There has been a profound shift regarding the nature of audit evidence as more than 90% of the documents are now digital (Marris, 2010).

The CAATs represent a key tool for the auditor to evaluate the control environment in an efficient and effective manner and process audit evidence and information (Table 6.7). The use of CAATs allows a broader audit coverage, more thorough and consistent analysis of data, and reduction in risk. According to Singleton et al. (2006), CAATs represent tools and techniques provided by IT to help auditors manage an organization's IS by performing the set of tasks they are entitled and more specifically, fraud detection. Because of their effectiveness, CAATs are useful in audit methodologies (Chapters 4 and 5) thus contributing to a good corporate governance, and hence, shareholder value creation (Chapter 3).

Table 6.7 Audit procedures for obtaining audit evidence*

Procedure	*On-site methodology*	*Remote audit methodology*
Inspection of records or documents, e.g., authorization	Pull a sample of purchase orders and verify authorized signature exists and matches authority list	Evaluate entire purchase order PO population in ERP and verify POs passed through approval workflow and possessed authorized user stamp.
Inspection of tangible assets, e.g., physical inventory count	Print a list of inventory, walk through warehouse, open boxes, etc.	Employ closed-circuit video monitoring, scales, other metrics
Observation, e.g., watching someone complete a process	Shadow a worker and observe procedure.	Use process mining to identify transactions that do not follow a standard workflow
Inquiry, e.g., written or oral interviews	Communicate electronically or in person as part of traditional audit	Monitor processes/controls. Automatically identify process owner when exceptions occur
Confirmation, e.g., verify account balances	Send letters or emails to banks, suppliers, etc.	Evaluate linked data streams from financial institutions, other businesses through IDE, etc.
Recalculation, e.g., using CAAT to recalculate figures	Manually extract data, run CAATs	Monitor transactions, run calculations automatically at standard intervals, perform process integrity reviews, monitor changes in processes.
Reperformance, e.g., aging of accounts receivable	Manually extract data, run CAATs.	Monitor accounts, run calculations automatically, replicate transactions.
Analytical Procedures, e.g., scanning and statistics	Extract data, scan for anomalies based on auditor judgment.	Filter real-time data through continuity equations, ratio analysis.

Source: Teeter et al. (2010, p. 78).

* Based on SAS No. 106 AICPA (2006).

Conclusion

The impact of the COVID-19 crisis on the economy as a whole, on society and organizations has been significant. The COVID-19 has exposed the vulnerabilities of individuals, companies, societies and economies. The crisis was not foreseeable and raises the question of medium-term and long-term forecasts (which may be called prospective analysis).

Further research should explore the impact of the COVID-19 crisis on auditing activities and provide valuable lessons that can be taken from the management of this crisis for the future. The world has changed. Internal audit must change too. Internal auditors were already experiencing changes before COVID-19 with the emerging technologies that challenged many internal audit functions in order to ensure data accuracy and transparency (The Institute of Cost Accountants of India, 2020). Internal audit must continue to manage a variety of risks.

Questions for discussion

Why does foresight matter in a time of crisis?

What are and will the drivers of success be in the post-COVID era?

How the pandemic crisis is accelerating the future of audit?

How the auditing profession is transforming to meet future challenges?

How will internal auditors react to digital acceleration and need for new skills, upskilling and adaptability?

Recommended reading

Bechtel, M., & Hickin, R. (2021). *Futurism is a means to see beyond COVID-19.* Here's how to time travel. https://www.weforum.org/agenda/2021/04/how-futurism-can-help-you-navigate-a-post-covid-future-gtgs21/

IFACI (2021). *Risk in focus 2022. Hot topics for internal auditors.* Retrieved November 13, 2021 from: https://www.ifaci.com/wp-content/uploads/Risk-In-Focus-2022.pdf

Kniffin, K.M., Narayanan, J., Anseel, F., et al. (2021). COVID-19 and the workplace: Implications, issues, and insights for future research and action. *American Psychologist, 76*(1), 63–77.

References

American Institute of Certified Public Accountants (AICPA) (2006). *Audit evidence.* Statement on Auditing Standards No. 106. New York: AICPA.

Appelbaum, D.A., & Nehmer, R. (2017). Using drones in internal and external audits: An exploratory framework. *Journal of Emerging Technologies in Accounting, 14* (1), 99–113. https://doi.org/10.2308/jeta-51704

Beale I. (2020). COVID-19: Lessons learned and next steps for internal audit. *Journal of Business Continuity & Emergency Planning, 14*(3), 262–274.

Böhme, K., & Toptsidou, M. (2020). *Scenario snapshots of a post COVID-19 EU: Recovery strategies shaping new normals.* Spatial Foresight Briefing 2020:14. Luxembourg. Retrieved July 11, 2021 from: https://www.spatialforesight.eu/files/spatial_theme/spatial/publications/Brief_2020-14_201119.pdf

Chambers, R. (2021). *5 ways COVID has changed internal audit forever.* AuditBoard. Retrieved February 20, 2022 from: https://go.auditboard.com/rs/961-ZQV-184/images/AB-AR-5-Ways-COVID-Has-Changed-Internal-Audit-Forever.pdf

Christ, M.H., Emett, S.A., Summers, S.L., et al. (2021). Prepare for takeoff: Improving asset measurement and audit quality with drone-enabled inventory audit procedures. *Review of Accounting Studies, 26*(4), 1323–1343. https://doi.org/10.1007/s11142-020-09574-5

COFACE (2021). *Country & sector risks handbook 2021. Major trends of the world economy.* Retrieved February 20, 2022 from: https://static.coface.com/202102CofaceCountry&SectorRisksHandbook2021EN.pdf

Eulerich, M., Wagener, M., & Wood, D.A. (2021). Evidence on internal audit effectiveness from transitioning to remote audits because of COVID-19. http://dx.doi.org/10.2139/ssrn.3774050

EY (2020). *Are you reframing your future or is the future reframing you?* June 19, 2020. https://www.ey.com/en_gl/megatrends/how-megatrends-can-reframe-your-future

EY (2017). *EY scaling the use of drones in the audit process.* https://www.ey.com/gl/en/newsroom/news-releases/news-ey-scaling-the-use-of-drones-in-the-audit-process

Federation of European Risk Management Associations (FERMA) (2020). *Risk management, recovery and resilience COVID-19 survey report 2020.* Retrieved November 21, 2021 from: https://www.ferma.eu/app/uploads/2020/12/Risk-Management-recovery-and-resilience-COVID-19-Survey-Report-2020_2020.12.01_final.pdf

Futuribles (2022). *Prospective and strategic foresight toolbox.* https://www.futuribles.com/en

Hancock, T. & Bezold, C. (1994). Possible futures, preferable futures. *Healthcare Forum Journal, 37*(2), 23–29.

IMF (2022a). *World economic outlook update.* January 2022. https://www.imf.org/en/Publications/WEO/Issues/2022/01/25/world-economic-outlook-update-january-2022

IMF (2022b). *Transcript of IMF media roundtable on Ukraine.* Kristalina Georgieva. March 10, 2022. https://www.imf.org/en/News/Articles/2022/03/10/tr031022-transcript-of-imf-media-roundtable-on-ukraine

The Institute of Cost Accountants of India (2020). *Guidance note on risk based internal audit.* Retrieved March 5, 2022 from: https://icmai.in/upload/IAASB/GNRBIA_21_07_2020.pdf

Liu, Y., Lee, J.M., & Lee, C. (2029). The challenges and opportunities of a global health crisis: The management and business implications of COVID-19 from an Asian perspective. *Asian Business & Management, 19*(3), 277–297. https://doi.org/10.1057/s41291-020-00119-x

Marris, D. (2010). Challenges obtaining audit evidence. *Economics of Networks eJournal*, 1–18. Published 28 February 2010. http://dx.doi.org/10.2139/ssrn.1590634

Martinelli, M., Friedman, A.E., & Lanz, J. (2020). The impact of COVID-19 on internal audit. *The CPA Journal, 90*(6), 60–63.

OECD (2020). *Strategic foresight for the COVID-19 crisis and beyond: Using futures thinking to design better public policies.* https://read.oecd-ilibrary.org/6b392c59-068b-4e1a-b861-ceb2cc98cf8f

PWC (2020a). *Post Covid-19: What's the role of Internal Audit after the crisis?* Melissa Ambühl. August 20, 2020. https://www.pwc.ch/en/insights/post-covid-role-for-internal-audit.html

PWC (2020b). *Seven key actions business can take to mitigate the effects of COVID-19.* Melanie Butler and Kristin Rivera. March 24, 2020. https://www.pwc.com/gx/en/issues/crisis-solutions/covid-19.html

PWC (2019, January 3). *PWC completes its first stock count audit using drone technology.* https://www.pwc.co.uk/press-room/press-releases/pwc-first-stock-count-audit-drones.html

ReportLinker (2022). *Video conferencing global market report 2022.* https://www.reportlinker.com/p06246506/?utm_source=GNW

Scoblic, J.P. (2020). *Learning from the future how to make robust strategy in times of deep uncertainty.* Retrieved January 15, 2022 from: https://www.ffcoi.org/wp-content/uploads/2020/07/Learning-from-the-Future-HBR-2020.pdf

Singleton, T.W., Singleton, A.J., Bologna, G.J., & Lindquist, R.J. (2006). *Fraud auditing and forensic accounting.* 3rd edition. Hoboken, NJ: John Wiley & Sons.

Teeter, R.A., Alles, M.G. & Vasarhelyi, M.A. (2010). The remote audit. *Journal of Emerging Technologies in Accounting,* 7(1), 73–88.

Voros, J. (2017). Big History and anticipation: Using big history as a framework for global foresight. In R. Poli (Ed.), *Handbook of anticipation: Theoretical and applied aspects of the use of future in decision making* (pp. 425–464). Cham: Springer International. https://doi.org/10.1007/978-3-319-31737-3_95-1

Voros, J. (2003). A generic foresight process framework. *Foresight, 5*(3), 10–21. https://doi.org/10.1108/14636680310698379

Wack, P. (1985a). Scenarios: Shooting the rapids. *Harvard Business Review, 63*(6), 139–150. https://rjohnwilliams.files.wordpress.com/2016/02/wack-scenarios-hbr2-1985.pdf

Wack, P. (1985b). Scenarios: Uncharted waters ahead. *Harvard Business Review, 63*(5), 73–89. https://rjohnwilliams.files.wordpress.com/2016/02/wack-scenarios-hbr1-1985.pdf

World Economic Forum (2020a). *Are we experiencing a K shaped recovery from COVID-19?* December 22, 2020. https://www.weforum.org/agenda/2020/12/k-shaped-covid19-coronavirus-recovery/

World Economic Forum (2020b). *The future of jobs report 2020.* Retrieved February 13, 2021 from: http://www3.weforum.org/docs/WEF_Future_of_Jobs_2020.pdf

Index